D1612748

BIRDS and ISLANDS

BIRDS and ISLANDS

Travels in wild places

RONALD LOCKLEY

Illustrated by
Noel W. Cusa

H. F. & G. WITHERBY LTD

First published in Great Britain 1991 by
H. F. & G. Witherby Ltd,
14 Henrietta Street, London WC2E 8QJ

Text © Ronald Lockley 1991
Illustrations © The Estate of Noel W. Cusa 1991

A CIP catalogue record is available
from the British Library

ISBN 0-85493-196-1

Photoset by Rowland Phototypesetting Ltd,
Bury St Edmunds, Suffolk
Printed in Great Britain by
St Edmundsbury Press Ltd, Bury St Edmunds, Suffolk

Contents

Preface

> O these endless little isles
> lying clad with soft verdure
> and in thine awful solitude
> Afar off in the lap of wild ocean –
> not to see thee with the carnal eye
> will be to have seen nothing!
>
> T. S. Muir

Why do the lonely little islands attract some of us, especially the young of heart, right into their old age? I have lived long enough, fourteen years, on one alone or with my wife, daughter and visiting friends, to have grown momentarily tired of the sequestered pioneering life. Yet when I have left it, I have longed to return. That longing remains.

In a pocket anthology for such friends (*In Praise of Islands*, published a good many years ago) I wrote:

> There is something about a small island that satisfies the heart of man. What fun we could have with it, we say. And we plan what we could do with a little kingdom of our own set in a silver sea. So much we could do, and no one would say us nay! We should build our little house out of driftwood – or pine-tree logs if any were handy to cut; rear a family of joyous sturdy children – or turn hermit if our philoprogenitiveness were weak; our amateur engineering and constructive ingenuity would have a gloriously free field for development, or we could merely laze in the sun and live on wild fruits, depending on the climate and natural fertility of the island of our dreams.

I remember discussing my passion for small islands with another good friend who had lived several years on the small one-house smuggler's islet of Jethou in the Channel Islands – handy to France. Like me Compton Mackenzie had had to abandon his beloved isle on the outbreak of the 1939 war. But afterwards, staying with him at his home in the Vale of White Horse, he offered me this contribution to my pocket anthology:

The real pleasure for me of inhabiting a small island is not as many suppose the satisfaction of being monarch of all one surveys, but of being granted what I may call the freedom of the compass. It is really the same pleasure which possesses a mariner, with this difference, that an island does not rock and that even the smallest island is a miniature continent with all the inexhaustible variety of land, including the perfume of vegetation for which above every-thing terrestrial the seafarer longs. Nobody can pretend to know much about the sea who has not spent some of the time looking at it from the top of a small island.

Because he had visited so many islands in his literary pilgrimage through life, from Shetland to Greece and beyond, Compton in-vented the word *nesophile* (island-addicted) to describe himself and me. Elizabeth Barrett-Browning was another nesophile dreaming of the ideal small island:

> My dream is of an island-place
> Which distant seas keep lonely,
> A little island on whose face
> The stars are watchers only.

But like Walter de la Mare, and many other writers, she desired the islet of her dreams to be scenically acceptable for living:

> Hills running up to heaven for light
> Through woods that half-way ran,
> As if the wild earth mimicked right
> The wilder heart of man;
> Only it shall be greener far
> And gladder than hearts ever are.

From time immemorial poets and writers have described the island of their dreams. Virgil (70–19 BC) wrote of the 'Fortunate isle, the abode of the blest.' The Fortunate (Canary) Isles are described in detail by Plutarch (AD 46–120).

In *The Man Who Loved Islands* D. H. Lawrence (1885–1930) pictures the great enchantment: 'Our islander loved his island very much. In early spring, the little ways and glades were a snow of blackthorn, a vivid white among the Celtic stillness of close green and grey rock. And many birds with nests you could peep into, on the island all your own. Wonderful what a great world it was!'

Celtic isles were usually inhabited by fairies, elves, witches, ghosts.

The romantic poets Shelley, Keats, Byron, Swinburne and Tennyson adorned many of their island tales with characters from the mythology of the Roman and Grecian pre-Christian centuries when kings and emperors were governed by pagan gods who dwelled in the sky – heroic, quarrelsome, jealous, noble or ignoble; and there was also a god of the underworld. I had been brought up on the translations of Homer's *Iliad* and *Odyssey*.

Robert Louis Stevenson was another man who loved islands. Little did I dream when as a boy I was given a copy of *Treasure Island*, after a casual visit to the Highland cottage where he wrote the book, that I would stand beside his monument on Mt Vaea, Western Samoa. His *Travels with a Donkey* inspired me to save enough money to follow that epic lone wandering through the mountains of France.

One day, lo, I was there, knapsack on my shoulder, sitting in that same inn of the stupendous Gorges du Tarn, with eagles and vultures soaring above, where – so claimed M. le Propriétaire – his father had revived the travel-weary Robert Louis Stevenson with *vin du pays*, and stabled the stubborn Modestine 80 years earlier.

With his *Travels* in my pocket I too slept out on that summer-scented height amid the alpine flowers, listening to nightingales answer the laughing waterfalls of the Tarn gorges; but without the old-fashioned pistol which RLS kept under his pillow to ward off the wolves he heard but never saw.

During wartime visits to London, enjoying the hospitality of the Savile Club, I found to my delight and youthful awe that Stevenson was one of the founders of this Brook Street club begun by a group of impecunious writers.

RLS was a solitary at heart, with itching feet, but longing to find complete harmony with kindred minds. His flowing narratives, the divine discontent of those soliloquies with his soul – and with the ass Modestine – suited my habit of lone exploration and observation of wild nature.

I never found that other inn in France, where, leaping through a window, Louis accidentally fell into the arms of Fanny Osborne, a little American artist. It was love at first sight for this man who until then had preferred male company. And for Fanny, ten years older, we can believe it was at first more of a protective motherly love for a penniless man stricken with tuberculosis. Undoubtedly Fanny saved Stevenson's life by their marriage in 1880 and by her loving care and courage. Until he met Fanny he believed himself a failure – his fine

books had been financially without profit. But love made their frugal
honeymoon in an abandoned silver-mine (described in his *Silverdale
Squatters*) a happy time of literary rebirth.

With money in hand from his first success (*Dr Jekyll and Mr Hyde*)
two years later the determined Fanny hired a yacht in which they
explored the warm coral islands of the Pacific, from Hawaii southwards through the Gilberts and Marquesas to Samoa. His accurate,
fascinating description of these islands and his encounter with the
decadent islanders – their ancient culture destroyed by white invaders and traders – in his book *In the South Seas*, was for me my
inspiration and guide in exploring those same islands, known today
as part of the Polynesian Triangle.

For, like Stevenson I retired to live where I write this, in the farthest
corner of that Triangle, New Zealand (*Aotearoa* in the Polynesian
language common to the islands of the Pacific Oceania). From
Aotearoa I can fly in a few hours to Western Samoa, where Stevenson
at last found joy and peace among a brown-skinned people still
worthy of his admiration for their honest caring and sharing way of
life close to the land and sea. Where, as I relate this book, money is
less important than happiness in what the average pakeha (white
man) calls poverty.

Here Tusitala (Story-spinner), as the Samoans called him, was
content to live and die among a people he described as 'the gayest and
the most entertained inhabitants of our planet. In a climate and upon
a soil where a livelihood can be had for the stooping, entertainment is
a prime necessity. Perpetual games, journeys and pleasures make
island life a smiling picture.' Polynesian culture is based on sharing
resources: all is for each and each possesses all. In return for
Tusitala's assistance in peace-making between rival tribes, local
matai (chiefs) gave their labour and materials free to build the
Stevensons a magnificent home (to his specification) which they
named Vailima – today a Government reception centre and showpiece of the island nation's first national park. Here RLS lies buried,
and you may visit his grave and read the epitaph he composed:

> This is the verse you grave for me:
> Here he lies where he longed to be,
> Home is the sailor, home from the sea
> And the hunter home from the hill.

My problem in composing this book on the islands I have visited is
which to include and which to leave out. There are too many for a

slender book. All are culled from my diaries written during those journeys and sojourns. Perhaps the most enjoyable were those undertaken as a lone traveller with no more than a back-pack and a camera; for I have found that the lone explorer is more hospitably received into a family if he or she appears on the doorstep as a humble, solitary and perhaps pitiable figure. It is so much easier to travel alone, uncluttered with companions and heavy baggage – even to reach the farthest Arctic and Antarctic islands. But I acknowledge here the advantages of using air and ship facilities to attain some of the more remote islands described, in particular on three voyages with companion naturalists aboard the *Lindblad Explorer* to the Arctic and Antarctic, under the skilful and genial Captain Hasse Nilsson, a great lover of little islands – he tells me he intends retiring to one he now owns: 'set in the silver Baltic Sea: you must see the log cabin I am building there.'

Eskimo Island

Barrow, Alaska, 550 km north of the Arctic Circle, is the most northerly inhabited land in the United States. The sun never sets between mid-May and early August.

In this sad, interesting large village sudden monetary wealth has destroyed the nomadic stone-age culture of Eskimo life which had survived the severe climate since at least a thousand years before Christ. The discovery of oil and gas on Alaska's north slope brought a horde of white exploiters, while the Pentagon's agonised dread of the USSR's increasing nuclear strike capability has resulted in the erection of yet another DEW [Direct Early Warning] station to brood like some immense steel-domed spider waving its antennae at this listening point so close to Soviet Siberia.

Thomas Brower, proud to be the whale-hunting son of a pure-bred Inupiat Eskimo by Charles Brower, trader, whaler, author of *Fifty Years Below Zero*, and the first white man to live permanently so far north, chuckled as he described to me how Uncle Sam, having bought the whole of Alaska from Russia in 1867, assumed that he owned not only the land but also the people on it and the oil and gold beneath it.

'After oil was discovered we were told that we could stay on the land if we paid rates and taxes. Uncle Sam would grant us a favourable lease for that privilege!' said Thomas Brower.

'No way! I am not a politician – I hate politics. But I advised the frightened 500 Eskimo people of Barrow never to lease, sell or buy back their own inheritance! The land is theirs, and the oil and minerals thereon. Let the Yankees pipe gas to Eskimo homes – as they have done in Barrow. I call that a guilt reaction.

'I told them to take no notice of Uncle Sam's wily offers, or his Pentagon politics trying to set us against our own flesh and blood across the Diomede Strait and Chukchi Sea in Russian Siberia. It's paid hands down. We've got them publicly scared, with troubled consciences.'

Most of the local Eskimos took the advice of the Brower family, their trusted trading friends and advisers over the eighty years since Charles Brower had established what is known today as Browerville,

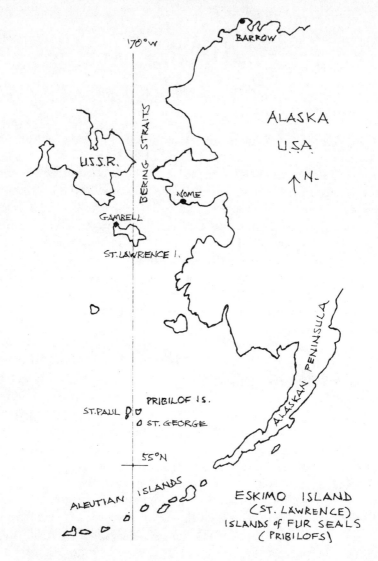

70°W

BARROW

ALASKA

U.S.A.

↑ N-

BERING STRAITS

U.S.S.R.

NOME

GAMBELL

ST. LAWRENCE I.

ALASKAN PENINSULA

PRIBILOF IS.

ST. PAUL

ST. GEORGE

55°N

ALEUTIAN   ISLANDS

ESKIMO   ISLAND
(ST. LAWRENCE)
ISLANDS of FUR SEALS
(PRIBILOFS)

a separate Inupiat community. But some land was sold to the white invaders, who produced paper deeds of doubtful validity, to be signed by Eskimos who could not read or write English, but were happy to be paid in cash.

My introduction to Thomas Brower had been through the Explorers' Club of America, of which we were both elected fellows. In response to my letter of intention to visit Barrow, he sent a fellow New Zealander to meet my plane.

'Jumper' Bitters from Napier in the North Island of New Zealand had worked both in Antarctica and in Greenland, I was to learn. He loved Greenland huskies and had achieved some fame recently as dog-handler to Wally (North Pole) Herbert's brave adventure of circling Greenland's ice-bound shore by dog-team in midwinter.

With no more formality than a handshake Bitters hustled me in a jeep through Barrow out to NARL, the United States Naval Arctic Research Laboratory, on the headland looking towards Siberia – also known as DEWS [Direct Early Warning Station]. A marvellous view over the Arctic Ocean, but the air was bitterly cold and I was glad of the central heating hospitality of this outwardly hideous complex of bungaloid shedding and Pentagon paraphernalia.

Here scientists and oil moguls of impeccable background are pampered, overheated and overfed at an inclusive fee of $78 per day. I did not realise that I was not in that impeccable category, that is to say, Jumper had not troubled to ask for my credentials. I had told him I proposed staying at the new large 'Top of the World' hotel in Barrow, but he said, 'It's far too expensive! A hundred dollars a day without grub, and anyway it's probably full up.' He carried my back-pack straight into the guest quarters at NARL at high speed (he is known as 'Expediter', apparently an official post at NARL), introduced me to the house steward, and departed hurriedly on his next assignment.

It was good to talk with scientists that evening, describing their fascinating projects of studying marine mammals (including polar bears, seals and whales), caribou, musk ox, wolves, foxes, lemmings, and birds. They are liberally supplied with air support of small planes and helicopters, largely paid for by the oil exploration companies employing seismologists and geologists. These men offered me a place in their camps and a seat in the plane or 'copter, if I was 'going that way'.

Oil moguls are accepted as paying guests; and like me must share a bedroom as necessary, and make their own beds – no female staff in this harsh wilderness environment. It seems that anyone connected with a project that will benefit Uncle Sam's business or scientific knowledge, for war or peace, is welcome.

Unfortunately the whole area around NARL is a chaos of discarded military and associated machinery, rusting barrels, pipes, miles of old wire, damaged coils of electric circuitry, boxes and bags split open. The 'city' of Barrow is no better. You must pick your way through paths bordered with middens of tin cans, polythene, discarded paper, dogshit – and worse.

'Quite disgusting,' agreed Thomas Brower over coffee in his tidy Browerville house and emporium overlooking the sea, with dozens of Eskimo kayaks and small boats on the beach, and some decked fishing boats anchored close-to. 'In father's day there was far less litter about, for the old Inupiat had virtually no inorganic refuse. They lived by the fur and flesh and feathers of their hunting, and any organic scraps were cleaned-up by the hungry sled dogs. But you should be here in winter, when all is hidden, even the sea, under the white beauty of snow and ice. That is the time we go visiting, and enjoy singing and dancing in traditional style. There's seal and bear and caribou meat in plenty, and the stored red flesh of the great bowhead whales, and frozen fish and sea-birds. Every genuine Inupiat family has cached away a ton or so of these main foods in the natural deep-freeze cellar dug in the permafrost a foot below ground level.'

For me the open tundra under the 24-hour day of continuous sunlight called irresistibly. On my long walks it glittered with bird calls and wings and low-growing rosettes of bright flowers. Thousands of wading birds were already feeding their precocious dappled downy young, although remnants of winter ice still floated on the water of numerous ponds and shallow lakes of this low flat peninsula. Despite the sunlight the sea air was cool, said to rise rarely above seven degrees Celsius.

I was amazed to see snow bunting, godwit, sandpiper and other long-legged waders apparently feeding on snow and ice. The reason was plain on closer inspection: they were actually feeding on layers of insects, seeds and berries, which, plentifully produced during last summer and early autumn, had been frozen under the first layers of winter ice, and so preserved in cold store. Layer by layer, as the sun thawed this manna just now, they could enjoy the still succulent insects and seeds sandwiched between. What is remarkable is that if the birds fail to devour some of these insects, seeds and berries, these can revive from deep freeze, and live to multiply again. They are not dead, and in the case of the insects, the tiny spark of life within, like the deep-frozen semen of some mammals (notably a stud bull), is able to survive intense frost and hibernate, apparently without heartbeat or breathing, in a way we do not understand.

A few days later the gold-braided Naval Officer in charge of NARL requested my attendance at his sanctum. Politely he demanded to know why I had entered his establishment and enjoyed its facilities without presenting my credentials. I apologised, explaining that I had been kidnapped at the airport by Jumper Bitters.

'Ah!' said the NOIC, with a smile that developed into a hearty laugh. 'Expediter Jumper! The old devil! But we have to put up with his Kiwi ways, can't do without him, he practically runs this joint! Anyway, reckon he thought you important enough to be given the VIP treatment . . .'

And much more was said over the inevitable cup of coffee, when I explained that I was just a lone curious naturalist enjoying the splendid wildlife of the Arctic tundra for the first time. He got me to fill in a NARL form with such credentials as I could think up, and said I could remain one more night . . . 'but we sure are a bit overcrowded just now.'

I was very willing to leave my room to the blissful snoring of two oil executives early next morning, pay my bill, and, on Thomas Brower's advice, proceed to a remote island in the Bering Sea where lived some of the last pure-blood Eskimos.

'I'll signal a genuine Eskimo elder there, the hunter Vernon Slovooko, to put you up. To get there take the plane to Fairbanks, and thence one to Nome, where a smaller one will fly you to Gambell, the only landing strip on St Lawrence.'

What courtesy and kindness! I shook hands with this gentleman of the smooth face typical of the half-caste Eskimo he was. He shrugged off my profuse thanks, saying I was welcome to ask for his help at any time, and gave me his card. This informed me that Thomas Paneahtak Brower is President of the Cape Smythe Whaling and Trading Company, established 1886.

'I am adviser to the International Whaling Commission, which wishes to prohibit the taking of the bowhead whale which they say is approaching extinction. Not true, I tell them, and I ought to know, having hunted them in umiaks since I was old enough to stand upright. They are still common in the Beaufort Sea nearest the northernmost Canadian Arctic islands. The largest my father and I ever harpooned was a female nearly 60 feet long. They are taken by Inupiat hunters as they migrate south in autumn before the Beaufort is frozen solid. I told the IWC whale meat is essential food for isolated Inupiat Eskimo communities. But they only allocated eight whales for slaughter this year. One has just been taken and cut up at Gambell on St Lawrence.'

Nome proved to be a former goldrush town, now a good deal decayed. It was 10 pm when I turned in at the Nugget Hotel ($62, b & b). Signs of the goldrush glory were apparent in a tatty double bed bathroom suite I was ushered into. Nome is now devoted to tourism, a decently kept town, no rubbish in the streets, and proud of the oldest newspaper in Alaska – the *Nome Nugget*, first published in 1901. Too many drinking saloons today, and alcohol at prohibitive price (for me) – the result I was told of the big oil compensation handout to all Alaskan residents, but sensibly controlled through selected corporations. That of Nome has set up a meat-cannery at Golovin Bay on Seward Peninsula where some 130,000 reindeer graze and provide a useful source of employment and profit.

At 09.00 hours next day I was flying above the Bering Sea, at 4,500 feet through low wisps of cloud above an almost calm sea. A six-seater plane, with four other men passengers, Indian hunters of caribou, seal and other Eskimo prey, on holiday to St Lawrence – so the white pilot informs me.

The pilot is very young. As he invites me to take the seat beside him, he warns me not to smoke. All the same, as soon as we are airborne he automatically lights a cigarette. He points out the instruments, lets me hold the co-pilot's joystick briefly. Airspeed is 155 mph, the distance is 170 nautical miles. 'These little machines carry no radar, depend on chronometer, compass and directional radio beacon signals, dead reckoning and sight. Which means we have to carry enough fuel to be sure of getting back if we can't find Gambell.'

The island was plain enough in increasing sunlight – a long bulging shape like a sleeping woman wearing a mantle of snow, reaching to the sea in places, except at the north end where the village of Gambell stood starkly naked with its wooden box houses and gaunt tall frames hung with red strips of meat curing in the sun and wind. We bumped to a stop on a narrow airstrip above a gravel beach.

Two or three villagers met the plane, and while the luggage and mail was being sorted, I was accosted by a genial talkative Eskimo I believed must be Slovooko, my recommended host. He had limited English but was abundantly hospitable, inviting me to climb into the back-saddle of his Honda motor-tricycle. He seemed to be in a great hurry, and chattered in broken English as I clung to his rotund anoraked body.

'You belong Kiwi tribe? I bin Australia. We Yupik top hunters. Put in special Marine Commando Corps fight Japs in Yankee war. I wounded Guadalcanal. Great fighters, them Japs – gotta admire 'em. I wounded, sent 'ospital Wellington – big Australia port, yes? Very nice strong beer . . .'

In a few minutes we arrived at his somewhat ramshackle cottage, a gift from Uncle Sam, complete inside with TV (non-functioning), bathroom-loo (no water – it freezes too easily), and other evidence of useful and useless modern status symbols I was to encounter in other Eskimo homes.

Inside the door were two wooden tables, one loaded with bottles of bourbon whisky and the other with soft drinks, sweets and chocolate. 'For the children,' explained my hospitable host. 'You like drop o' bourbon?' Without waiting for my reply he filled two teacups and motioned me to sit on a wide dilapidated sofa with him. It was to be my bed or sleeping couch for the rest of my sojourn in Gambell.

He told me his Yupik name was Aningayou. 'You name Ronal'? OK. You call me Winnie James – more easy, yes? When I go join Commando Corps, recruitin' sargun ask my name. 'E roll 'is eyes, say no unnerstan' Yupik. 'E say "OK. I write down near-enough English for you name. I write Winfred James – name o' me girl friend. Nice name," 'e says. So white man call me Winnie James.'

When I mentioned Slovooko he looked grave for a moment, took another gulp of bourbon and said rather scornfully: 'I am strong 'unter, better than 'im! [giving Slovooko's full Yupik name, impossible to reproduce here] I no charge dollars like 'im. 'E keeps boardin' 'ouse. You my guest, pay nothin'. I ver' rich man, worth hunner thousan' dollars.'

He offered me another cup of bourbon, but did not drink the second he had poured for himself. Perhaps because at that moment his wife walked in, a stocky plump matron with a seamy weathered face, which was yet beautiful from the kindly look in her slanted Yupik eyes. She bowed politely to me, and immediately began to cook *muktak* (seal or whale meat), fried in its own blood – a dish I found delicious, like a tenderised beefsteak. But I was hungry. So was she. With some of her children she had been up at dawn, digging for walrus ivory in ancient middens.

Curious neighbours were crowding in, all wearing modern Yupik summer dress – fur cap, fur-lined anorak and jeans, feet encased in knee-length rubber boots. As Kulukhon spoke good English, I got her to write the names of her family in my diary. She explained that English names were given to children when they entered school – a Yankee custom, although Yupik remains the language spoken between Gambell Eskimos at home: Under Kulukhon (Anna) she wrote:

Winfred Aningayou James, husband
Ugalog – Dennis
Urregu – Winfred Jun. (a professional ivory carver)
Tutemquilngoug – Elsie
Annalonggha – Gloire
Nuut – April

A fourth daughter's name was indecipherable, English name Veronica. Dennis added the names of his children: Kassa – Ila; Aghven – Joel; Uukaaghhnil – Junior; Uulagi – Tami.

A youth from the only other inhabited St Lawrence village, Savornga, inserted his name – Horace Akeya. It seems he was courting one of Aningayou's pretty daughters.

A fine quiverful of a family. None of the younger generation seemed to go to bed during the midnight daylight in this high latitude. As I lay on my sofa couch in the living-room, the young people were ceaselessly visiting from house to house, snacking, smoking, giggling, gossiping, one playing a melodeon, having a thoroughly sociable time, sitting on the floor, even on the edge of the sofa (I of course pretended to be fast asleep enough to let out a gentle snore, fearful I might be intruding on their fun, but with one eye not quite shut). The talk was all in Yupik, not one word comprehended by me. I was glad when from time to time the chattering laughing youngsters abandoned me, and I could sleep.

Mother Kulukhon drank less bourbon than Aningayou, who was befuddled and half asleep by midnight, when he was shoved and belaboured up the ladder to the loft bedroom by his wife, as if he was a naughty older son. Both were soon snoring.

Now that the snows of the long winter had melted, the main excitement – and no wonder – is digging for walrus ivory. The ancient middens of both existing villages are being mined feverishly with pick and shovel, as well as those of long-abandoned settlements miles distant along the shore. Walrus tusk, fresh, white and maybe only a few hundred years old fetches around $50 a pound. Fossil and semi-fossil tusk, iron-hard and golden in colour, is worth double.

Sometimes mammoth ivory is uncovered, relic of the glacial period when the island was part of the land-bridge joining Siberia with Alaska. Urregu, who has a separate hut where he carves exquisite

walrus tusk ivory miniatures of Arctic animals, showed me one of a
polar bear with a seal in its jaws – it was for sale at $500. I coveted
but could not afford it.

'No matter,' said he, 'I sure can't sell it for less. The New York
merchants come to Gambell each spring and buy up all the good
carvings at around that fee. But perhaps you'd like this walrus penial
bone – they sell for $100 just now.'

Bone from freshly-killed walrus and whale is of much less value
than tusk ivory. As I was leaving his studio, which I enjoyed visiting
for a chat with this educated man (it was also warm on dull, cool
days), Urregu said he would carve me a sea-otter out of a spare length
of old walrus ivory. This he did within one day, but refused my offer
to pay for it. I have it on my desk as I write, a graceful miniature of the
long-bodied, thick-tailed sea-otter now rare in the Bering Sea. I am
sure he could have sold it for $100. Before I left St Lawrence I sent
him a $50 note by the hand of his sister Nuut – or perhaps it was
Annalonggha (Gloire)? To me the sisters were like pretty peas in a
pod.

I began to realise that happy-go-lucky Winfred James was probably as rich as he boasted. His attitude to his material wealth was
typical of Eskimo men. When a Honda motor-tricycle, or an outboard engine or skidoo (motorised sledge) broke down it would be
taken to bits; and the bits usually left – when more interesting events
intervened; the mishap would be forgotten, there was always a new
machine to be bought at the central store. Eskimo villages are littered
with abandoned machinery and household throwaways, hideously
revealed when winter snow melts.

I made my apologies to Slovooko, who proved to be a gentle soul,
agent for the air company, collector of mails, and owner of a
bunkhouse for tourists. He shrugged his shoulders amicably, saying
that he should have apologised to me for failing to pick me up at the
airport, 'but I had to pick up the mail. I don't mind in the least that
Winfred James got to you first, he is a most hospitable man, perhaps
too impulsive.'

In further visits to Slovooko's house and hostel I was glad that I
had been snatched up by Winfred James and taken into the bosom of
his interesting family, rather than to the Slovooko hostel, which was
somewhat drab and empty at the time. It was soon plain that Winfred
Aningayou James was a little jealous of Slovooko – over the matter of
the recent capture of a bowhead whale.

Slovooko took me to the site where this giant had been hauled ashore and described the occasion, as we stood together inside the great curving upper jawbones of the bowhead. They measured 6.3 metres from beak-tip to skull-socket. They had been scraped clean of meat, and the green baleen plates (normally 350 in number, each 4.5 metres long) had been taken away for drying and storing for sale. In fact nothing had been wasted; even this jawbone would be used, as of old, as part of the framework of a hut or cabin convenient to some distant hunting beach, or beside the interior swamps where wildfowl were taken during the autumn roundup of moulting swans, ducks and geese.

'I was lucky on this whalehunt,' said Slovooko. 'My umiak was first to lance this whale, I heard it blow while repairing my umiak on the beach here, so I got away first, having first raised the alarm. Aningayou was next to launch with his team, but failed to overtake me.

'Of course these bowhead are slow swimmers, never in a hurry. You can sometimes jump on their back from your umiak. They don't have a chance today, with the modern harpoon gun, fired from your shoulder. As you must know, the first man to lodge a harpoon becomes owner of the whale. That is to say, he has the choice of certain delicious entrails, liver, heart, brain. But of course by custom he must share the meat and blubber and bone with every man, woman and child who helped to bring it ashore. This female measured nearly 20 metres (65 feet) in length. It took a hundred men, women and children to haul it up here. I suppose it yielded around ten tonnes of meat. Some of it is still curing on village racks, most is underground in the permafrost cellars. I suppose a quarter of the grand old lady will have been eaten fresh, some at the usual feast celebrating the first bowhead taken this year.'

The International Whaling Commission had authorised no more than two bowheads to be taken this year at St Lawrence.

'For myself,' said Slovooko, 'I would abide by that rule, but it's ignored by some of our younger men, who ride far out to sea in pursuit of any passing whale, a trigger-happy breed of boys. I was one myself once. The only rule which is going to save the bowhead is absolute protection, impossible to enforce. As you can kill grey whales regardless as they pass on migration, an unscrupulous hunter will say he killed a bowhead by mistake.'

Slovooko and Aningayou were both proud of their umiaks built on a wooden frame covered with walrus hide, which is thick and almost hairless. Each is roomy enough to hold a dozen persons and their

utensils and weapons for hunting-expeditions after walrus, seals, sea-birds and their eggs, and taking fish on hand-lines.

Just now Winfred James was gearing up for the autumnal battue of moulting wildfowl on the interior lakes, which might involve more than one night's absence. He seemed secretive about this and did not invite me; in any case my week on the island was drawing to a close, and I wished to explore the enticing bird-thronged wilderness of tumbled cliffs along the north coast below the snow-capped central mountains. Thither he conveyed me on the back of his Honda with its broad tyres, admirably adapted to surmounting the rough gravel ridges of the foreshore, as far as the base of the cliffs. He carried his gun slung over his shoulders (a bumping nuisance to me at each jolt). He would leave me there for the day, and go inland to shoot

wildfowl, collecting me later if I had not arrived home before he did.

Thousands of burrowing and hole-nesting sea-birds occupied these screes and ice-shattered cliffs. New species to me were horned puffins, rhinoceros and other auklets wearing strange facial decorations of horns and crests; and the tiny nocturnal murrelets I tried but failed to unearth with my hands to identify them. There were lemmings popping in and out of the maze of burrows, suspicious of me until I remained perfectly still, when they resumed browsing upon the vegetation, jaws champing voraciously.

This terrain is a rock garden of unique beauty, made fertile with bird-droppings and melting snow; luxuriously-growing varieties of common wild flowers resistant to salt and wind thrive in the warmer microclimate between huge boulders multi-coloured with moss and lichen. Scurvy-grass, roseroot, coltsfoot, lousewort, dandelion, oxeye daisy, sunflower, an aromatic wormwood, white fragile anemone, low grazed grasses, and here and there the taller blue-purple spikes of monkshood, the so-called aconite which yields a poison formerly used by Eskimo and Aleutian hunters to tranquillise large sea mammals by dipping their spears in a concentrated extract.

So said Slovooko, from whom I gathered other snippets of Yupik lore and history. He spoke of the small dark lemmings of the island as 'little red rats'. They periodically swarmed, as this year, and died out to a low population early in the winter, devoured by the Arctic foxes, which bred the more numerously in a 'Lemming Year'. I found the lemmings' runs numerous, extending far up the mountain slope above the sea-bird colonies, their burrows unroofed with the melting of the snow.

Here too were snow buntings, carrying mosquitoes and other insects to feed young in nests under scattered boulders. The high screes between the deep drifts of old snow were the haunt of the turnstone, more familiar to me as a winter visitor to New Zealand, and to my native Wales.

Late in the afternoon of my second day of cliff exploration I walked back across the two miles of shingle spit, to find Aningayou fast asleep on my sofa couch. At his feet was a handsome duck he had shot. I recognised it as a Steller's eider.

As I was very hungry I woke him up. I rather expected we might have the pleasure of eating duck that evening. But he had other ideas. He removed his hunting jacket, exposing naked pink arms and a pink singlet.

'What you call a feast, yes? Kulukhon far away, gone dig tusk far away in old Yupik derelic' village. I good cook, show you . . .'

In the next half-hour Winfred Aningayou laid on a wonderful meal. Assisted by a cup of bourbon at his elbow, he broiled on the stove (bottled gas) a delicious steak of tenderised grey whale meat, stirring in rice. This was followed by *Australian* grapes, seedless and fresh. He explained that the mail plane had landed with the usual weekend groceries and other supplies ordered from Nome.

His eldest son, the carver Urregu, joined in this feast, and presently some of his daughters came in. They had been digging for ivory nearer home. They too were hungry, and the grey whale steak having been eaten by the men, they set about their own supper – imported chicken from the cold store, garnished with rice and herbs.

There is no school during the midsummer months, a long-standing provision enabling the children to help in gathering the winter store of food. But at Gambell it is more profitable for them to dig for ivory.

They sat, mostly on the floor, eating their dinner from plates in their laps. Aningayou and Urregu joined in an argument I could not understand. But part of it Urregu translated:

'My sisters are angry with the old man for drinking whisky almost non-stop. Did you notice how Elsie has been quietly watering the bourbon when Winfred asks her for another cup? Good for her. But she does it out of love for her dear pappa. She hates alcohol – the bane of Eskimo society today.'

Presently Urregu and his sisters departed, leaving Pappa and me to drowse on the sofa, Elsie first removing the cup from Aningayou's nerveless grasp.

Much later I was roused by the return of the sisters, presumably to sleep in the loft upstairs (Urregu slept in his separate studio). The girls were quarrelling over something, raising their voices, and the youngest, the pretty rosy-faced Nuut, was soon in tears – terminated by her running outside, shouting hysterically. The uproar did not wake Pappa, who was snoring, oblivious to any noises.

About 06.00 hours Winfred Aningayou woke up, yawning, went outside to pee, then put on coffee for us. While it was brewing he went up the ladder to discover who might be sleeping in the loft. Returning to hand me coffee, he said anxiously:

'Why Kulukhon not home? Think she got trouble far away in ole village, bad place in swamp. I walk-talk 'er.'

All grown Yupik carry walkie-talkie radio. I had also learned that every active person, from young school-children to grandparents, possessed their own Honda tricycle. And most families have several snowmobiles, for winter transport.

There was no reply from Kulukhon to her husband's several efforts to walk-talk his wife. He shrugged his shoulders, still clearly anxious:

'Think she on way 'ome, yes? It's Sunday, she not miss church, you bet!'

When Urregu came in for coffee I asked him why Nuut was so upset last night. He said dryly that it was over something her sweetheart from Savornga, Horace Akeya, had, or had not, done. 'Poor darling little Nuut, she thinks the world is coming to an end if she doesn't get her own way!'

Virginia, the white spouse of the white priest – both have strong Yankee accents – had invited me to attend the eleven o'clock morning service in the corrugated-iron-clad Presbyterian church. I estimated about forty Yupik villagers present, with a few miscellaneous whites or half-breeds. Older people were wearing dark clothes, younger were in brighter modern 'best jackets'; all were bare-headed – the church was centrally overheated.

The parson gave a short sermon. He called out two young Yupik girls to read the Lesson in turn, which they did shyly, prettily I thought, in English at the lectern beneath the one stained-glass window. One woman carried two sleeping babies, one in her hood, the other in her arms.

Meanwhile, without a word to me, Aningayou had gone off to look for his wife, but carrying his gun to shoot the odd wildfowl. Urregu fried a couple of hamburgers for our lunch, and promised seal muktak for my last meal tonight, in case his mother did not return. 'Momma is daft about ivory digging, but also I know she likes to get away from the family . . .'

In the afternoon I walked alone on the other coast, following the motor-tricycle tracks through a well-worn route leading to the distant lakes famous in ornithological literature for a huge population of emperor and snow geese. Vernon Slovooko, shaking my hand in farewell, said he was about to join the annual shooting-expedition lasting three to five days.

No time for me to walk so far, but I was happy to botanise and watch birds that afternoon in the low swampy habitat, where godwit, golden plover, redpoll, turnstone, semi-palmated sandpiper were feeding fledged young among low-growing Arctic willow, cotton-grass, cowberry, a dwarf pink, etc.

Back at the house Aningayou had not returned. I never saw him again, or his wife. For one thing I wanted to thank them for their wonderful hospitality, and pay for it. But Urregu, cooking our muktak supper at 9 pm, said his parents would never accept cash, it was an honour to have a Kiwi-Welsh naturalist to stay.

At that moment the eldest daughter came in. She took over the cooking, serving orange juice and biscuits as a first course while the seal meat was unfreezing and cooking in the frypan. She said she had brought home five kilograms of good ivory from a new midden near Savornga assisted by Horace Akeya.

When Horace Akeya joined us over the delicious muktak, I wondered where Nuut (April) was. Was not Horace her sweetheart? And where were the other sisters – Sally, Veronica, Gloire? I was confused by the comings and goings of this delightful Yupik family. Apparently they were supping with relatives and friends elsewhere.

As I don't care for whisky, my head was perfectly clear that evening, to enjoy the good English spoken by Urregu and his sister Elsie with the impossibly long name which I got her to write down again – Tutemquilngoug.

Elsie revealed a sweet, caring nature towards her family, constantly smiling as she talked. The seal meat was just a trifle tough, I thought, but went down well with canned potato and corn. They were curious about New Zealand, and envious of my lone wandering that had brought me to their remote island, which lies forty miles nearer to Siberia than to Alaska, Urregu said, measuring the distance on a map.

Urregu declared he was not a hunter by inclination. He was a great reader. He wore glasses, was short-sighted. He had ridden on dog-sledges with his grandfather, '. . . far out over the winter ice, when the polar bears come down from the frozen Arctic following the seals and beluga. My grandad loved to shoot all three, and trap the silver foxes which follow the bears for the sake of their leavings and dung.

'But the iron-dog – the snowmobile skidoo – is nohow good to smell out and avoid a crevasse or tide-crack like the husky team grandad hunted with. Did Pappa Winfred tell you of his adventure when, far out to the north, hunting bear and beluga and seal, his benzine gave out, and he would have perished if he had not kept his matches dry, and knew how to build an ice-shelter over his skidoo, and light a bottle-gas stove to keep him from freezing? Poor Pappa had broken a leg in extricating himself and the skidoo from a hidden tide-crack.

'He was very lucky that his battery in his walkie-talkie was strong enough to keep calling for help. He could never have walked so many miles back to Gambell. The rule is never to leave your vehicle when it breaks down so far from home. But Pappa is a loner. He is too impulsive and headstrong.'

Islands of the Fur Seals

In the long ago when history was recorded in song, Igadik, a great hunter of whale and seal, was storm-driven in his fine large kayak from his home island of Unimak in the long Aleutian chain which encloses the chill waters of the Bering Sea.

During the fog which ended the storm he heard the cries of millions of fur seals. Paddling in that direction, he discovered islands so packed with them that he had great difficulty in finding space to pull his kayak ashore.

Many moons later Igadik loaded all the skins he could carry in his kayak and returned south before a favourable north wind.

The story of his discovery of Amiq, as he called the seal islands, is celebrated in the folksongs of the Aleutian people. They kept its location secret although they seldom visited there because of the long voyage over the misty sea.

These people of the Western Aleutian islands are said to have originated as an offshoot of the 'Hairy Ainu' tribe of Hokkaido, the northernmost island of Japan, whom they resemble in their physiognomy, hairiness, dialect and habits of acupuncture, massage, and use of herb medicines and poisons.

The oldest Aleut I met in Amiq (now known as the Pribilof Islands) shrank back when I brought to his house a bouquet of the handsome purple-cowled monkshood flowers I had plucked from the wild cliff gardens which make these fur seal islands enchanting with colour in the brief sub-Arctic summer.

'If one drop of juice from those plants gets into a cut in your flesh, you're a dead man!' he exclaimed in a mixture of Yankee English and Russian overtones. 'As a boy born in the westward Aleutians I heard my grandfather tell how he hunted the big sea-mammals with lances dipped in a mixture of the root-juice of that plant and putrid flesh. When attacking a small beast like a sea-otter or harbour seal a float was attached to the lance so that it could be followed when it dived. It soon died from the poison.

'But it was much harder to kill the great bowhead and grey whales – they took much longer to die, and were too dangerous to follow. As soon as one or two poisoned lances had been struck home the kayakman fled to escape the monster's wrath. From the shore the hunter watched and waited, perhaps for several days, for the whale to sicken and be washed ashore. Then there would be great rejoicing in the village, and the proud hunter, claiming the whale by his mark on the lance in its body, would by custom have the first pick of the meat and bone; the rest he would share with every family.'

Hunter Mikaelof had been a baby when his parents were transported from the Aleutians to the Pribilofs to make up a population dwindling under the harsh rule of enforced labour, imposed first by the Russian, and then by the American, fur-traders.

He had an Aleut name which he had almost forgotten. On arrival he had been baptised by the Russian priest. The only good the century-long Russian occupation of the islands seems to have achieved was the conversion of the pagan natives to the Orthodox faith. The priests gave Christian comfort to the living, in place of the ancient (Siberian) shamanism of Aleutia, and Christian burial to the hundreds that died of white man's diseases – smallpox, tuberculosis, influenza, venereal infection. In the century of Russian exploitation the Aleutians dwindled from some 18,000 to 4360 by 1867, in which year Uncle Sam bought the whole of Alaska from Russia.

'Grandpa said they died so fast here on Amiq the survivors could hardly dig their graves, let alone mark them with crosses,' said

Mikaelof. He waved his hand towards the cemetery outside his village on St Paul Island.

'A few driftwood crosses and a few wild flowers are all the poor souls get even today.'

I had enjoyed walking in the neglected cemetery, collecting the midsummer wild flowers amid the few recent crosses – monkshood, a vivid pink and purple lousewort, yellow poppies, all twice as luxuriant as those of St Lawrence Island much farther north in the Bering Sea. This luxuriance is said to be the result of untold centuries of sole occupation by the fur seals covering the whole plateau of St Paul, the soil being a fertile volcanic red. No trees can grow in this ever-windy place, but hardy finches sing and nest – snow and Lapland buntings, grey-crowned rose finch and a grass sparrow.

Mikaelof recalled: 'My father used to say we were better off in the Pribilofs than in his home island of Adak in Aleutia. For here we at least had enough to eat – seal, seabirds and fish. But the sea-otter, walrus and whales had all been exterminated by our people, driven by the Russian bosses planted by the fur-traders. It was pure slavery, and it was not much better under the American fur-traders when Uncle Sam bought Alaska in 1867. In fact it was worse.

'Why, even in the last war we here on St Paul were herded about like animals, and after Pearl Harbor we were evacuated to the mainland and forbidden to leave the miserable draughty wooden huts we were thrown into.'

Mikaelof had retired on an old age pension, and told me he was writing up the history of the Pribilofs, which he delighted to expound. Apart from the tradition of the kayakman Igadik, the written history begins with the Russian explorer-navigator Gerassium Pribylov coming on the islands (now named after him) when seeking new grounds for fur-traders in 1776. 'In a dense fog his bowsprit touched the rocks, and when the mist lifted the shores glowed golden with thousands of fur seals, sea-otters and walrus.'

To protect this remarkable harvest of furs and ivory, Russian fur-traders planted a garrison of young Aleuts collected from the over-exploited chain southwards, 'promising them 40 cents a skin, or the equivalent in Russian goods and liquor. But took care to imprison them on St Paul without boats.' The new settlers could have survived and even prospered by their natural hunting skill. They built their own homes in the traditional Aleutian style, large barn-like dwellings for each extended family, with turf walls and roof supported on baulks of driftwood, thatched with grass and mud, half well below ground level, warm and weatherproof.

However, the greedy Russian overseers made sure that they remained in debt by building for each family a small wooden house above ground, bitterly cold and draughty in winter, for which they charged a rent. If they refused to work for the fur company they could be dispossessed and forbidden to take seals for food. Their dogs had been forbidden and killed on the excuse that these animals interfered with the peaceful breeding of the fur seals. No guns were allowed.

Catherine the Great of Russia had established a monopoly of this Alaska fur trade, of which the sea-otter was considered the most expensive and exclusive fashion at that period of the eighteenth century. Captain James Cook on his last voyage to the Pacific in 1778 described the Aleutians as 'dirty, but good-looking. As to honesty, they might serve as a pattern to the most civilised nation on earth.' We may note here that Cook and his crews in the *Resolution* and *Discovery*, during the exploration of the Bering Sea and passage through the Bering Strait to the Arctic Ocean, took every opportunity to acquire by barter from the inhabitants of those coasts the cured skins of seals, bears and sea-otters, which they sold at a vast profit in China on the way home.

When the Russian company's lease lapsed in 1864, Tsar Alexander, hearing of the traders' brutal treatment of the Aleutian tribes, hesitated to renew it. He was a humane man and in difficulties with war in the Crimea and other fronts.

At this juncture an enterprising San Francisco businessman interested in the fur trade of the whole of Alaska offered the Tsar $5 million cash down.

Seward's name is perpetuated in the vast Seward Peninsula on Alaska's west coast, now largely a profitable reindeer ranch.

It was a marvellous investment for Uncle Sam. Subsequently the private profits of the fur-seal production of the Pribilofs during the lease held by the Hutchinson Company of the USA, added to the revenue levied by the Government, amounted within ten years to the total figure paid to Russia for the whole of Alaska. Yet the islanders continued to be paid low wages and were not allowed to vote in elections or leave home. At that time US law regarded Indian and Eskimo as inferior citizens, in effect supporting the Hutchinson Company's monopoly of the fur-seal skins and control of the islanders who produced them.

'Yes,' said Mikaelof, 'it was almost total bondage under virtual prison conditions. By 1887 the population was down to 233, and eighteen of these died in that year. The statistics for that year showed that the Aleutian community, which by custom shared its wages among all, received only $40,000 from the Company (about $170 per head). But the fur-traders made a clear profit of $1 million and in addition the Federal Government collected $300,000 in dues that year. By my calculation the islanders received only one thirty-third of the receipts of their labour of slaughtering, skinning and dressing the skins of the fur-seals for export – at that time London was the main market for seal fur.

'But at least, once Uncle Sam became the sole proprietor and exploiter of the islands, we were treated a little more humanely; no longer were the overseers allowed to ravish our daughters and young wives employed as servants in their luxurious homes.'

Despite the island's history of long servitude to greedy Russian overlords, Mikaelof preferred his Russian name to the vulgar 'Mike' used by his mates of the fur-processing factory. He was a quiet, gentlemanly person, who spoke Russian fluently, taught by the Russian priest, who still presides over the spiritual welfare of the Pribilof islanders.

This priest showed us the ornate beauty of his church, a golden temple glowing with its icons, altars and gilded ceiling. From the pulpit he lectured us (including a few non-resident tourists): 'Everyone in our church must stand or kneel. There are no comfortable pews. Christ had to walk or kneel on his way to his Crucifixion. We must follow him humbly.'

His concluding remarks after the benediction surprised me: 'Please, all of you, come and have dinner at my house. Follow me. Nothing is above $5.25, I promise you.'

Very good it was too, at the price – fish pie of halibut, fresh-caught, or pan-fried fur-seal steak (which I did not fancy); and home-made tart of wild cranberry, all prepared by stout, bustling Pribilof women helpers.

In his role of café-keeper, a very different pastor emerged, clocking up our dollars in his cash register with a beaming smile. The café was much patronised by the residents, despite the fact that they had their own government-built, co-operatively run restaurant and hostel elsewhere. The food I sampled there seemed less glamorous, on self-service lines – lacking the warmth and geniality of pastoral prestige?

Mikaelof, a devout member of the Orthodox Church, had been noted in his youth for his skill in killing the seals.

'Looking back now, as an old man,' he sighed, 'it seems strange that I was so eager and proud that my first blow with the cudgel always broke the skull.' He remembered how hard he had practised on a football jerked about on a string by his father, 'for the seal is forever swaying his head around when you approach it. I must have killed over a hundred thousand as a young man. But not so many years ago, I had several bad misses and knew I must give up. You need the keen eye and muscle of young manhood. I will take you to the killing tomorrow. You will see how it is done by our young experts. It is well paid, so long as you kill with one blow of the long bat.'

The Pribilof islands of St Paul and St George are said to form the largest fur-seal rookeries in the world, estimated at several million head before the exploitation began a century ago.

All is changed today. In place of the indiscriminate slaughter of the herds lasting to 1910, said Manager Dick to me and a couple of US visitors invited to tour the processing factory, the seal population is stabilised at approximately 1,250,000 due to the policy of killing only surplus young non-breeding males, but also because of the development of offshore (pelagic) hunting of the seals by the schooners of other nations, notably Japan, Canada and Britain, chiefly in ex-whaling vessels. The latter harvest was extremely wasteful, for a lanced or shot seal invariably sank. The American Government countered by sending armed Coastguard cutters to arrest the poachers, who nevertheless often got away in the almost perpetual fog which covers the islands in the midsummer breeding season. Some of the poachers were equally armed, and at intervals sent raiding parties to loot the St Paul factory of its store of skins.

Although at the present time this pelagic killing in the Bering Sea is much reduced, by a treaty signed by Russia and Japan by which these two nations are given a small proportion of the total skins harvested at St Paul, or the equivalent value, there is now a considerable new threat to the survival of seals offshore. They become entangled and drown in the fishing nets of a now numerous fleet of many nations exploiting the rich fishing grounds. This was soon evident to me on studying the breeding beaches on St Paul, and finding some of the bulls and cows carrying the evidence – segments of nets draped about their necks and shoulders, seriously hampering their efforts to indulge their normal social life of mating and suckling their pups. Many more must have been drowned.

July is the time to kill what is now considered to be a sustainable yield of 30,000 to 40,000 males annually. It was a long walk by dirt tracks to reach the killing field on Wednesday, July 26, having been granted a permit to do so because Dick wished to prove that the slaughter was done as humanely as possible, and I was allowed to take photographs provided I stood well clear of the action.

First of all a gang of younger islanders was sent to that portion of the main breeding beach where the immature males assemble, on the outskirts of the main herd; the latter consists of groups comprising a master bull and the harem of cows and their pups which he has gathered around him.

Young islanders (of both sexes) carry 4-litre tin cans attached to long wooden poles. Rattling these, they scare the young males and drive them inland, over a flowery heath to a flat area where small groups of a dozen or so seals are separated from the main muster. As no dogs exist on the island, the young tin-rattlers must act as a sheepdog does in helping to sort out each small batch. This requires some experience of detecting and releasing the odd immature females, which can look very like males of the same age – although the male head and shoulders are larger. The adult female fur seal is less than one quarter the size of the full-grown master bull.

The time-honoured plan is to harvest the majority of these young males, which are surplus and a nuisance if allowed to mature. A master bull can inseminate up to a hundred cows in the breeding season of about two months of midsummer, and does so the more easily if the competition from other bulls is thus reduced.

Each batch of selected young males is coaxed and scared by way of the poles and noisy rattles, until it is ushered into the arena of smooth ground, where the killing gang of half a dozen trained men await their chance to make a lethal blow to the head of the nearest seal. This stunning-weapon is a five-foot-long rounded stick – like an elongated baseball bat.

Dick informed us that the stunners, robust men aged between twenty and forty years, are highly-paid, earning between eight and twelve dollars an hour, according to their accuracy in landing a first killing blow – not easy because the alarmed victims keep swaying their heads from side to side, rolling their bold eyes to seek an avenue of escape; but the tin-can herders keep up the pressure.

Why not herd them into corrals? 'Because they would fight each other and damage their much-prized young skins,' said the foreman supervising the operation. Generally the stunning was successful the first time, and the seal slumped to the ground with scarcely a quiver of its long limbs. The object was to smash the skull in one blow; if this failed – the blow glancing off slightly – a second was necessary.

Meanwhile a second batch of a dozen or so young bulls was waiting a little distance off, detached from the main muster nearer the beach. The foreman whistled this batch to approach, and the pole men moved accordingly.

Each felled seal was inspected to make sure it was dead before a party of expert skinners moved in. These dealt with the carcase expeditiously, opening the body with a sharp knife from the neck to the lower belly. With special tongs to take a firm grip on the neck skin, one man in front and one behind, a third man pronging the neck to the ground with a two-tined fork, the tongs holder stripped the pelt neatly and cleanly away from the carcase – in two seconds flat – by a vigorous tug.

A visiting biologist examined most of the naked raw red bodies, looking for parasites, he said. He also said that at present there was no sale for the flesh.

'Quite good eating – if you pick a really young one. The males taste rather strong from about four years onwards. Normally they are sold to the Japs, probably to be processed as pet food. But this year the Japs haven't turned up.'

He talked later of his work, reporting on the health of the herd. He had found some infestation of lung and tapeworms . . . 'all marine mammals have them in some degree.'

Milk was oozing from the teats of one carcase – a young pregnant or lactating cow had been killed in mistake for a male. After she was skinned the foreman marked her with a white ribbon, for separate treatment at the processing factory.

It was a sunlit day, rare in this misty climate, and I was eager to prowl around the whole island in search of birds and flowers. I did not linger long on this blood-spattered slaughter meadow. Just long enough to interrogate some small boys who were moving from one carcase to another, each carrying a pocket knife and a half-gallon tin. They were cutting off the genitalia of the butchered bulls. English is now the spoken language on the island, and in a few minutes the most articulate of the five-year-olds had explained haltingly that they were allowed to collect these grisly scraps which, when dried or frozen, could be sold at a useful price as an aphrodisiac to buyers in Japan, China, Korea and Hong Kong.

Next day at breakfast at the hostel, the American scientist ate an enormous plateful of syrup flapjacks, and put jam into his boiled egg, and declared himself ready to accompany me on a tour of the cliffs, having ascertained I was knowledgeable about sea-birds. We were joined by a young man from Greenpeace, who had come to study the seal-harvesting and told us it seemed reasonably humane, but it did pose some ethical and other problems.

It was sunlit and beautiful out there on St Paul's highest cliffs, up to 400 feet above the sea. Aggregations of both common and thick-billed murres (guillemots) crowded in the broken rocks at the top of the cliffs, taking little notice of us as they brought little fishes to their half-grown chicks. In burrows below there was a vast coming and going of tufted and horned puffins, and a few least and crested auklets. Red-billed cormorants craned their necks upwards at us from seaweed nests on the ledges, and I had clear views for the first time of North Pacific fulmar petrels (browner on the wings than Atlantic fulmars) and red-legged kittiwakes. At the foot of this cliff, as the tide ebbed, red-coloured foxes now and then trotted along the sand, probably waiting to snatch up fledgeling sea-birds accidentally tumbled from the cliffs. They are scavengers of all flesh, and in the summer feed much on seal placenta and dead seal pups. They turn silver or white in winter.

The whole of the uneven plateau of the island is a wild flower garden of large pink-purple lousewort up to a foot tall, interspersed with yellow arctic poppies, white oxeye daisies, stitchwort, cinque-foil, blue lupin, silvery scurvy-grass, little blue gentians, eyebright, fronds of yarrow, and the northern marsh violet. The only really tall plants were monkshood, alexanders and dwarf willow. Lately intro-duced reindeer, few in number, had not yet had any effect on this midsummer riot of wild flora.

Now and then we almost stepped on a lone young fur seal, which had climbed high up from the sea and fallen fast asleep among tall flowers inland – probably starting its annual moult, suggested the scientist. Or was it one of those allowed to escape from the round-up and the killing as too young or female?

The Greenpeace visitor was worried that if, as now seemed possible in the near future, public opinion would compel the closure of the skin factory and the cessation of marketing fur seals at Pribilof, the seals would increase to their former maximum numbers as described by Gerassium Pribylov in 1776.

'We conservationists are succeeding in our propaganda to stamp out the trade in wild fur. At the last auction of sealskins in New York and other big cities, their value had sunk below the cost of producing them. Women are becoming ashamed of wearing animal fur, and have gone in for synthetic hair coats.'

At the factory Manager Dick confirmed that from 1978 onwards, the American Treasury, now responsible for maintaining the business, had reported an increasing loss due to costs spiralling upwards and market returns downwards.

'What Uncle Sam is going to do about that will not concern me; I'm due to retire at the end of the year. And so far, despite my warnings, the Treasury has failed to send a competent replacement I could help to train in this highly-specialised job of managing the seals from birth to death, and the final product of first-class fur.'

Pribilof women are now the principal labour in the factory, well-paid to process the new skins as they come in, scraping every bit of fat and meat from the pelt and passing it through a succession of bleaching vats, and finally a drying and storage shed. The factory is an old building no longer fully used. Part has become a museum of the early days, with try-pots for rendering whale blubber, and out-of-date flensing tools. The meat is no longer processed, even for pet food; there is no modern abattoir to keep it frozen.

'Everything is going to pot,' Dick shrugged, 'since the community, quite rightly, has been given the vote and full citizenship, and the right to elect the island council and make the rules. After the great oil strike on Alaska's North Slope the Government finally had to grant all Alaskan natives their right to ownership of their native land, and substantial compensation for exploiting the oil. I think the total figure for the whole state was close to a $1000 million. This was distributed through regional and village corporations set up for the purpose by the natives – a sound arrangement, I mean, not to give the money to individuals. Here in St Paul all the land, except the seal rookeries, was returned to the original owners or their descendants. But come to my house this evening and I will run a slide show of island life I have made.'

At the slide show, Dick told us he had got his present job as a result of research on Pacific salmon in British Columbia, ageing them by the rings on their scales.

'You can age a fur-seal in the same way by the rings inside its fangs, if you cross-section them. It is important to cull males when they are immature up to six years; this gives harem bulls about sixty females to inseminate each season, which they do very easily. If you kill a harem bull, experimentally, his territory is immediately occupied – I have timed this – in less than half-an-hour by an observant bull waiting to take his place. We normally cull up to 35,000 young bulls, about as much as the herd can stand. But in fact it is never likely to increase just now because the feeding grounds offshore are over-fished all summer by hundreds of boats from many northern Pacific nations, and this overfishing makes it much harder for the lactating cow to produce milk for her pup, or provide nourishment for the unborn foetus. And hundreds, as you have probably seen, get entangled in drift and other nets. Some break free but most of them eventually choke to death.

'Mothers and pups swim to southern California in winter, where they stay together and normally grow fat. But again there is over-fishing there, where fishermen find seals drowned in their nets. Immature bulls and cows don't travel quite so far south. The beachmaster bulls, which never feed during their two months ashore, hardly migrate at all, merely avoiding the winter ice by swimming as far south as the Aleutian Chain.'

Armed with this information I spent my last day ranging the several beach rookeries, and trying to photograph activity in a typical thick mist, getting a lift in a ramshackle car borrowed by Greenpeace. There are wooden blinds (shelters) set up conveniently on the inshore edge of the principal rookeries for the comfort of visitors and students watching the domestic scene, of loving mothers returning from sea and finding their pup, not by sight recognition but by its individual scent – a remarkable feat in a crowded rookery that stinks to heaven of their body odour and excrement. Yet the pup soon recognises his dam's whine and hungrily makes its way up and down the tumbled boulders to greet the source of nourishment. If an overhungry pup attempts to suckle an incoming mother not its own, she grabs and flings it aside.

Mating takes place a few days after parturition. It was slightly pathetic to watch an oestrous cow sniff her way to the prominent rock on which each harem bull was poised, awaiting the arrival of lady suitors. If he was asleep she might paw him awake, then crawl into his embrace – lovesick indeed to suffer what followed. With his now lean but lengthy flanks he was huge enough to bury her completely, except her head peeping from between his long fore-

flippers astride her shoulders. During the copulatory thrusts, discreetly hidden under his huge body, the lord of the harem kept his
head erect, ever watchful for a rival bull who might dare to approach
and kidnap one of his wives. An exhausting business, and in the end
the fasting beachmaster, lean and usurped, must retire too spent and
hungry to roar defiance any longer.

In the middle of each main beach there is a raised open platform
some four metres tall, accessible by ladder for counting the number
of breeding seals at the spring and summer census, or at any other
time: excellent for photographing the mass of seals from above,
although a notice forbids the visitor to enter a rookery. Other notices
warn you that seals cross the road at certain points. 'Purely for the
benefit of tourists,' said Dick somewhat sarcastically, 'now coming
in droves since the council built an airstrip.'

But my favourite place to be alone was the high cliffs apart from
the noisy, smelly rookeries. Here I could look down on the pageant of
nesting birds and wild flowers and watch the sleek seals playing,
washing and feeding in the heavy swell with great *joie de vivre*,
sometimes coming up to chase and tease an oldsquaw duck or puffin
or auklet; while still at the foot of the cliffs the red foxes ran, vainly
trying to catch wading birds such as the tattler, rock-sandpiper and
ruddy turnstone which feed on the insects and molluscs of the
seaweed zone, but nest high up on the flowered plateau.

Savai'i, Western Samoa

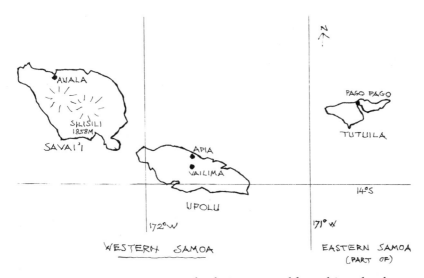

Are not young Samoans, with their rose-golden skin, the best-looking of all Polynesian people? And now, since we have lived a while there, we know that the best beauties are from the more remote western isle of Savai'i.

Someone was needed to guard the New Zealand Ornithological Society's expedition foodstores and gear while other members ranged the unexplored coast to identify sea-birds and make a scientific record. Outside the empty forest workers' lodge on stilts, far inland from the sea, the ancient lorry unloaded and departed as the swift tropical twilight faded, leaving my new home to darkness and to me.

I felt quite tranquil, rediscovering the truth of Thoreau's observation that there is no companion so companionable as solitude. I was glad to have escaped from the insistent, over-generous hospitality of the hamlet of Auala, by the sea far below, provided by the plump, smiling Reverend Amosa and his splendidly curvaceous wife, as pretty as her name, Fa'ananu, with hibiscus in her raven hair.

They had talked of their mission to teach the illiterate parish children, of how they had appealed to New Zealand firms to send more food to relieve the winter malnutrition they had found on settling here a few years earlier.

Although there is really no winter in Samoa. It was now August and the land yielded abundantly. The Amosas had fed us prodigious meals of starchy taro, roast banana, pork (scores of black piglets roamed the hamlet), land crab (tasty claws), yam, rice, washed down with home-grown coffee and the somewhat intoxicating *kvass*, ceremonially presented in a half-coconut shell. I had felt myself laying up fat.

But as he placidly strummed the guitar after each meal (*Silent Night, Lili Marlene, While the Moon her Watch is Keeping* were his agreeable favourites), Mr Amosa said it was essential for Savai'ians to get fat . . . 'it's an insurance against hard times when crops dry up, even get burned down, in our dry waterless summer.'

Even when rain falls it immediately sinks into the lava and pumice of this volcanic island. The sole permanent fresh water in Auala is a spring which issues on the beach, accessible only at low tide. Up in the high inland forest conditions are moister, although I noted that there is only roof water to drink, and an artificial reservoir of polythene behind the lodge to collect the dew and scant rain for the tree-nursery close by.

I was not entirely alone that night, after the graceful white-rumped swiftlets which had so obligingly devoured mosquitoes late into the dusk had departed in a squeaking cloud to roost in distant sea caves. There was a buzz of nocturnal cicadas. When I lit the hurricane lantern I could watch geckos walking upside down on the ceiling, deftly snapping up moths and other insects attracted to the light.

I made coffee and sat on the veranda. Rats – the tame little Polynesian *Rattus exulans* – scuttled across the lane, to scavenge food-scraps left by the day-workers in the tree-propagation shelters.

Suddenly an unearthly shriek rang out, followed by a ghostly form floating past, chilling my blood until I recognised a white owl on noiseless wing, usefully hunting the rats.

When presently real footsteps stealthily approaching alerted me, I picked up a broken balcony rail. I had been warned that pilferers might want to investigate our stores. Among tribal people, such as the Samoans and Maoris, what's yours is mine is a good Christian rule for sharing; however, stealing ought to be done publicly – so that you can steal back in return.

The soft-footed intruder revealed under torchlight halted, and mumbled a greeting. He was a night watchman, it seemed. To make

sure, I got him to record his name in my diary: a scrawling 'Hetau Pestage Hope'. He had almost no English.

He began to light a fire to cook his supper, tearing off the pages of a discarded paperback he picked up from the rubbish-bin. I rescued what was left – three-quarters of a book of short stories by Albert Wendt.

During our week's stay I was to read every one of the stories avidly, my first encounter with this 'vivid Samoan author, highly effective and libidinous story-teller' as my diary criticises; a great change from the no-less-vivid and literate Samoan stories of Robert Louis Stevenson (whose grave I had visited on the main island of Upolu). 'The Samoans are the best and gayest inhabitants of our planet,' wrote Stevenson when living, and dying, in the lovely Vailima House which the Upolu matai (chiefs) built near Apia out of gratitude for his wise help in settling their bloody feuds a century ago. And next morning I could but agree with his verdict.

At 09.30 hours two lorryloads of chattering, laughing women and children arrived. They swarmed into the bungalow for ten minutes, intensely curious to examine the Palagi (white visitor) who sat so possessively atop a huge pile of stores, trying to keep them intact. Fortunately their woman boss Lotu, hibiscus behind one ear, shooed them away to the tree nursery opposite, to their paid job potting and planting exotic saplings (teak and eucalypts) which are to replace the felled endemics.

Wendt's pen vividly depicts and forbodes the present native Samoan dilemma: 'There is no returning to island innocence.' It is the old story throughout Polynesia.

In Samoa from 1830 onwards the London Missionary Society brought Christianity to feuding tribesmen, made them cover their nakedness and attend church. Alcohol was banished and a curfew established – all young people had to be home to the *fale* (opensided house) by dusk. These rules still apply in theory today.

Years of plantations for copra export followed, chiefly under German settlers. But one New Zealander acquired 30,000 acres cheaply, which he managed (1972–77) with 'blackbirded' Micronesian labour. Happy at that time with their own self-sufficient horticulture on inherited land, the Samoans were not prepared to be indentured slaves.

Today big timber companies, mostly Australasian, have leased and clear-felled most of the tall endemic forests essential for Samoan old-time subsistence – food, firing, *fale*-building, spiritual needs – which preserved an equilibrium with the ancestral environment. The profit having been creamed off, the Palagi profiteers depart, cleverly (from their point of view) leaving it to the conscience of the protecting power (New Zealand) to help the Samoans replant, at Samoan cost.

This is called grant-aid, to be repaid by the Samoans. New Zealand Forestry Service personnel supervise this replanting, and have – of course – advised the inexperienced Samoan forest owners to plant quick-growing eucalypts, teak and pines. Unfortunately these create a greater fire-risk as they mature, killing the damp ferny understorey which is such a feature of mature tropical Samoan forest. (It is sad to record here that this replanted area of exotics of several hundred acres was burned down completely in a recent drought.)

Our party was glad of the loan of this Forest Service Nursery lodge, from which we made our forays far up beyond the tree-line to reach Savai'i's highest peak, volcanic Silisili, 1870 metres. Our main object was to try to rediscover certain rare species of birds and flowers, some of which have not been seen in this century, in particular the flightless Savai'i forest rail. We carried mistnets and sampled bird populations at all levels; we met the now rare forest thrush but decided the rail must be extinct.

There were plenty of common birds around the tree-nursery, especially the noisy honeyeaters. The competent overseer Tegania Lotu was deeply interested in us – the Palagi bird people.

On Saturday there was no work in the nursery, the villagers tended their own plantations – taro and other roots, banana, paw-paw and coca bush. But Tegania, coming to water the newly pricked-out tree seedlings, enjoyed the morning round of the mistnets with me. She was delighted when I ringed and released a wattled honeyeater, which immediately perched on her head, enabling me to get a snap photograph.

'Smiling, thoughtful, reliable brown-faced Lotu,' I wrote in my diary, 'must have been a beauty once; she is still nice-looking, with a few lines to her forehead and the typical broad rather flat Samoan nose' (our peaky European noses, she later told me, are very ugly in Polynesian eyes).

In conversation over coffee as we watched the mistnets I learned that the word Savai'i means Homeland; that the ancestors of the present Polynesians arrived from Malaysia centuries before Christ was born, sailing their large canoes, and, bypassing the hostile black tribes of Micronesia and Papua, they discovered Savai'i. From Savai'i as the Savai'ians multiplied in this beautiful island, they colonised far and wide, even to Hawaii in the north, Easter Island in the east, and last of all, New Zealand in the cool southwest.

'Since when,' Tegania Lotu chuckled merrily, 'New Zealand belongs to Samoa, not the other way round, as you Palagi like to think! We speak the same Polynesian language in all the islands, though the Maori have a rather rough accent – or dialect – to my ears. Poor devils, the Maori have a lot to put up with, such a cold climate, even in Auckland, where many friends and relatives of mine have worked. I have an aunt in Auckland, and went for a holiday with her – never again! So cold, and unhappy for us Samoans. If they stay, our young people are cut off forever from making a real home. Palagi city life destroys Samoan innocence, like Albert Wendt says.'

Towards the end of our stay in the Savai'i forest the Rev. Amosa invited us to yet another feast in his large home-built assembly hall, an open-sided building which is also the school and dance hall at Auala. Here we met a young American couple investigating 'the ancient matai system of male government of Samoa,' still operative at that moment.

'It is badly tainted with personal graft and greed, especially in Apia,' they insisted. 'If he has enough money and children a man can buy a matai-ship, entitling him to a seat on the local council, his first step to becoming a Samoan M.P.'

I turned for comment to Tegania Lotu's sister, as she squatted on the floor of the Amosa *marae* – we were all squatting here, between dances and other performing jollities of this warm-hearted Savai'ian get-together.

On my other side was a stout matron who had just made me jog with her (compulsory when Amosa announced a 'ladies' invitation-only dance'); she leaned towards me, pointing to my stomach, and laughed: 'Fine you get large fat, then you be matai. You get plenty children [she was mother of seventeen, she said]. Then children do all work, so you belong matai, you get large, fat, no more work, be lazy, make talk-talk, give orders.

'Everybody 'bliged work plantation, bring food, serve matai or husband, all same he eat first; wife she like – how you say – bottom dog? She born hard worker, she like work, matai too fat, no more health, soon die, see!'

'So? What has happened to all your children?'

'Two-three go New Zealand. Make big money Otara place, come home for holiday. Sisters help mine babies. No like Auala no more. Men like beer, motor bike, TV, cinema. Go back Otara.' (Otara is a suburb of Auckland, dominated by Samoans.)

Remote Savai'i villages were swarming with children. The country birthrate remains as high as the high fertility permits, until recently about one child each year for a married woman between the ages of twenty and thirty-six, Amosa told us. This fecundity results naturally in Polynesian people from generations of selective breeding of the most fertile women to counteract the high deathrate of the Stone Age existence two centuries ago and provide the labourers and warriors essential for survival in the competition for the limited island food supply.

Today, thanks to modern hygiene and medical care, the infant survival rate has soared. Samoa's population has quadrupled to about 150,000 within half a century. But today, alas, the outlet for surplus population is virtually closed. Polynesians who wish to obtain work and homes in New Zealand must now obtain a special work-permit. Samoa has suffered this restriction as the price of declaring complete independence as a sovereign nation.

There was a tragedy on the night before we left Savai'i. The one shopkeeper in Auala described it to me: 'Young woman in Auala lose job in Auckland, no more work permit, she come home. She get sick – what you say depressed. No work, no TV, no cinema, 'bliged sleep same home *fale* along snoring old people, father, mother, uncle. Strict matai rules. Go bed curfew time. Plenty dull prayers, God-talk.

Smelly dogs and pigs sleep under *fale* floor. Night time too long. This morning she found in sea.'

It seems the suicide rate in the remoter villages is abnormally high, the victims are those returning emigrants who cannot adjust to the strict early-Victorian religious code taught by the missionaries, and still largely enforced by the matai and clergy.

'The predicament is still the philoprogenitiveness of the matai,' said our Peace Corps student. 'Naturally the matai want large families – to increase their mana, their personal wealth. They are resisting attempts to teach contraception – the matai tell you that's a religious sin. But not all matais are selfish. A few we've talked with are genuinely anxious about the suicides, want to provide better entertainments to keep the young people in the villages, build village halls and form women's committees, plan birth control, and so on.'

Sunday. We are all obliged to our warm-hearted Rev. Amosa, who last night served kvass to us and the grown-ups of his church, and made all of us contribute to the entertainment individually. I sang part of *The Foggy Foggy Dew*, convinced that its naughty nuances would pass over the head of the Savai'ians, and having a Welsh accent as well. *Ten Men Went to Mow* was a howling success as we each fell down in turn. There were prayers at 23.00 hours, and Amosa with his seraphic baby-face smile bid us to attend without fail morning service in his fine large windowless church by the sea.

My diary records: 'All the golden-skinned ladies looked beautiful but strange in white hats and dresses. Their natural swagger as they enter would do royalty credit, carriage so upright, yet flowing

gracefully. The men wear dull black trews – a coloured lava-lava (normal wear skirt) would not be considered decent in church?

'The harmonium has a dirge-like accent. Children go in and out, play in a tidal pool in sight of the windows. A bent old man in the distance is laboriously tottering, hand on a steadying stick, to reach the thunderbox, which in Auala lies at the end of a little pier, extended above the tide. (No doubt he supposes this is an opportunity to escape notice of this advertisement of his need to perform a natural function, while the grown-ups are gazing at the altar?)

Dogs stroll in, sit awhile or scratch, wag their tails at us, and go out again. For our benefit there is a long harangue in broken English by a stout lay preacher who reminds me of a giant panda. To announce each hymn, the genial Amosa briefly appears in the pulpit, like a jack-in-the-box . . .'

Capricorn Flight, Tahiti

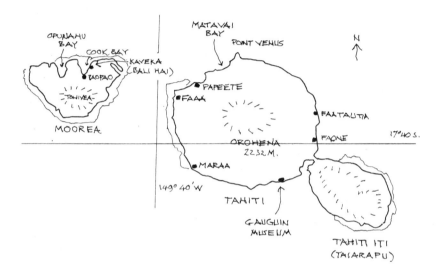

To attain the Falklands and South Georgia from my New Zealand home involved a series of flights across the South Pacific Ocean, via Tahiti, Easter Island, Santiago and Tierra del Fuego. From Punta Arenas in the Strait of Magellan the good ship *Lindblad Explorer* would follow the track of some of the earliest explorers, notably the redoubtable Captain James Cook in the *Resolution*, who was first to circumnavigate the South Polar ice-cap, 1772–75.

In our minds too was the exploit of Ernest Shackleton in January 1908 of reaching farther south than any party had achieved previously; Shackleton had been with Robert Falcon Scott in the *Discovery* Expedition attempt of 1902 to reach the Pole, which had failed from sheer inexperience and amateur planning, and, it was said, by differences of temperament between the introspective Scott and the extrovert Shackleton. So Scott had refused Shackleton a place in his second expedition to reach the South Pole, successful but fatal – Scott's party had died on the return trek, after finding Amundsen had planted the Norwegian flag at the Pole a month earlier.

50   *Birds and Islands*

Of which more anon, related in the chapter on South Georgia, where Shackleton, after his attempt on the Pole from a landing on the Weddell Sea coast of Antarctica from the *Endurance* in 1914, died on yet another expedition in 1922, and is buried there – on South Georgia. His Weddell Sea adventure failed dismally. The *Endurance* was crushed in the ice, but Shackleton achieved fame by the success of the amazing voyage he made with part of his crew in a small open boat sailed across 800 miles of stormy winter sea between Elephant Island and South Georgia.

Diary. 31 December 1984 Crossing the international date line makes this the longest New Year's Eve of my life. Leaving New Zealand at 20.00 hours, the plane ascended to 35,000 feet and touched down at Tahiti's airport alongside a coral lagoon – at 08.00 hours *the same day*, local time!

The half-full plane left plenty of room to stretch out, snooze, drink the free wine, and talk. My seat neighbours were Norman and Eileen from England on their first crossing of the equator, keen admirers of Captain Cook – born in their native Yorkshire.

'Eileen dabbles in painting,' explained Norman. 'I am an amateur historian. We want to enjoy a bit of sunshine away from the cold Yorkshire winter, tha' knows. . . . Thought to explore Gauguin's Tahiti, and go on to Robert Louis Stevenson's *Vailima* in Samoa.'

As I knew Tahiti from previous visits, and we had a two-nights' stopover, it was agreed we would hire a mini-cab and drive around the island by the only road, which circles the 2240 m tall jungle-clad and virtually impenetrable volcanic centre; and in the evening they wished to visit the dancing-dens and eating-houses of the Papeete waterfront.

We had been identified as tourists, having been garlanded on arrival at the airport with the traditional *lei* by a bikini-clad maiden in a grass skirt who lovingly placed a single tiari tahiti flower behind one ear.

'If behind your right ear, it's a signal you are already engaged, married or feeling unsociable. Behind your left ear it means you are free,' I warned the couple – conversationally but unsure that it was not the other way round.

'And if I wear a flower behind each ear?' queried Eileen.

'It must mean you are fancy-free, if not promiscuous. I note most of these beauteous maidens wear flowers behind both ears . . .' this from Norman.

'Tahiti is noted as a paradise of free love,' I said. 'You have only to read the journals of the first literate Europeans to land here to realise that they had discovered an arcadia of innocent love, an Eden before the Fall. You will find the story retold in a book I am reading – *Lost Paradise, the Exploration of the Pacific*, by Ian Cameron. I will lend it to you.'

Captain Sam Wallis, RN, was first in HMS *Dolphin* in 1767, followed by the Paris-born explorer Antoine de Bougainville next year, and Captain Cook and Joseph Banks in 1769. Of these the scholarly Bougainville was the most openly enchanted. He wrote, 'I thought I had been transported to Paradise. Everywhere we went we found hospitality, peace, innocent joy, and every appearance of happiness.' They were given fine tropical fruits to cure the scurvy which his men had contracted during the stormy passage of fifty-two days through the Magellan Strait to reach the open Pacific.

Above all Bougainville records his amazement at the free love offered by the Tahitian women:

... who for agreeable features are not inferior to European women, and who in beauty of body often surpass them. Many of these fair females were naked, and their men pressed us to choose a woman to come ashore with her; and their gestures denoted in what manner we should form an acquaintance with her. It was difficult to keep at their work our 400 young French seamen who had seen no women for six months. One young girl came aboard and placed herself on the quarter-deck, then carelessly dropped the cloth which covered her, and thus appeared to the eyes of all beholders as Venus showed herself to the Phrygian shepherd.

Bougainville's favourable impression was echoed by Captain Cook, though in less elegant terms, who records in his Diary how, as soon as the *Endeavour*'s anchor was dropped in Matavai Bay in the lee of Venus Point (so-called not because of the Tahitian Venuses, but because of the Royal Society of London's request that Cook and Banks should observe the transit of the planet Venus at this place almost exactly on the other side of the earth from London): 'It was a hard matter to keep the Natives out of the Ship as they climb like Monkeys, and it was harder still to keep them from Stealing every thing which came within their reach; in this they are prodigious expert.'

As the *Endeavour* remained three months in Matavai Bay, where Cook built and maintained a fort, 'in order to observe the passage of the planet Venus over the disk of the Sun' and to refit the ship for the westwards search for Australia's unexplored coasts, there was plenty of time to record the habits and morals of the Tahitian inhabitants.

Captain James Cook, now over forty years, with a wife and six children in England, might well have been one of the few of his expedition who did not succumb to the invitation to sexual intercourse with these beautiful and nubile Tahitian women. Susceptible young bachelor Joseph Banks wrote that 'their bodies and souls are moulded to perfection' and he early experienced – as he put it – the joy of 'persuading a pretty girl with fire in her eyes' to sit beside him.

In his diary Banks omits to describe an even closer acquaintance he enjoyed with the beauteous maidens. We quote from the very factual diary of James Cook:

> *Friday. May 1769* Cloudy weather with Showers of Rain. This morning two young women came to the Fort, Mr Banks as usual at the gate trading with the people, when he was told strangers were coming, and stood to receive them. The Company had with them about a dozen young Plantain Trees [i.e. bananas]; these they laid down about 20 feet from Mr Banks, the People then made a lane between him and them; and when this was done a Man (who appear'd to be a Servant of the 2 Women) brought the young Plantains Singley and gave them to Mr Banks, and at the delivery of each pronounced a Short sentence which we understood not. After he had thus dispos'd of all his Plantain trees he took several pieces of cloth and spread them on the ground; one of the Young Women then step'd upon the Cloth and with as much Innocence as one could possibly conceive, expos'd herself intirely naked from the waist downwards; in this manner she turned her Self once or twice round, then step'd off the Cloth and drop'd down her clothes; more Cloth was then spread upon the Former and she again perform'd the same ceremony; the Cloth was then rowled up and given to Mr Banks, and the two young women went and embraced him, which ended the Ceremony.

Commenting on this extract in his book *Lost Paradise*, Ian Cameron is in no doubt about the significance of this ceremony: 'The banana as a phallic symbol was ritually presented, dowry in the form of cloth was offered, the sexual parts and the tattooed thighs and buttocks invitingly displayed, and to make their meaning absolutely clear the two girls came up to Banks and embraced him.'

Wallis, Bougainville and Cook had been annoyed at first to find that the Tahitians, who had given them such a welcome, and many gifts of food (fruit, fish and pigs), helped themselves freely to whatever they fancied and could carry away from the ships or camps. But during his long stay Cook gradually accepted that the Polynesian notion of private property was virtually non-existent; everything belonged to the family and the tribe, to be used, taken or given freely, by all, although on a reciprocal basis, and this seemed to include the favours of the young and unmarried women. However, in general a young woman would not favour an inferior suitor, or one she could not love.

Of course the arrival of the giant sailing ships, with their officers and crew in splendid uniforms, and the panoply of their death-dealing guns and every kind of mechanical device and tool for comfortable living, quite dazzled the unworldly islanders at first. The older chiefs and their priests were more cautious, and saw in the Europeans the opportunity to use the white man's power for their own aggrandisement. Cook was invited – but refused – to help the Matavai chief to revenge himself upon the tribe's neighbouring enemies for alleged insults of territorial raids and killings, which were part of the eternal *utu* [an eye for an eye] practised on almost all small Polynesian islands which had become overpopulated, and thereby had become short of food and living-space.

Cook and Bougainville estimated that some 150,000 Tahitians lived on this comparatively small island in surprising harmony, basically due to its fertile soil and warm moist climate, providing a sufficient plenty of seasonal fruit, fish and pigs. All was shared, so that none need go hungry. It was a truly Christian concept of these pagan yet deeply religious people, and in the end Cook came to admire their happy way of life which produced such physically splendid-looking men, women and children who obviously had few cares as they idled in the sun, swam and fished in the coral lagoon, and did the minimum of work necessary to cultivate their gardens and harvest their breadfruit, and other tree and root crops. Every family had a canoe (or borrowed one).

Laughter, clean air and sea, song, dancing, and love – what more could a man or woman want?

As for *stealing*, there was probably no such word with the white man's meaning in the purely oral language of the Tahitians at that time. Cook came to accept the endless petty thievery as incurable and not to be punished – the Tahitians could not understand why they might be punished; they invariably returned items when the white owner demanded them back. And when Cook punished his own seamen for crimes against the islanders, the latter were horrified to hear of these offenders placed in irons or flogged. 'They burst into lamentations and begged Cook to stop.'

It was an irony of fate that indirectly Cook was responsible for the collapse of the Tahitian paradise. His own reports of thousands of whales and seals unhunted in the sub-Antarctic seas he had visited attracted in the next hundred years whale and seal hunters there from the depleted northern oceans, to operate in the southern summer. Inevitably these ships visited the tropical islands of Polynesia during the southern winter, to reprovision, rest and repair. And with them they brought the infectious viral and bacterial diseases of their crews. The islanders had no inbuilt resistance to these lethal diseases, especially tuberculosis, syphilis and gonorrhoea, 'Within three generations the population of Tahiti plummeted from over 140,000 to under 5,000,' wrote Ian Cameron.

Even more traumatic than the physical impact of whaling and trading crews was the arrival of Christian missionaries in Polynesia, which destroyed their paradise of loving-and-giving-happiness and introduced the concept of Original Sin, Satan and Hell. In March 1797 the schooner *Duff* landed a party of thirty-nine clergymen and lay-preachers at Matavai Bay. They were sent out by the London Missionary Society to convert the 'Noble Savage' (as conceived by Bougainville and Cook) to (the white man's) God's grace and His forgiveness of sin, or else . . .

Cameron wrote that these Londoners were of little education, selected from the dregs of the city; most had never left their native parish, and even supposed they might be killed and eaten – but if this was God's will they were courageously prepared to accept martyrdom. Instead the Tahitians overwhelmed them with hospitality, provided all the native food they required, offered them land to grow crops and to build homes, and a selection of young girls were made available for the pleasure of the white males according to need.

'Their generosity is boundless, and appears excessive,' wrote one missionary. 'Some of us have received surprising abundance of gifts, without return being expected or even thought of.'

James Wilson had been appointed master of the *Duff*, and in due course wrote a detailed account of the expedition entitled *A Missionary Voyage to the Southern Pacific Ocean 1797–1798* – a factual summary of the history and civil state of Tahiti compiled from the journals and reports of the officers and missionaries who took part in those years. It was printed in London in 1799 for the Missionary Society, and edited by a committee of the Society appointed for the purpose by the Society's directors, who made sure that it was in accord with the probity and honest propaganda of the Society's aims.

This fascinating volume of 420 pages, with maps and illustrations, reveals much of the story of the mutiny on the *Bounty* which took place off Tahiti in 1789. Lieutenant-Captain Bligh had been seconded to collect breadfruit food plants at Tahiti (where he had been a master under Captain Cook in the *Endeavour*) and convey them to the West Indies. But Fletcher Christian, the *Bounty*'s mate, dissatisfied by the over-strict rule of Bligh, and above all by the departure of the *Bounty* loaded with the breadfruit plants after five months of living in the comfort and hospitality of the Tahitians and their paradise and free love, persuaded a majority of the crew to seize the ship, and turn Bligh and a minority of 18 officers and crew adrift in the ship's launch.

During his stay collecting and preparing the young plants (much helped by the Tahitian belles mingling with his men), Bligh had built the largest pavilion so far erected on the island – as a residence and protection for the tender young breadfruit. Now, typically, when the *Duff* mission arrived in 1797 it cast envious eyes upon the empty structure, which Wilson describes in detail:

> Standing on the extremity of Point Venus, it was called *Fwharre Pritane* (The British House) by (King) Pomarre, who said he had built it for Captain Bligh who had said he intended to come back and reside there. It is a large and spacious building ... one hundred and eight feet long and forty-eight wide. In the middle are four large wooden pillars about eighteen feet high on which the ridge-tree is supported. About three feet within the sides stand pillars all round, about nine feet long and six feet distant from each other. On top of these a plank is let down which runs round the whole house; from thence to the ridge large poles are set up, about eighteen inches asunder, handsomely bound round with fine matting; on this the thatch is laid, of palm tree leaves most beautifully worked ... Thus hath the Lord appeared to set before us an open door, which we trust none shall henceforth be able to shut.'

The chief of the district, an old man named Pyteath, said the house was theirs and would be cleared for their reception next day. 'He then shewed them the picture of Captain Cook, upon the back of which were written the names of His Majesty's ships and their commanders who had visited Matavai since that great navigator's time . . . He made a long oration, descriptive of all these ships and captains which had touched at Otaheite (Tahiti).' This old man, being the chief priest of the island, concluded his oration by linking the names of these English captains with those of the pagan Gods of the island, acknowledging the British God to be the best, and that he should request the island king and people to worship the Christian God.'

But when the aged high priest paid a visit aboard the *Duff* he brought with him five of his wives, 'not one of which exceeded fifteen years, and desired he might sleep in the cabin, and according to the custom of the country, very cordially invited Captain Wilson, his *tayo* [friend] to take his choice.'

'Surely it was very careless of Britain, having been first to raise the flag here,' said Norman, reading a guide-book, as we started out on our island tour, 'to have yielded these islands to the French. It says in this guide that after many conflicts with other European powers the natives of the archipelago became French citizens under the reign of King Pomare V. There are at least 100,000 people living permanently on Tahiti today, of which half are believed to be true descendants of the original pre-European population, and the rest are a mixture of half-breed [*demi* is the word] Polynesians, Asians and Europeans. Indian and Chinese labour was early imported to assist agriculture, but they soon abandoned the land in favour of commerce, and form the wealthiest business community today.'

'So long as we get to see something of the Gauguin Museum, please,' pleaded Eileen, 'though it's the other side of the island.'

'Can't go wrong, there's only one road, less than eighty miles long around the whole island.'

So we left Papeete, population 40,000, and its colourful harbour full of trading and pleasure schooners, and drove northabout, as I did on my first visit in 1961. As first impressions are usually best, I shall quote (my sister and I had arrived in the *Rangitoto*, a mailship from England):

9 *December* 1961 For £5 hired a car for the day at Papeete. The only road goes around the whole island, following the beautiful lagoon inside the coral reef. Inland the 2241 metre volcanic Oropena peak was lost in the morning clouds. The shore is lined with trees of many kinds, chiefly coconut and pandanus,

sheltering the little homesteads from the heat of the day – it was already 73°F in the shade at 08.00 hours. The lagoon perfectly calm, but outside the Pacific swell burst with an incessant roar on the reefs. Apart from some expensive-looking modern houses close to the town, the country homes of the Tahitians are lightly built of bamboo, thatched with palm leaves, and most had no glass or doors – no need of these in this delicious climate – you see the half-naked men and women and stark naked children happily at their work and play. So easy to live here, every home has a garden-orchard with every kind of tree and root crop – mango, citrus, breadfruit, banana, paw-paw, vanilla, coffee, melon and watermelon, etc., such a profusion that ripe fruit falls unharvested by the wayside. We were told to help ourselves to the sweet ripe mango by the smiling natives.

The average Tahitian has a yellow-brown skin of smooth plump texture, the nose broad and rather flattened, expressive, mobile but not thick lips, large black-brown eyes, and ebony black hair, brows and eyelashes. Having read a good deal of their history and supposed origin, one sees, or imagines one sees, much of the North American Indian in their handsome oval faces, but with none of the haughty disdain you may see in pure-bred Haida and Alaskan natives of that Pacific coast. It has been lost in the centuries of thriving in the Tahitian cornucopia of abundant food and ease of living.

1984 Our route today was lined with the same wild and planted flowering shrubs and tropical plants as I had recorded over twenty years earlier: jacaranda, bougainvillaea (named after the redoubtable explorer Louis de Bougainville), hibiscus, acacia/laburnum species, frangipani, lilies, irises.

First stop was at the tall white lighthouse on Venus Point, above Matavai Bay. Here beside the monument to Captain Cook, tourists and islanders alike were picnicking, lazing, or swimming in the lagoon, some snorkelling, some out riding the surf from the ocean swell washing over the reef at high tide.

'One could spend a whole year here,' sighed Eileen, happily up to her neck in the warm lagoon water. 'Such utter peace and beauty.'

'I shall buy you a bikini,' was Norman's response.

We dawdled so long at Venus Point, Eileen and Norman falling asleep after their swim and eating the squelchy mangoes we had half-filled the car with. I brought my diary up to date, squatting under a coconut palm. Noted the furtive noises of animals in burrows at the root of the tree, threw a slice of mango and a biscuit there, and was rewarded by the sight of a small rat (surely the Polynesian *kiore?*) which dashed to claim it, just in time before a sizeable land-crab emerged from another hole. (They can both climb trees, and enjoy ripe coconut.)

Other wildlife: plenty of large pied butterflies flitting from blossom to blossom, but I could not identify them. Very few birds, except the tiresome Indian mynas; these have been introduced, and colonised almost every Polynesian island from Panama to New Zealand. Actually I once thought they were quite handsome with their white-flashing wings and tail, cinnamon breast, and yellow-gold beak and long legs. Experience of this myna in New Zealand, however, has shown it to be a ruthless predator of the nests of small birds, throwing out eggs and chicks though rarely eating these. Just territorial jealousy, I suppose. They are clever enough to avoid a gun, yet ready to snatch the crumbs at your feet. Withal a model garden pest destructor, living much on grass-grubs and other unwelcome insects.

Thus I mused until Norman and Eileen woke up, and clamoured for Gauguin. We drove on. The day was slipping by, and we barely had time to glance at the much-advertised east coast waterfalls – cascades falling down valleys inland into deep pools where graceful young brown bodies dived and bathed with shrieks of joy. The inspection of a dark natural cavern going far into the mountain was ruined by a raucous party of tourists drinking canned beer with transistor radios blaring at excessive decibel strength.

The Gauguin Museum, although set in a beautiful garden, was a disappointment. The Keeper had just locked the door. He was going home, but invited us to come tomorrow. In any case there were no original paintings on display. They were too valuable to risk damage or theft by the new element of criminal visitors to the island (who slipped in and out so easily via the International Airport). But he would show us full-size reproductions tomorrow – of the great artist's paintings of Tahitian women and life . . .

Back at Papeete the white facade of the clock tower and spire of the old cathedral glowed pink in the last light of sunset. A noble little building in the colonial style of the London Missionary Society which erected it. For despite being ruled by a French governor, the majority of Tahitians remained Protestant. It was cool and inviting inside, its windows and great door wide open to the evening zephyr.

Not so tranquil when I piloted Eileen and Norman into the red light area of *buvette* and *maison de tolérance*. The streets here were crowded with New Year's Day revellers making merry with radio, song and jiving. From my diary of my first visit I quote:

10 December 1961 The friendly steward of the *Rangitoto* offered to guide my sister and me to the local hotspots. One we entered (*Quins* was painted on the door) was packed with crew from our ship and seamen from the waterfront, and other 'foreigners' dressed in light summer attire, clutching in their arms the more than half-naked Tahitian belles as they danced drunkenly (most of them) to the thump of native drum and hollow log and their exuberant singing. At intervals the partners adjourned to the ring of tables around the walls. The atmosphere was thick with tobacco smoke, the lights dim and the noise deafening. One wall was lined with curtained alcoves, raised a step or two above the floor. Near the door was the long bar, propped up by the older habitual drinkers, neatly dressed serving-boys in lava-lava skirts attending to the tables with laden trays.

1984 I could see little changed in the intervening years. Perhaps a greater lewdness in the bottom-wriggling and hip-swinging of the dusky women so heavily made-up with lipstick, rouge and mascara. After all such dens of drink and prostitution are sanctioned by licence in all the main French towns . . .

'If you notice,' had said our steward guide in 1961, 'it's the men get drunk – the seamen and dockies. Hardly any Tahitian men drink alcohol, they simply work as waiters and musicians. And the native girls drink coca-cola or diluted beer. They wouldn't be employed if they got drunk. Their job is to get visitors drunk, give them a bit of the genuine *amour en cachette* in one of those curtained boxes, for which a large fee is charged. If the lady is clever enough she'll win a handsome tip from her client's pocket . . .'

It was stifling, and to me, as boring after a few minutes as it had been in 1961. We walked in the balmy evening air to the Hotel Tahiti, a modern domed and thatched reconstruction of a Polynesian great house or *marae*. We were hungry for a large supper, as a pleasant ending to a happy day. The Nash couple chose *poulet*, peach melba, and a good French wine. Afterwards Eileen confessed she had wanted to dance at Quins, had loved dancing all her life. She instantly succumbed to the music of the visiting drum and log band which started up as she spoke. She swept Norman on to the big floor as other guests joined in the New Year celebrations under the dim yet decorous flashing lights.

'This is the real thing!' Eileen whispered later, as she dragged me from our table for Auld Lang Syne.

Moorea

Diary. 1 January 1984 Sunday 08.00 hours. Coffee by the Hotel swimming pool in the tidal rocks of the lagoon where last night Tahitians were fishing throughout the dark hours. This morning I watched a multitude of little coloured fishes and crabs: the tide was ebbing from the higher small pools, threatening to dry out some of these.

But lo and behold, most of the tiny fishes made a spectacular escape in good time. They leaped or flipped several feet to reach a deeper pool! But how did they know which way to leap? Probably they have memorised the position at high tide when all the little pools are covered by the sea? If they fail to leap in time they are certain to be snapped-up by the big white reef heron which came stalking into the pools as we ate our breakfast on the veranda. Paw-paw and croissants for me, Norman and Eileen couldn't resist bacon and eggs.

09.30 hours. All aboard MV *Keekee*, a fast passenger boat to the spectacular craggy island of Moorea. Another perfect sunlit day, just a light tradewind. Tourists from France, UK, Australia, Japan, even

Norfolk Island. Much critical discussion on Gauguin, who lived at
Moorea for a while. His paintings were beautiful; they were avant-
garde; they were invariably sad, his women, even ugly, they never
smiled . . . 'But the colour, so rich, and the simplicity which added
mystery to his outlines of the human form!' – Artist Eileen rhap-
sodised over this man who arrived here in 1891, seeking the ancient
Polynesian art and culture he had read about in his fellow-
countryman's account of Tahiti, the romantic visionary Louis
Antoine de Bougainville.

But like Robert Louis Stevenson, in his classic *In the South Seas,
being an Account of two Voyages (1888–9)* in small schooners to the
Marquesas, Paumotus and other islands, Gauguin found that Christianity under the London Missionary Society, plus the diseases
introduced by trading and whaling ships had utterly destroyed the
true ancient Polynesian art, religion and happy paradise of living and
loving under the sun. Stevenson and Gauguin found the people of the
Marquesas almost all died-out, chiefly of smallpox; and the rest
waiting to die. They had given up hope and will to live, more than
half their homes were empty, crumbling to dust. Suicides were
common. The only successful men were the white beach-combers
(some were ex-convicts) who were living with one or more
Polynesian women, and traded in goods, alcohol and guns.

No wonder Gauguin's paintings are sad. Alan Moorehead in *The
Fatal Impact* (1966) wrote that 'In Gauguin's Tahitian paintings no
man or woman ever smiles; supine, defeated, despairing and beautiful, his people gaze in a reverie into the lost past. They see nothing but
the broken stones of their marae, their fallen idols, the great legendary war-canoes with their tattooed warriors in their elaborate robes,
and the forgotten dances and rituals of the *Ariori*.' The title of
Gauguin's most effective painting of this utter despair is simply
Nevermore, depicting a nude young Polynesian woman forlorn on a
couch.

The Ariori were a caste of high-born priests who practised infanticide, approved of cannibalism and homosexuality, and as a result
were much feared for their power over the common people. Since
they killed their own children at birth (if they had fathered any) they
were obliged to recruit future Ariori from the most promising of the
sons of high-born families.

On leaving Tahiti in 1769 Captain Cook took with him a young
Ariori named Tupia, trained and articulate in the customs, language
and navigation of the Society Islands (so-named by Cook after the

Royal Society of London). By his diplomacy and interpretation of the Polynesian language Tupia proved invaluable to the great explorer in making their several peaceful landings elsewhere.

But the Ariori have long vanished. They were subject to the same infectious diseases brought by white sailors, traders and whale-shipmen – even more lethal than the infanticide and cannibalism of the Ariori shamanism. These ancient witch-doctors of Polynesia died out for lack of victims. They had arisen in the first place as Nature's answer to overpopulation?

'Do you believe in an Almighty God, sir?'

This question, whispered in my ear by the ebullient courier of the Paradise Tour aboard the *Keekee* startled me as I sat in the stern, quietly observing the sea-birds following the ship on its half-hour crossing to Moorea. This gentleman, who spoke with a strong Los Angeles accent, had been forward, talking to a group of young nuns, and now sat relaxed beside me, smoking a cigarette. He smiled benignly, awaiting an answer with arched brows.

Presently I replied, groping for a sincere reply: 'I often ask myself that question – as a naturalist. I find some sort of answer when I see great beauty in a bird's wing, for instance in the grace and perfection of the flight of these sea-swallows following and fishing in the white wake of the ship. I am prepared to believe that their perfection must have been the work of a divine inspiration; they are noddy terns, I believe.'

'Shure thing! The Almighty God which make all creatures great and small!'

There was no need for me to expatiate. Jake Schneider, as he introduced himself, was a compulsive talker – it had got him this present occupation as a tour leader. He enlightened me with much of his own background, guided by a few interjections from me.

'Those Sisters of Mercy up in the bows – delightfully naive, very young, dedicated souls, don't talk much – gather they've been sent by their Mother Superior to report on an old abandoned Catholic chapel I'll be showing 'em on Moorea. 'Tis in a way, a nice little spree for the innocent young angels.'

'And you are a Catholic?'

'That I am not! I am a Seventh-Day Adventist. I was born on Long Island, New York State, and have loved islands ever since!'

'Curious – for I met a man on Norfolk Island recently, who also said he was a Seventh-Day Adventist and loved islands, and was about to live on Pitcairn Island at the invitation of some Pitcairners living on Norfolk Island. They had children left on Pitcairn but the priest there – I think he had been an old missionary – had died or left . . .'

'"Curiouser and curiouser" as Alice in Wonderland said. For I too had applied for the post as Seventh-Day pastor on Pitcairn, just too late. That Norfolk Island priest got the job. He's there now, with his wife and family. Lucky fellah. You bin there?' enthused Jake.

'No such luck. But a friend of mine – Alan Bangor Jones – has, says it's delightful, such hospitality, simple healthy home-produced food in abundance, no alcohol, but plenty of prayer and bible-reading, he says, and no work on Saturday, which is their Sabbath. Said he'd be happy to live there forever, but the Pitcairners have a rule never to accept an outsider as a permanent inhabitant.'

'Quite right, too. Otherwise 'twould be overrun with sinful money-makers and modern machinery, just as Tahiti and Moorea are. And after seven years even the Seventh-Day Adventists have to leave – unless they get a Special Dispensation from the Pitcairn Island Council to stay on for a further period.'

Half an hour to reach the south coast of Moorea and its calm encircling lagoon behind the coral reef. And another half-hour skirting the reef to enter the main lagoon and landing-place, variously named Bali-Hai or Kaveka on my map.

Here the forceful Jake ushered us into an open-sided bus, a converted lorry. He had explained to me that he was not allowed to wear his priest's dog-collar and vestments for fear of alienating tourists – he wore a bright T-shirt and a flower-draped Australian sombrero labelled 'Paradise Tour', and his short trews were as blue as and longer than mine.

The onshore breeze was just the right temperature to encourage those who had not been afflicted with mal-de-mer to bathe within the lagoon below the Bali-Hai hotel, before the Polynesian feast was ready.

I made the mistake of walking a little way off, to swim near a group of attractively thatched houses on stilts – partly because I wore only my blue underpants and there were few to witness the sight. The mistake was to find the shallow water an unhealthy clinging brown with seaweed and worse – the debris of tourism washing around me, and several sooty terns tamely scavenging what I had stirred up.

I followed the terns back to dry land, to the tall coconut palms in which they were nesting, or resting, some sixty feet up and impossible to see into their nests, if there were any. The flight of these long-winged graceful birds was a pleasure to study, but even more beautiful were the pure white fairy terns (*Gygis alba*), remarkable for laying an elliptical egg, which form is less liable to roll out of the non-nest it is laid in – a crease in the stem or bark of a palm leaf or tree. They were safe, so high in the trees, but aggressively they descended, to buzz around the faces of spectators beneath their nesting trees, and make mock attacks as if they were about to stab with their sharp-pointed bills. Fairy birds in truth, ivory white, wraith-like, with large dark eyes ringed with ebony shadow.

Much higher, on the sheer thousand-foot wall of the central mountain, ethereal against the brooding sky, the splendid tropic birds glided in pairs close to their hidden nest-holes, flashing their black and white wings, and seeming to caress each other with the long streamers of their very long tails.

Back at Hotel Bali-Hai, Jake was declaiming in his broad US accent at top strength to overcome the roar of gossip and small-talk of the rest of us assembling to witness the opening of the Tahitian *umu* (ground oven feast), a metre-deep pit in the sand under a palm-thatched shelter. First the canvas covering was removed from this earthen mound, then many layers of palm and banana leaves were stripped away, no earth allowed to fall on the food beneath – the steaming hot cooked head of a boar, tusks gripping a small avocado fruit. His body was finally uncovered by removing layers of cooked kumara (sweet potato) and wild banana.

All very delicious, if you knew how to handle such food, melting in the mouth as you accepted the squishy mixture offered in a wrapping of green leaf. I noticed that some non-Polynesian whites preferred to go to the table for the alternative – cold beef or chicken, and pineapple slices.

It was meant to be a surfeit and so it was. Stomachs swelled, and meanwhile there was a display of belly- and bottom-wriggling by scantily-clad maidens and lads, dancing and singing for our delight. All part of the Paradise Tour we had paid for, but as some of the performers were out of step and out of tune I returned to watch the gyrations of the aerial fairy terns.

At 15.00 hours a minibus collected fourteen of us for a tour of the one tar-sealed road by a fair-headed youth who introduced himself as a French-Swiss by a Tahitian father. He stopped to show us local wonders. The tiny sensitive plant which closes its little parasol of leaves instantly if you touch it. We walked up a bowery rock glen under the highest mountain to cool our bare feet in a pool at the foot of a long white waterfall. He explained the rural economy of this surprising tropical island, taking us past fields of pineapple in orderly regiments, and lush meadows where Charollais and Friesian cattle grazed contentedly. Normally he worked on a farm here.

He loved Moorea, that was certain, where he lived with his widowed mother, and, on learning of my interest in birds, said he would be happy to take me up to the central precipice where he knew that certain noisy night birds nested in burrows, for now and then a young fledgeling fell into the valley in taking off from the heights. 'An insular species of the *Pterodroma* petrel or shearwater, such as are found today only on such difficult places, where like the tropic birds, they are safe from predatory man.'

Just as we were about to part he took me aside, and whispered that there was a cockfight that evening in an enclosed farmyard near his house. 'You probably know that the sport is a speciality of France and Polynesia? The fighting cocks of Moorea are noted for their ferocity. People come to the regular contests every month here.'

I was very glad to decline: 'I shall be in the air this evening, en route for Easter Island.'

Easter Island

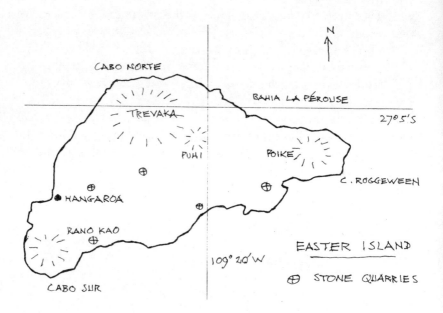

A six-hour flight from Tahiti to Easter Island. The Lan-Chile 747 was only half-full when we took off about midnight. Once more, plenty of room to move about, excellent food and free wine loosened the tongue and started up fleeting friendships.

There had been an alleged suicide by drowning in the pool at our hotel while we had been at Moorea – a brief talking-point before we introduced ourselves as curious travellers to Easter Island. Peggy Thomas, mother of five, is a New Zealand graduate on sabbatical leave to study the famed Easter Island statues. Lyman Kipp, a sculptor from Hunter College, New York, was similarly excited, and revealed he was – small world – a friend of a friend of mine – Bill King, likewise an American sculptor; I related Bill's delight when some rude-looking large beach pebbles he had picked up on Cape Cod and other beaches, won handsome awards at his exhibitions. He had done nothing to them, except to polish them, he told me, and set them up on a base plinth to hold them in suggestive attitudes – 'they could suggest anything in your head – a preggy woman, a bunch of grapes or testicles, the more sexual these natural stones looked the more praise or damning the critics give me, and the better they sell.'

'I'm much more conventional,' groaned Lyman, 'but Bill King goes ahead like the genius he is, earns thousands by expensive avant-garde murals for the big banks and city councils . . .'

Artist Valerie Allen told us she was returning to her birthplace in the long-settled Welsh colony in Patagonia where her brother maintained the family estancia, breeding horses, cattle and vicuñas. She was sixty and wanted to get away from her present existence married to a Queensland businessman. She produced a portfolio of her paintings – almost Welsh-looking landscapes of the wide-open Patagonia pampas. By contrast she had some Picasso-like abstracts of grotesque human and city forms which she had painted in Australia. The pampas and estancia paintings appealed to my romantic Welsh-born imagination. But she would not sell them – not yet. She wanted to let her brother have first choice.

'But please do come to see us; my brother loves to entertain intelligent company on his lonely estancia. I hope you can ride a horse?'

We exchanged addresses. The talk veered to the strange stone statues of Easter Island. We had all read Thor Heyerdahl's books, and I had met him very briefly on his recent lecture tour of New Zealand, but none of us had visited Easter Island. Peggy Thomas believed that Heyerdahl's test of sailing a balsa-raft on his amazing voyage west across the Pacific had proved beyond doubt that Easter Island – so-called by the first people to record landing there, the Dutch explorer Roggeveen and his crew, on Easter Day 1722 – was colonised centuries earlier from the east, from Peru and the west coast of South America. On landing the Dutch found the great statues already in position, showing evidence of being erected many centuries earlier. They were being worshipped by a large population of natives of two distinct types: one was tall and fair-headed, the men bearded; the majority were typical yellow-brown beardless Polynesian types.

In *Aku-Aku* (1958) Thor Heyerdahl describes the effects of a succession of visitors to Easter Island following the Dutch, whose stay had been brief because of the necessity of anchoring their vessel offshore of this tideswept, harbourless island. The Dutch had been hospitably received, no weapons in sight, and an abundance of sweet potatoes available. But the islanders had no boats save tiny canoes used in fishing in fine weather.

They were great thieves; one who came aboard the Dutch ship was shot in the act of stealing, and 'a dozen others were shot ashore' when they stole a few hats from the white sailors. After this the Dutch departed in haste.

Gold-seeking Spaniards were next, landing from two armed ships in 1770 under Don Felipe Gonzales. Invited ashore by smoke signals, the Spaniards marvelled at the number of tall stone men (wearing gigantic 'topknots' of red stone) standing upright along the coast as if to guard the island, which seemed to be governed by tall fair men with beards 'quite like Europeans', but also no women or children – they had been hidden in caves. The Spanish invaders landed two priests and a large party of soldiers. A cross was planted, the priests gave God's blessing, and Gonzales declared the island annexed to the Crown of Spain under a new name – San Carlos Island.

When Captain Cook arrived in 1772 in the *Resolution*, his men were suffering severely from scurvy, and he himself from a 'serious Colic', so that, to save the great man, his servant sacrificed the ship's dog. Boiled dog, supplemented by sweet potatoes and other edible island plants, cured his party, which set about a brief but interesting survey. They found that the stone statues were no longer being respected or cared for, but regarded as useless objects of an ancient cult of unknown origin. The islanders appeared fearful of the white invaders with guns, and Cook realised that the majority of the women and children had been hidden from sight in the numerous natural caves underground, their entrances concealed by stones.

The islanders had good cause to be afraid of the white man's ships subsequently. Until well into the present century Easter Island was subject to predatory raids, notably by captains of ships commissioned to 'blackbird' natives of remote oceanic islands to serve as indentured labourers for small or no wages. In one operation 1000 were forcibly rounded-up and transported in a fleet of Peruvian ships, to dig the rich deposits of guano on the Bird Islands off the coast of Peru. During untold centuries of nesting and roosting by myriads of cormorants, boobies, pelicans and penguins on these comparatively small waterless islets, a stratified mass of solid guano had built up several hundred feet high, well-known for its value as fertiliser to coastal peasants. But not until the advent of large sailing and later steam-driven cargo vessels was it exploited for export to

European and other countries. On that rainless Peruvian coast the nitrogenous and phosphatic concentration improved with age.

Dumped on the exposed, waterless and stinking islets with little provision for shelter, the displaced Easter Islanders sickened and died rapidly of despair and disease. Too late the remnant was returned home, only to die of the smallpox, which they brought back with them. The Spanish authorities made slight amends by supplying a Catholic missionary priest and introducing maize, pigs, poultry, cattle and sheep. But the lone priest was robbed even of his clothes, and such crops as were planted were unfenced and quickly devoured by the introduced livestock running wild, until most of these were slaughtered and devoured by the hungry, leaderless surviving natives.

In his more recent book *Early Man and the Ocean; the beginning of navigation and seaborne civilisation* (1978) Thor Heyerdahl summarises his considerable research into this subject, backed by his remarkable voyages in both the Atlantic and Pacific oceans. Always following the world's trade winds, he shows that he and earlier navigators (of whose voyages there are records) made good speed downwind, assisted by the accompanying currents. All known attempts to return in the same latitude, against the prevailing wind and current, had failed.

Thus it is probable that the earliest explorers sailing from their supposed Asian homeland of Indonesia and the Philippine Islands were first swept across the North Pacific Ocean by the clockwise tradewind currents to reach the north-west coasts of North America. Those who settled in the forested Queen Charlotte Islands of British Columbia developed into the powerful Haida Indian tribe, famous in its heyday as builders of large canoes of cedar wood, used in hunting the abundant whales, seals, sea-otters and salmon of the sheltered Sounds.

What is remarkable about the Haida Indians is their close resemblance in physique, physiognomy, colour and culture to the Maori of New Zealand. Both were a maritime Stone-Age people, using large wooden canoes, with carved prows and stern-posts. Both erected tall totem-poles in their villages, with images of men and animals, the Haida specialising in crowning these with a carving of an eagle – so abundant still along the north-west coast of North America – as described in the next chapter.

But who erected the Easter Island statues? There are, or were, some 600, all more or less of one type. Excavations and carbon-dating of human remains and artefacts in the ground under or near each statue indicate that most were a memorial or tombstone of a chief and probably his family grave. There were a few exceptions. One in particular, now in the British Museum, was a beautiful basalt statue from a solar observatory of an earlier period, a miniature kind of Stonehenge for observing the solstices – what is left is now quite destroyed. Unfortunately, with the arrival of Christian missionaries, most of the statues were thrown down, and many broken.

What should we find?

On arrival at the gravelly airfield at Easter Island we were immediately herded into an enclosure for a brief Customs inspection, and warned we had only an hour before the plane took off for Santiago in Chile. But luckily Peggy Thomas was met by appointment by an Easter Island guide, who told us the plane would be at least two hours grounded, and she could run us around the whole island in that time.

Anna Tepano Paoa told us she was Polynesian, not in the least Spanish:

'We speak Easter Island Polynesian dialect. My people dislike the Chilean language which is official here, although most of us speak United States English. First we go to my home. I keep a Guest House, Taheta One-One, phone 57 in case anyone would like to stay. We welcome all of you to plenty of our simple entertainment – Polynesian style.'

Anna chattered away, as she drove her minibus to points of interest on this rolling, grassy island intersected by the hills and craters of dead volcanoes. Tiny villages of tin-roofed houses lay among planted trees. She told us that originally the island had been heavily forested – in the days when fair-headed 'kings' first settled unknown centuries ago:

'They were tall men with golden beards, and ears elongated with gold and silver weights they brought with them from the great cities their fathers had established in the High Andes. They were full of wisdom in building their stone temples and cultivating the fertile soil, having brought kumara (sweet potato), taro and manioc, capsicum, gourd, tomato, maize – you name it and we, their willing slaves, planted and grew it. They even brought papyrus and reeds to plant in the wet valleys here, to make paper, and reed-boats which we used to keep us afloat in swimming around the island cliffs for fish and sea-birds. But you can see everything in the new museum.'

Anna Tepano Paoa had it all pat, and it was interesting. There was now a keen desire to reconstruct and re-erect and preserve, helped by the numerous archaeologists who were coming in greater numbers, following the published findings of Thor Heyerdahl and others, and the new 'international' airport.

Today was some kind of holiday. It was warm, the locals were in flimsy summer dress, even when riding their horses – a principal means of transport. We stopped to admire a group of six giant statues, each wearing a red stone topknot a metre tall and broad, planted perfectly upright in a straight line, about twenty paces apart, on a raised ridge close to the sea beside the main road from the village of Hangaroa. This is the island's main centre, with shops, a tourist office, and Government House. There is also a Leper Station, which we did not visit, although we peeped into a cave in that direction. Most of the villagers paid no attention to us; they were enjoying a football match across the road from the six enigmatic tophatted statues, which we tourists photographed. Anna agreed that the 'six old kings' had been resurrected for that purpose, and we could obtain postcards in colour at the tourist shop.

The cave along the road had been explored by Thor Heyerdahl, and the Governor and Island Council, said Anna, had preserved its contents for the benefit of visitors. There was no time for us to do justice to the dark interior and its display of artefacts, guarded by a middle-aged woman.

It was time to return to the plane. But I came away with a miniature of a typical Island statue, well worth the ten dollars I paid to the doorkeeper. Sculpted in variegated green, brown and black native obsidian, it stands on my desk as I write, the streaks of black in the heavy rock cleverly exposed to mark the typical beard, peaked nose and long ears of an aristocratic Island ruler. Barely ten centimetres tall, it makes a companionable paperweight, evoking memories of that all-too-brief visit to Easter Island.

Humpbacks, Hawaii, and Haida Indians

The world is too much with us; late and soon,
Getting and spending, we lay waste our powers:
Little we see in Nature that is ours;

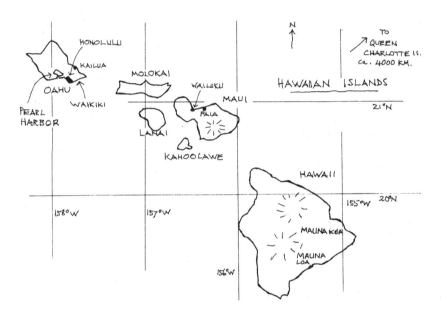

So wrote William Wordsworth some 200 years ago. So felt I, standing at the rim of the world's largest (cubic content) volcanic crater, Mauna Loa on Hawaii, greatest of the Hawaiian Islands. A huge tourist party from Honolulu had suddenly arrived in a gigantic bus, utterly out of place, with noisy children throwing their picnic paper and rubbish into the red-veined lava, cracking and molten at intervals under the sullen mountain mist.

My mood of claustrophobia had begun on arrival in Honolulu's mad world of hype and bustle – everywhere sleek limousines going to and from nowhere on this jumbled island of Oahu, with its highrise rabbit-hutches and jam-packed Waikiki beaches, mass-spending, and mob excitement . . . and a concussed roar of humans on holiday.

No-one walked, it seemed to me. The much-advertised Woodland Outing, a few hundred yards, had to be accomplished in a smelly diesel train to reach the hardly spectacular Waimea Falls.

It caught up with me halfway, as I watched a mongoose chase a guineafowl in the bush. The driver shook his head pityingly when I refused to jump on.

No, not for me sophisticated Oahu. I had really stopped off to see the well-known Sea Life Park, where wild dolphins and false killer whales had long been trained to perform games and intelligence tests in enclosed sea-water pools. But did they enjoy them? They seemed to be remarkably affectionate towards their bikini-clad girl trainers rewarding their antics with doled-out fish. Spectators clapped appreciatively.

The central channels, between Lanai and Maui Islands, are the winter breeding grounds of the North Pacific humpback whales. A marine sanctuary today, where underwater photography is popular. Innovative Sir Peter Scott has even sketched these gentle giants as he swam under water close to their graceful courtship gyrations.

It was now midsummer. The main industries of too-popular Oahu Island seem to be tourism and the military presence – an unholy alliance. There is more room to breathe and enjoy the view on the Big Island (as it is called) – Hawaii itself, where at the airport an advertised tour drives through spectacular black lava scenery to the beach where Captain James Cook was slain in 1779.

To be struck dead at the height of great fame was a good way to leave this troubled world, I mused, listening to the patter of our pot-bellied Hawaiian courier (a half-caste Japanese like so many present-day islanders). His stream of old chestnut tales had made our minibus party from Tennessee and Ohio laugh uproariously.

'You know, our friend Ronald here,' he wound up more soberly [he had demanded our first names as we entered the bus] 'tells me he has seen a marvellous collection of the bits and pieces of Captain Cook's voyages of discovery through the Pacific, from the Arctic to the Antarctic, in the Bishop Museum. I guess you'll be seeing it when you get back to Honolulu, folks. Tell us about it, Ronald. Take the mike . . .'

When the minibus stopped at the James Cook memorial plaque I gave a brief account of the Bishop Museum's comprehensive display of the artefacts and diaries gathered, many on loan, from all over the world, and cleverly arranged to emphasise the spirit of scientific adventure and exploration of Cook's *Voyages*.

At this point I left the minibus for the high plateau of Hawaii, which is largely a cattle ranch below the volcanic peaks. I knocked on the door of the Polynesian cowboy deputed to guide me to enclosures where the Ne-Ne geese were – hopefully – breeding. This gentleman, by name Wiliobi (Williams), gave me a map and the choice of a pony or a Honda motor-tricycle. I preferred the look of the broken-winded roan nag Rosamund – promising a quiet day of ambling and bird-watching by meandering paths through the lava-fields. The sky was rich with singing larks.

Mauna Kea, the island's other volcano, is well over 4000 metres high but inactive. It is the original home of the curious tawny-plumaged Hawaiian or Ne-Ne goose, remarkable for the lack of webbing to its toes, an adaptation to living on the bare black lava heights. Thirty years ago it was close to extinction, hunted to the remotest crags by local gunners.

A few survivors were collected by Peter Scott and his Severn Wildfowl Trust team from Slimbridge, England, leaving a tiny remnant with little hope of recovery despite protection – applied too late. My mission was to assess this remnant, which had lately been reinforced by a small consignment of Ne-Ne bred at Slimbridge. There, through devoted nursing and foster-care of the original geese brought from Mauna Loa by Peter, a strong population has been bred in captivity. These are now so tame that they walk about with Slimbridge visitors along the enclosure paths, and some fly free-winged.

The route to the Mauna Loa sanctuary lay through a spectral landscape of lava, with pockets of flowering hibiscus, mimosa, frangipani and other native shrubs. This area is declared a Forest Reserve, whose Chinese warden Ah Fat Lee manages the aviary, incubator and nursery for the Ne-Ne. The breeding adults live in grass pens with vermin-proof netting fences.

Lee said Ne-Ne are naturally prolific, laying three clutches; the first two he places under bantam hens. Surprisingly, other pens contained wild mouflon and small Polynesian black wild pigs.

'The trouble is,' said Ah Fat Lee, 'we Hawaiians are born hunters. You'll have noticed every kind of exotic species introduced – not all exactly good for the future of the Ne-Ne.'

They include chukor partridge, pheasant, quail, Indian mynah, sparrows, etc., escaped ship rats, feral dogs, goats and Axis deer. I did not see any wild dogs, but on returning the nag Rosamund to Wiliobi's cottage, where a tarsealed road begins, a car awaited my pleasure and a note from Herbert C. Shipman — wealthy cattle-rancher, meat-packer, orchardist and aviculturist — inviting me to dine at his seaside home. 'I keep Ne-Ne-, jungle fowl, doves and other birds . . .'

Shipman was a large man, seventy-ish, a bachelor with a big stomach, immaculately dressed, a kindly glance, but with a glint of steel when he talked of his dislikes. Before we sat down *à deux* to a huge meal of lamb, venison and abundant tropical fruit — all from his estate — he handed me a glass of old ripe sherry (he does not drink or smoke). The huge rooms were furnished in typical early Victorian style, but lacking a feminine hand to relieve their air of musty bygones, a real bachelor colonial establishment. All the servants were imported Philippine 'boys'.

He talked endlessly about Hawaii, of his ancestry; his grandfather was a Presbyterian missionary in the days when the islands were a British colony.

'You will have noticed that our Hawaiian State flag carries a Union Jack in place of the stars on the same field of stripes.'

After dinner, we walked awhile to examine the Ne-Ne geese in their palm-shaded grass enclosures beside his own private lagoon, sandy beach and freshwater pools: 'They don't breed well so close to the sea, and I send any goslings I manage to hatch up to Ah Fat Lee on Mauna Loa. You must stay the night, like Peter and Philippa Scott did.'

Shipman retired to bed at 8.30 pm., saying that he had recently suffered a stroke. He was also diabetic: 'For which reason I have

never married, and that made my two old sisters angry – because there'll be no children to leave my fortune to. My brother, who inherited this place from our reverend grandfather, died young. I didn't want it at first, but I have grown to love this island. I shall take Peter Scott's advice and leave his World Wildlife Fund a fat endowment in my will.'

Next day Shipman was stirring at 5 am to warn me that it was a rare cloudless morning and he would drive me around his huge estate. He is breeding Brahmin humped bulls on Red Poll cows, which he finds are a much hardier cross than the traditional Herefords popular on Hawaii. His lands are divided into paddocks averaging 1000 acres, simple to manage:

'The trouble is we have Portuguese smallholding settlers who rustle cattle, secretly killing and skinning them at night under the shelter trees. They also steal about ten per cent of our sheep.'

During this drive of over 150 miles (the Hawaiian State Flag on the bonnet) around the whole 'Big Island', by public and Shipman's own private roads, I learned some surprising facts about Hawaii, which I condense here:

'The wild deer are everywhere. Everyone shoots or poaches them around the villages. Up on the heights and in some of the woods (bush is the local term) there are too many exotic goats eating the grass, or – as Peter Scott said – "drinking the morning dew belonging to the endemic Ne-Ne geese". And there are feral dogs co-existing cleverly alongside the goats. These dogs rest peacefully with the goats, following them wherever they go. When the dogs are hungry they quietly pull down a young kid and devour it. But they never kill more than they can eat. In return they warn the goats of the approach of a hunter. It's a very successful partnership. But a damn nuisance to cattle and sheep ranchers.

'Just before you came we ranchers co-operated to make our annual drive from the mountains to the sea, using helicopters and mounted ranch hands. Several hundred goats were forced into a cattle corral with extended wings of tall netting. It's quite an occasion for the villagers on foot. If they help in the roundup and slaughter, they are entitled to take home some of the meat free. Otherwise we defray our expenses of time and materials and helicopter hire by selling the flesh and skins to the Polynese-Japanese of the poorer districts ... the riffraff which, with the immigrant Portuguese, originally imported as labour in the sugar-cane and pineapple fields, breed like rats, and are taking over control of our town and rural councils.'

Not that the new autocratic democracy would bother him; not at all. He was too old, too wealthy, he sighed. But he did loathe the insidious way the British colony had become a Japanese empire since Uncle Sam had seized the islands.

Looking down from the ten-seater seaplane on its half-hour crossing from Prince Rupert in British Columbia to the Queen Charlotte Islands it was exciting to recognise the distinctive white head of 'Old Baldie', America's rare eagle and national emblem of the USA.

The huge bird perched unmoving atop a stag-headed cedar close to the seaplane ramp at Masset on Graham Island, largest and northernmost of the Queen Charlotte archipelago of more than 150 islands which lie in a north–south chain 280 km long. To the north across Dixon Strait lay the dim outline of the steep cliffs of Prince of Wales Island which, despite its name, is part of Alaska and thus US territory.

Captain Cook dropped anchor off this coast in 1778, followed by

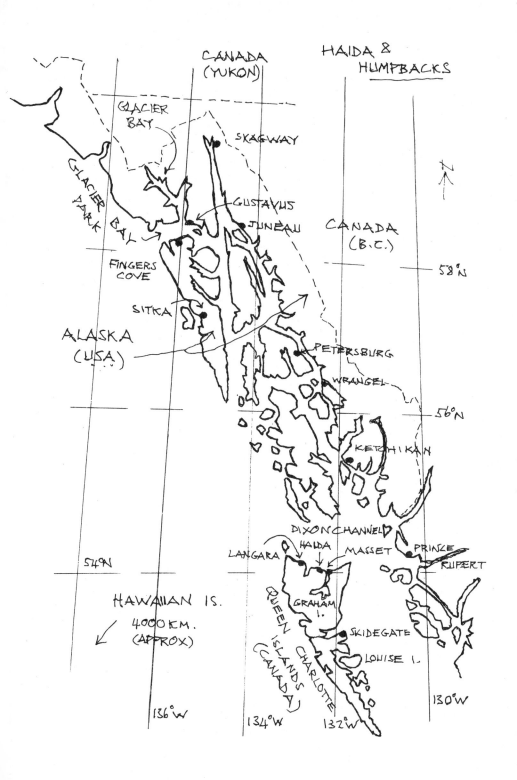

HAIDA &
HUMPBACKS

CANADA
(YUKON)

GLACIER
BAY

SKAGWAY

GLACIER PARK

GLACIER BAY

GUSTAVUS

JUNEAU

CANADA
(B.C.)

58°N

FINGERS
COVE

SITKA

ALASKA
(USA)

PETERSBURG

WRANGEL

56°N

KETCHIKAN

DIXON CHANNEL

LANGARA

HAIDA

MASSET

PRINCE
RUPERT

54°N

HAWAIIAN IS.
4000 KM.
(APPROX)

GRAHAM
I.

QUEEN CHARLOTTE ISLANDS
(CANADA)

SKIDEGATE

LOUISE I.

130°W

136°W

134°W

132°W

N

Captain Dixon who surveyed these islands in 1787 and named them after his ship and his Queen, wife of George III.

These mountainous islands, full of lakes and indented sea-fiords, had been surveyed last year by naturalists who counted 144 nests of the bald eagle, the greatest known concentration in the world, as well as numerous pairs of peregrine falcons, buzzards and smaller birds of prey. They feed on the abundant chinook salmon and other fish, and on the immense numbers of cliff-nesting seabirds.

The lordly eagle swoops upon gull or osprey rising from the water with fish, and forces the great-winged osprey to drop its prize, and the gull to disgorge, and in its same thunderbolt dive catches the fish in its long talons before it hits the sea.

Few people visit these islands today. Masset is a sad dreary 'city', untidy with derelict cars, untended gardens and rubbish blowing in the wind. It has the neglected air of a remote Hebridean or west coast Irish fishing port. Even to the same flora – rowan trees (which keep away witches), rosebay willow-herb, buttercup, dandelion, and white and yellow clovers. Potatoes seemed to be the only crop, not yet flowering – if they ever do. No sparrows or starlings but a short-tailed swallow hawking flies, and a flock of tufted duck in the dammed-up harbour basin.

At dinner in the Singing Surf Inn I was invited to join the twenty-first birthday celebration of a handsome Haida Indian boy, with lank black locks and faint chin hair, dark eyes and chestnut-brown face reminiscent of the Polynesians of Tahiti or New Zealand Maori. His two young sisters were in high festive mood and insisted on plying everyone with imported champagne.

We were enjoying ourselves, the giggling girls perhaps a little drunk by the time we dispersed after midnight, I to bed in the annexe to the Singing Surf Inn.

After breakfast next day I walked to the museum at Haida, a hamlet at the mouth of the entrance to the Masset Inlet Lake, a winding waterway bordered by cedars where bald eagles seemed to be perched watchfully or asleep on every other tall cedar. The museum was shut, but was opened at my knock by a polite curator, a grey-haired Indian, who detained me half the morning by his excellent discourse on Haida history and folklore, going back to the discovery of the Queen Charlotte Islands by the Spaniard Juan Perez in 1774.

Every third house in Haida village is derelict. The majority looked unoccupied, with dirty windows obscured by opaque polythene curtains. But the rain had stopped and I happily resumed my listing of birds and flowers, adding mimulus, tall crowfoot, briar and other roses, forest cranberry – yellowish berries just ripening with a tasty raspberry flavour. Birds new to me were a pipit-like bunting with a yellowhammer song, many barn swallows, a creeping hedge-sparrow species, a large kingfisher, robins and unidentified warblers, ravens and crows flying overhead, and canvasback ducks moulting along the shore.

By good fortune, birding and botanising along this wild and beautiful coast, I was given a lift in a utility pick-up by a fisherman living at Langara, forty miles west of Masset. He was French-Canadian and would take me to see a colony of harbour seals (*Phoca vitulina*): 'The tide is just right, a spring tide with a twenty-six foot fall exposing their lying-out sands.'

His seven-year-old pigtailed daughter spoke little English but at my suggestion scrawled her name in my diary – Let Endje.

I had seen a minke whale skeleton in the museum, and Let's father said they were still common in the main channels around this coast. There were also plenty of orca (killer whale), and grey and hump-back whales passed on migration. All marine mammals were now protected, but the sea-otter had been exterminated.

And he told me what I already knew: that the sea-otter was one of the few animals that could use a tool. It lived exclusively amid the immensely long tresses of bull kelp seaweed, feeding on abalone and other shellfish which it brought to the surface where, floating belly-uppermost, it smashed them open with a stone, using its stomach as an anvil.

'Possibly there were 10,000 Haida living a good subsistence life on these islands before white traders, and whale and sea-otter hunters brought their guns and diseases here. Gold was discovered too, that soft metal that the Haida had thought little of save as an ornament; but prospectors rushed in and none is now left. The only metal – iron ore – mined today is on the west coast, inaccessible by land; it is exported to Japan in bulk carriers.'

Endje lived in an old, comfortable wooden house close to the beach facing the island of Langara, noted for its sea-birds, a source of seasonal food for the Haida. But rats had destroyed the burrow-dwelling species, puffins and auklets.

'A melancholy story,' admitted Endje, 'but it's peaceful here now, we live simply; chiefly by salmon and other seasonal fishing, and all the arts my Haida wife Ellen has taught me. I met the dear lady when

I was working at a Prince Rupert shrimp-processing factory. We both wanted to come back to her old home, and live more independently.'

I ascertained that they had a spare room for the occasional paying tourist, but otherwise were busy and content to live off the sea and their well-planted garden. A warm current washes the Dixon Channel, offshoot of the trade-wind-driven Californian current moving clockwise through the subtropical zone of the North Pacific. 'We seldom get a hard frost,' said Endje.

That evening over our salmon supper cooked in a wood-fed stove, Ellen talked freely of her memories of the tales her grandparents told. At that time Russian fur-traders were actively competing with the Hudson Bay Company, to buy up the valuable sea-otter pelts: 'In the end the Company ran out of stock, and into debt with the Haida, having bribed them with large advances. By the end of the last century the post was closed down.'

The Haida hunting way of life ended with the extinction of the sea-otter, and reduction of seal and sea-lion colonies throughout western North America. The fine Haida cedarwood canoes, in which their fathers had hunted whales and with their superior metal weapons raided neighbouring tribes, rotted on the beaches. Their villages became deserted and their tall totem poles swayed to the ground.

In the next two days Endje drove me south by pot-holed roads and two ferries to Skidegate in sight of lofty Mount Kermode, towering over 1000 metres tall above the fiords of Louise Island.

Endje knew most of the older people along the road, few enough in villages of largely empty houses, each with one or more totem poles askew or fallen to the ground. But we would call at the house of a noted carver of totem poles, modelled on decayed poles he studied in his village.

'I am trying to interest the young people in the art, but most of them think it's an old-fashioned gimmick. They get jobs ashore in Prince Rupert factories, and come home for weekends, carrying blaring transistors, driving cars or bikes at high speed on our limited roads, smoke tobacco and drink gallons of beer, dump rubbish as they go,' he told us.

Looking at his new carvings and those of old totem poles during my brief sojourn in these abandoned Haida villages of the Queen Charlotte Islands, it was clear that the motif generally adopted by the Maori carvers in New Zealand was much the same: grotesque human figures in war-like attitudes, the tongue extended (as in the war dance), each figure squatting on the head of another. Such decorated poles were, and still are, placed as gateposts each side of the Maori *whare* (tribal meeting house) entrance. Today, with metal carving tools available, the art has been strongly revived in New Zealand, and extended to the decoration of the interior, using and improving on the traditional and striking hieroglyphic style and patterns of colour.

Thor Heyerdahl's studies point to the colonisation of Polynesia 'the easy way' – from south-east Asia via the trade-winds and east-going currents of the North Pacific to the west coast of North America, whence surplus population migrated (sailed, rafted or canoed) southwards along the coast of Mexico to Panama and Peru. Around AD 250 there appeared among the pre-Inca inhabitants of Central America, known variously as the Aztecs, Mayas and Toltecs, who had based their civilisation on that of Mexico's earliest recorded culture, that of the Olmecs, a sophisticated people of sun-worshippers who built pyramids, had a calendar system, and kept written records. Their appearance on the Atlantic shore of the Gulf of Mexico with their fully-developed culture indicates their arrival from the east, from North Africa.

It seems clear that long before the Spanish conquest of Central America (begun in 1492) the Olmecs had carried their superior Mediterranean culture, with its engineering skills in building in stone – pyramids, temples, roads – far south to the high Andes. Heyerdahl traces them to Lake Titicaca (Bolivia) and beyond. But it is certain the Olmecs were not the first colonists of South America. They had encountered and enslaved or absorbed a sparse population of no-madic hunters and primitive settlers, whose ancestors are believed to have crossed from north-eastern Asia via the Aleutian land-bridge following the last Ice Age, gradually occupying all lands southwards to Tierra del Fuego and Cape Horn. The Fuegians, as observed by the earliest European explorers, from Magellan to Darwin, were the most primitive Amerindian people ever encountered, as well as the most hardy, surviving perfectly naked in a hostile mari-time climate, under glaciated mountains. (See chapter on Cape Horn.)

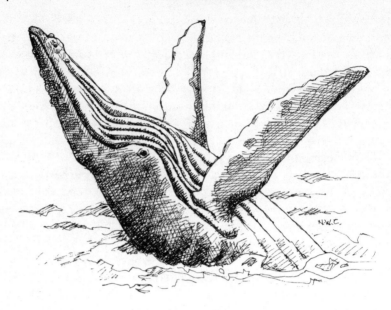

Humpbacks at home

Ravens were croaking above the fir-clad slopes of Prince Rupert city
when the MV *Malaspina* left the wharf at 07.15 hours, and began to
thread her way north to Juneau through the narrow Marine Highway on a nearly cloudless mid-July morning.

Nothing to do but relax for twenty-four hours of continuous
daylight in the comfortable observation saloon forward, admire the
stupendously beautiful scenery of glaciers above forested fiords, and
watch birds and whales; or snooze, waking up at intervals when the
ship hoots to a stop at sundry villages and small towns. We are in
Alaska, in seaways formerly the hunting grounds of the Tlingit
Indians, a proud nation now as fragmented as their ancient rivals the
Haida. We touched at Ketchikan, Wrangell and Petersburg, timber
and fish-cannery ports.

At the outfall of waste fish from the canneries, bald eagles were
two a penny, squatting in groups in overhanging stag-headed trees
after glutting on rejected salmon sluicing into the sea. 'A bit sordid
for our national bird?' remarked one US tourist, at the rail with me.

'But see how neatly old baldie scoops up fish dead or alive, with a
forward strike of its long talons, never diving, always rising dry-
winged from the water on the same beat of its huge wings. T'would
be waterlogged if it dived under like a kingfisher.'

Genial schoolmaster-scientist Charles Jurasz (Chuck) awaited me at the quay of Juneau, founded as a mining town, now Alaska's State Capital. He devotes his summers to studying the humpback whales which enter the sheltered fiords of Glacier Bay (a National Park today), so-called from the wall of ice which descends from the highest Alaskan mountain chain (Mount Fairweather tops all at 4663 m) direct into the sea. From Juneau we took a float-plane to reach the little settlement of Gustavus, which has a large and handsome log-built inn, beautifully situated at the southern end of Glacier Bay.

Even as we descended we spotted the tall spouts of humpbacks misting the distant air, and now and then a leaping form flashing a long white flipper in the evening sunlight.

Chuck is a handsome, robust figure, with a pigtail and a splendid smile. His wife and two children awaited us at the inn with others of the weekend whale-watching party, including Clemence of the BBC (we had last met in Wales on a climb of Snowdon). Clemence said he was working on a film for David Attenborough's series on the evolution of life on earth.

'The cetacean brain has developed in a way uniquely superior to ours,' Clemence pontificated over our quick supper at the inn with the Jurasz family and scientist Bill Lawton, come to help Chuck with hydrophone recording of the underwater talk of marine animals, and with assessment of the effects of ship noises on whales. Bill had recently spent months recording the songs and vocalisations of whales and fishes under the winter ice of the Arctic Ocean.

An early supper in order to make a brief run in Chuck's diesel motor-boat *Ginjur* (from his wife's name Virginia Jurasz). The Bay was alive with shrimps and capelin, pursued by hundreds of auks and murrelets, Arctic terns and three gull species from above, and humpback and minke whales below the surface.

Chuck explained that he had at least thirty individual humpbacks under study; a few had been darted with numbered tags, but as tagging seemed to annoy the whales, he had given that up. He found it far more satisfactory to recognise the individual by the shape of its back fin, sometimes with a stub, or bent forward or backward, or by the notches or the position of the large barnacles on the tail flukes.

'They also differ in size and colour with age, and the shape and height of their spouting. Some are as tame as you could wish, but others swim away if you approach too closely. And by the way, as we shall be cruising for perhaps a whole week, I like to maintain a routine on board which interferes as little possible with the scientific studies.'

Part of that routine was to conserve drinking water, and to keep the ship squeaky clean. Every morning before breakfast every one of us had to dive overboard 'starkers naked – no room to dry clothes aboard ship. You can get back aboard and dress as soon as you like, and dance about on the poop until you are dry and warm again.' My first plunge took my breath away; the sea is only a few degrees above zero. But I got used to it, a good way to exercise, with up to ten of us living aboard, sleeping in narrow bunks, or on the floor.

The 45-year-old wooden *Ginjur* was really very comfortable and warm, the Jurasz ladies – Virginia and fourteen-year-old Susan – efficient cooks as well as note-takers. We were each given an observation post next morning – bow, centre or stern – a perfect day with a rising air temperature, reaching 12°C at noon.

'Mark – Mark! Thar she blows!' presently shouted Peter (ten-year-old Jurasz junior).

'It's Old Lonely!' announced Ginny, spinning the wheel, as Chuck from the bow directed by hand signals the course we should take to anticipate Old Lonely's next breach and spout.

The savoury odour of new-baked bread rose from the galley where Susan was today's cook. She appeared with a pencil and graph paper to help record each breaching, while Peter marked the exact spot on the day's chart-tracing, and Chuck identified each whale and sang out its given name.

I was quite lost at first – lost in wonder at the beauty of our surroundings as, propelled by its specially muffled engine, the *Ginjur* glided quietly into Fingers Cove, yet another branch of these ice-strewn fiords.

Hemlock and spruce grew to the waterline of the moraines under the glaciers. And here we caught glimpses of black bears browsing on the blueberries and wild strawberries, which before dusk we gathered for our own supper, using the dinghy to go ashore. Handsome alpine harebells flourished in this fertile ground.

Many thousands – no exaggeration – of those dainty waders, the lobe-footed phalaropes, skimmed the water like painted toys before our bows, momentarily disturbed from their furious dabbling and pirouetting and pecking at the surface to capture their almost invisible plankton food. Shoals of smelt and capelin puckered the smooth sea like summer wind, pursued by cormorant and salmon below, and flocks of puffins, murres and murrelets above.

Gulls and terns circling and dipping low invariably indicated a shoal of capelin or sand-lace being rounded-up by a humpback, sometimes a pair working together. Thither the *Ginjur* was quietly steered.

Chuck is convinced that, in order to concentrate this food so that it can be swallowed half a ton at a gulp, the whale deliberately emits a ring of air-bubbles as it circles, scaring the fish into the centre. This procedure I, an amateur whale-watcher, was able to follow from observing the ripples made by the submerged circling of the leviathan.

Then came the emergence of the huge mouth, the pleated throat swelling enormously to suck in the ball of fish, giving a glimpse of the long curtain of baleen pleats each side of the upper jaw which act as a sieve to retain the food while the vast tongue rises to expel the water.

'Two orca coming in from the south!' sang out watchful Bill Lawton. The tall black fins of a pair of killer whales approached at a leisurely pace, but passed us and the feeding humpbacks without pausing.

'They're not interested in attacking the big whales in these waters, so long as the salmon run is on.' Chuck was anxious about his beloved humpbacks.

Bill related how from a spotter plane above the Beaufort Sea, north of Barrow, he had watched a pack of orca attacking a lone grey whale, first of all wrenching out its huge fleshy tongue . . . 'a nasty business!'

'Probably an old, perhaps dying whale,' commented Chuck. 'Everything in nature that grows too old must die when it gets too feeble to resist its predators. I have seen orca test out a large old female humpback here one day. She was peacefully browsing on capelin with a young calf at her side. Presently we noticed she seemed to be following two or three orca swimming ahead of her, their black fins showing above the surface. It was so odd that we came in quietly astern of her – to discover that another small pod of killer whales was actually almost under her tail! The whole convoy began to swim faster; it was not easy to observe exactly what was going on, but the orca at her tail seemed to be darting at her belly – at her ventral slits in which her teats are hidden – the vulnerable soft parts. At each darting attempt the whale beat her tail downwards, but when the orca persisted she leaped into the air and sounded, the baby calf tight under one long flipper. The whole lot – orca and humpback mother and child – disappeared below. But not for long. Just a few seconds later the cow humpback reappeared, this time rolling over violently, so that the orca had no chance of biting her vitals. At the same time – in fact all the time the orca pack molested her – she uttered squealing groans which we could plainly hear. She was calling in distress, and half a minute later two other humpbacks came to her rescue – as humpbacks will, swimming alongside. Whereupon the orca quietly disappeared. Looking back now, I believe it was a planned attempt by the killers to molest the mother, but almost as a playful game. How else explain the trick of half the orca party luring the mother to chase them away, while the other killers attacked from behind?'

It was agreed that all healthy whales are playful, especially when young, disporting themselves in leaping and diving and pursuit games in the sea, when full-fed and otherwise idle.

'Good practice, keeping fit by exercise, as humans do,' said Bill. 'I've watched an orca playing with a harbour seal it had caught, like a cat playing with a mouse, just wounding it sufficiently that it couldn't swim fast enough to escape. In the end the orca tired of tormenting its victim, and left it alone. I've often found harbour seals with healed wounds along the shores of these coasts – since there are no polar bears and few sharks, they must have survived orca attacks.'

Over pre-supper cocktails later, Chuck (who liked to make our drinking water from frozen snow and ice 'hundreds of years old' by bringing aboard and melting portions of clean glacier snow and ice floating in the fiords, freshly calved from the terminal wall of the ever-moving glaciers as these crumbled into the sea) related the moving story of watching a young orca playing with a half-grown harbour seal. The young seal, released from the tip of the orca's formidable fanged jaws, swam feebly to the *Ginjur*'s dinghy, and tried to climb aboard over the stern. But the orca plucked the seal away and dived with it, releasing it deep under the water. This game continued for some minutes, the Jurasz family almost weeping as they watched.

'It was terrible to watch,' said Virginia. 'I wanted to get in the dinghy and rescue the poor seal. But Chuck quite rightly refused to interfere. So we up-anchored and left the orca still playing its deadly game. We never saw that wounded seal again. Chuck says it probably survived when the orca tired of playing with it.'

Fresh salmon was daily available for meals aboard. Not caught by us, but gifted by one or other of the pelagic Indian fishermen who in summer enter the bay in their cabin work-boats; they are just another link in the sea-food chain of Glacier Bay, and help Chuck protect his whales.

The week slipped by all too swiftly in perfect weather. Every morning the night's mist lifted and it was warm and calm in the shelter of the glaciers, pancake ice, and noisy sea-birds and whales. Most of the time as many as ten whales were within hearing distance, shooting their tall spouts explosively. Each blow was instantly followed by a swift inhalation, snapping shut of the nostrils and sleepy submergence of the massive head.

'Why, I do believe it's young Garf!' declared on-duty Susan one afternoon. 'She's on her mamma's old feeding pitch!'

Garf was a calf last year. Now she was almost weaned after a year of suckling, but where was her mother Garfunkel? She might have mated off Hawaii last winter, in which case she would be undergoing another pregnancy of a year. Or was she taking a sabbatical year off maternity duty? Chuck was accumulating a lot of information on the life cycle, breeding age and longevity from years of study during which his named humpbacks had become so tame and accustomed to the friendly presence of the *Ginjur*, herself not unlike a tubby, peaceful whale.

One noon, cutting the engine altogether at lunch time, the *Ginjur* drifted alongside Garfunkel's huge body, fifteen metres long – longer than the boat. She was fast asleep, so close that Peter was tempted to stand on her broad shoulders, his legs already dangling above her from the edge of the deck.

Even the clicking of cameras did not wake her. We counted the warts on her lumpy skin. Each has a single bristle, relic of the days, millions of years ago, when whales were fur-covered mammals walking on four legs on dry land. Attached to her drooping sub-merged head and tail we could see, through the murky plankton-filled water, fat cup barnacles each 8 cm in diameter and 5 cm tall. Fastened to the hard shell of some of the cups were two or three long-stalked goose barnacles and some living seaweed.

Unlike lampreys which will attach to whales and suck their blood, these barnacles are harmless passengers, and derive sustenance from the minute free-moving plankton they intercept with their waving whiskers (cillia), from these advantageous positions.

'Garfunkel – Garfunkel! Welcome home!' sang our exuberant host, jigging barefoot on the deck. 'You ugly old woman! But we all love you!'

Garfunkel, at last awakened by the broad whale-shaped hull of the

Ginjur touching her near flipper, twisted slowly over, opening the nearer eye in a surprised but sleepy stare.

As she rolled away her three-metre barnacled flipper rose clear above the surface as if to salute us, but probably as a signal to her nearest neighbours, most of them females with calves, or pregnant, or merely on a fattening diet during a year of grace between pregnancies, that she was back on her favourite summer browsing grounds, ready to have fun, be friendly, and if necessary protect and act as an auntie to lactating cows in need of a wet-nurse.

'Of course,' said Chuck as Garfunkel slammed the long flipper with a reverberating crash upon the smooth sea, 'humpbacks have the longest flippers in the whale world for a significant reason, not only to signal their presence visually and audibly to friends and enemies, but you will note that the underside is pure white, and smooth as snow. Have you guessed why?'

Chuck looked quizzically at me, but as I could not think up an acceptable reason, young Peter Jurasz piped up: 'Chuck says he believes that humpbacks use the whiteness of their flippers to attract their fish food towards them, so that they can round them up with their open flippers. Minke whales have a clear white patch on their flippers, probably for the same reason, although they have very short flippers. They say that fish are always attracted to the flash of whiteness under the water, and I read somewhere that the sunlight reflected from the head of a diving cormorant under water will lure a herring or other sizeable fish into the gape of the cormorant.'

'But why does a humpback sometimes hold one fin up in the air for a very long time? Just for fun, or to warm it?' asked Susan.

'Certainly not to warm it. Heat is the last thing the whale's body needs. A healthy whale has its own internal combustion central heating, under layers of blubber fat,' Virginia said. 'Maybe it's just pure *joie de vivre*, they love to show off to each other. It's bound to be an important signal, like we used when we put up our hand in school to ask or answer the teacher.'

Time to part, to leave this wondrous place and hospitable family. They to pick up fresh provisions and crew, awaiting at Bartlett Cove. The BBC had engaged Chuck for more underwater diving. 'Just five minutes of whales underwater to tack on to the David Attenborough film,' said Chuck with a grin.

At Bartlett Cove burly red-faced Al Giddings, famed diver camera-man of the shark film *Jaws*, came aboard with marine biologist Sylvia

Earle, a very handsome woman just a little pale at that moment – a combination of air-jetlag and 'having danced with a dolphin in the West Indies' – so Sylvia said, giving this old naturalist a big hug because she remembered me; very welcome from such an enthusiastic and pretty lady whom I have no recollection of meeting before – except in her scientific articles in sundry journals and the *National Geographic*.

Chuck insisted on a farewell party on board – the newcomers had brought a case of malt whisky with them. Great tales until the light faded around eleven pm.

Virginia organised the older guests to sleep below deck, ladies in the bunks, Al on the galley floor with two cameramen, Peter and I on the bridge deck. All others went ashore to sleep in the Park Ranger's quarters.

The last thing I remember of that party was Chuck's loud singing.

He wanted us all to forgather in the winter at Hawaii, where we should help him study his beloved humpbacks playing, mating and singing in warm tropical waters.

Canadian Arctic

'You goin' Yellowknife on y'way to North Pole?' queries a loquacious Stetson-crowned old-timer at the Hilton Hotel in Anchorage,
where I have been cleaning-up after days with whales.

'Best is to bus your way over the Rockies, three long days and two
short nights. Don't miss best God's-beautiful country in world – one
two hunnerd (1200) miles by the Alaska Highway. Goin' meself.'

Why not? What a cheerful motley party scrambles aboard. A
big-bellied Texan millionaire and his plump self-satisfied wife; a
smooth-faced young pigtailed Japanese boy in blue jeans whose only
word of English is 'Yes'; a Jewish woman who suffered World War II
hiding in Holland (now made good as a metallurgist to a Canadian
car firm); a tiresome French-Canadian who drones on about politics;
a bearded naturalist (the author) – about a score of us in the
half-empty coach.

Up and up by Uncle Sam's tarsealed highway, soon crossing the
controversial pipeline, said to be 1000 miles long between the oil

wells at Prudhoe on the frozen Arctic Ocean and the export wharf of
Valdez on the open Pacific.

Stop to photograph this fat silvery snake winding through the
hummocky spruce forest. 'The caribou won't cross the big pipe – too
scared. The wolves know it – they crowd the deer against the pipe an'
slaughter 'em,' announced our driver.

True or false? I am sceptical, but ask politely: 'Where are the
caribou?'

'Far, far away, nibblin' the reindeer moss under that snowline, fled
from mosquitoes and blackflies, the wolves and the Injuns.'

The big blackflies are biting us. Into the bus, shut doors and
windows. Turn up the air-conditioning. Makes some of us sleepy.

Stop on the high glaciated plateau, gaze in wonder and snapshot
the pure white mass of the Wrangell Mountains, dominated by the
snow dome of Mt Stanford, 5000 m tall, unbelievably etched against
the clear blue sky.

One hundred miles of high-level foothills, draped monotonously
with black spruce, a narrow dwarf conifer never more than seven
metres tall – the only sort that survives the severe Rockies climate.
No mosquitoes. . . .

'Even a bear finds it hard to live here, but Rocky Mountain sheep
roam these barren heights, moving into the spruce in the winter. The
hunters are gettin' ready – there'll be the usual fatal accidents if they
don't wear luminous pink.'

This statement by our driver is inspired by glimpses of gun-toting
parties, a few wearing reflective scarlet jackets, some driving field
trucks carrying detachable dormobiles pig-a-back, and capped with
canoes and fishing gear, the movable home-from-home of United
States and Canadian wilderness holiday explorers, a vigorous,
independent, trigger-happy breed.

On this lone highway the exchange of information between coach
and truck is by way of short-wave radio, tersely polite.

'Don't pass yet, there is some moose ahead. I'm slowin' down.'

'OK. Thanks, my passengers would like a peep – before you shoot
'em . . .'

'Ye're sure jokin', buddy – that's an offence – shootin' on a public
highway. Reckon I'm stoppin' anyways.'

'OK. I sure was jokin', sir. But we'd like to see the elk. Thanks for
stoppin'. Shall we overtake now?'

'Go ahead, road's clear, but hurry. The elks is quittin'.'

A glimpse of huge spatulate antlers of the bull as he sweeps the hornless cow and calf into a willowy swamp, while cameras click hopefully.

Coffee and comfort stop at Glennrich, a wayside wilderness hamlet where some ate lunch prodigiously. With the Japanese boy I wander in search of birds and bears, lured by handsome bluejays, chickadees, and wild flowers hard to identify: five-petalled cardamine, downy-seeded senecio, long-leaved stellaria, cinquefoil, orache – all slightly different from the same genera at home.

The boy is no help, saying 'Yes' to each one I name, but politely smiling with his slant-eyes. I name to him the familiar dandelion, yarrow, oxeye daisy and cotton-grass which delight both of us. Scarlet fireweed (rosebay willow-herb) spectacularly fills the ground where the spruce forest has been lately burned.

All aboard, and soon the heavy eaters are slumped and snoring, oblivious of the glorious panorama of forest, glacier and craggy peaks under a vivid sky. They wake up only when the brakes are slammed on. The driver shouts that he has spotted a bobcat, lynx, or cougar slinking across the highway.

'A mountain lion!'

We tumble out, but all I can see is a very fine rainbow over a splendid precipice.

'Pot of gold, if only we could find it!' sighs the sleepy Texan millionaire wistfully, soon snoring again.

Is that white blob on the cliffs above the interminable black spruce possibly a Rocky Mountain goat or a Dall sheep? 'Yes,' nods my monosyllabic friend when I point it out to him.

We eat tart wild strawberries. Three overloaded cars pass, caribou or moose antlers lashed to the roofs.

'The bucks and bulls shed 'em in the spring. You can pick 'em up free anywheres here. All aboard or we'll be late at Beaver Creek.'

Into Canada, show passports at a tiny hut, where you can buy coffee at one US dollar a cup. The dunny nearby has a large book of art-paper chained to a side wall, and labelled 'BOOK OF THE LOO. Kindly confine graffiti to these pages.'

The road is no longer tarsealed, but metalled and uneven. Bump, bump!

'Hey, is this the almighty Alaska Highway?'

'Sure is,' answers the driver over the loudspeaker. 'Gotta thank the Japs for it, made to rush supplies to Alaska in the Big War. Canada can't afford to keep it tarsealed after big winter frost damage. Forty degrees below freezing and snowed to the roof come Christmas time.'

Our host at Beaver Creek is an Athabascan Indian with a hawk nose and long lank black hair, who traps beaver, wolf, bear, wolverine, fox, muskrat and ermine in winter, and subsists, he says, on caribou, blacktail deer, white hare, mountain goat and sheep. A romantic figure in hunting dress, with ravens tamely hopping around, feeding on the scraps of food from the kitchen of his hotel.

Our supper was large chinook salmon, fish which had travelled hundreds of kilometres up the Yukon River tributaries to be hooked on his guests' rods.

The second day was a repeat of the first; dirt highway lined with black spruce, with hemlock, willow and wild cherry in lake-filled valleys below crumbling crags and alpine snowfields. A dream-like fairytale world, not a single town, hardly a hamlet . . .

Late in the afternoon a shrill whistle develops – signal that the engine is overheating. It's at the rear of our coach; the experts congregate to discover the fanbelt has broken. The driver radios for a replacement – we are many miles from nowhere.

The boy and I watch birds, collect flowers. Two hours later, with no replacement, but with the freely-given advice of the rich Texan and the practical help of the Stetsoned old-timer, the fanbelt is sufficiently patched-up for the coach to limp grudgingly into the next hamlet, Pine Valley, consisting of a bunkhouse, gas station, coffee shop – all closed.

Hammering hungrily on doors produces a young couple who hospitably open their cafe. We devour the last doughnuts and ice-cream. I count forty-four mountain swallow nests, adobe cradles plastered under the eaves of the log cabin, each filled with young about to fly, and thriving, thankfully, on the too-abundant mosquitoes.

Night is not dark in this latitude in summer. At last a new belt is delivered and fitted. As we drive on, singing songs sleepily, the moon rises gloriously over Kluane Lake, with magnificent views of Canada's highest mountains: massive Mt Logan, 19,850 ft, and other snow-capped giants – Lucania, 17,148 ft, Mt Wood at 15,885, Mt Vancouver, 15,700 ft.

30 July Whitehorse City. It is bitterly cold at 03.00 hours in this frosted city under the moon. I take pity on my shivering Japanese lad preparing to doss down on the pavement, head upon his large back-pack. He is glad to share the last available room in a boarding-house. We register our names and addresses at the desk. His reads simply 'Jose, Tokyo, Japan,' and gives his age as sixteen. We flop into separate bunks to our well-earned sleep.

'Yes!' he says to my offer to take him with me early to see the famous Whitehorse Rapid Dam Fishway, the longest fish ladder in the world, enabling chinook salmon, rainbow trout and grayling to bypass the hydro-electric turbines on their way to their spawning-grounds in the Yukon headwaters.

But he is fast asleep when I prod him a few hours later, with the sun already high above the mountains. My three-mile walk is exhilarating in that sweet sharp air. Fascinating to watch the big glittering fish leaping in vain at the white rapids, then successfully ascending the ladder, as seen through the underwater viewing windows.

Back at the boarding-house there is a note in stilted English, signed Jose. 'Thanks kind sir for helps. I no go Yellowknife. Go Skagway for Vancouver and Tokyo. Good wishes.'

'Yes,' says the receptionist on morning duty. 'Your girl-friend left half an hour ago. Going to Skagway I think. But she paid for her bed. Your share is ten dollars, please.'

She seemed discreetly amused, unaware that this old naturalist, considering himself expert at identifying species, had signally failed to recognise the sex of a migratory bird in blue jeans.

1 August Resolute Bay, Cornwallis Island. Eskimo people of the high Canadian Arctic are torn between the devil of modern civilisation and the snow and ice of their ancient hunting way of life.

It seems there is no going back so long as oil is being sought and discovered in ever-increasing yield under the permafrost of the far northern islands.

From Yellowknife in the Northwest Territories you may fly to the hub of the oil search, Resolute Bay on desolate Cornwallis Island, 75 degrees North. Here the Canadian Ministry of Transport has set up a comfortable subsidised hotel, run (fortunately) by enterprising private enterprise, but under MOT rules.

Here you may shelter from frost and snow in American-style luxury (make your own bed, and self-serve in the canteen), and hobnob in central heating with oil tycoons, highly-paid maintenance men, Eskimo attendants, Italian chefs, and wandering tourists, for the modest cost of $44 a day, including as much as you can eat of the best food procurable by air. The club beer costs $3 a pint.

From one ice-capped island to another I shall roam, largely by courtesy of the oil and associated survey parties which charter small planes and helicopters to land on rough gravel beaches and barren dirt airstrips. There is a sound law that test-drilling may not take place before an environment impact report, paid for by the oil company, is completed and the site certified as unimportant to the wildlife and archaeology of the region.

Making these reports hardy young graduates earn money (and possibly a Ph.D.) and learn useful field experience. Discussing their research with me (some were British scientists I had met before), they offered free rides to their remote island camps.

Nevertheless one sheds a sentimental tear on finding that the admirable independent subsistence Eskimo way of life, so graphically described by my boyhood hero Peter Freuchan, explorer and trader, has vanished. Early this century this Dane lived with the farthest north Eskimos. He married an Eskimo maiden, and took part in their hunting.

Save to buy gun and ammunition – for which they traded furs – Freuchan's in-laws lived without money, exclusively by their skill in utilising every part of the animals they killed. They dressed in animal and bird skins, built temporary homes of driftwood, whalebone, turf and stones, or iceblock igloos, and constructed canoes, sledges, ropes, implements, clothes and boots from these natural resources of animal bone and sinew, fur, feathers, stone and wood.

They loved to visit each other and indulge to the full their arts of singing, dancing, story-telling, and carving of walrus and narwhal ivory, and soapstone. They roamed great distances between their winter and summer camps with their dog teams in an exciting, often dangerous pursuit of their livelihood. But they were free and independent, unfettered by the white man's laws and monetary system. When necessary they took the law into their own hands, as Eskimo survival custom demanded.

Freuchan describes how when a man troubled a community with madness, bad temper, murder or rape, the others drew lots to select an executioner who went forth privately and killed the offender.

Eskimos love children, but infanticide was sometimes necessary in times of great stress and starvation. Then, if it was a girl the new-born was exposed to the frost. But a boy-child was generally saved – males were necessary to assist the hunt. Sometimes a milkless starving mother would cut her fingers for her baby son to suck her blood until the father brought home meat.

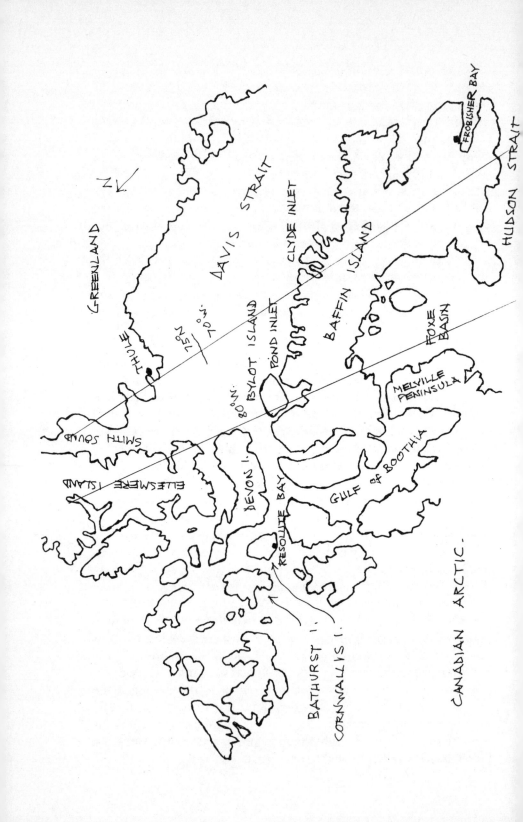

GREENLAND

T.K.

DAVIS STRAIT

CLYDE INLET

BAFFIN ISLAND

HUDSON STRAIT

FROBISHER BAY

THULE

75°N

70°W

BYLOT ISLAND

POND INLET

80°W

FOXE BASIN

MELVILLE PENINSULA

SMITH SOUND

ELLESMERE ISLAND

DEVON I.

RESOLUTE BAY

GULF of BOOTHIA

BATHURST I.

CORNWALLIS I.

CANADIAN ARCTIC.

This led to a shortage of women, and the comforting accepted practice of sharing wives. Marriage was the simplest ceremony: the man, having secured the consent of the parents, moved into the bed of his virgin bride.

Old people who had become too feeble to follow the dog-team accepted philosophically that one day they would be abandoned to die peacefully in their home, which became their tomb when the family moved seasonally to distant hunting grounds. Freuchan tells the story of how one abandoned grandmother remembered a deep cave in which it was customary to store surplus animal meat for the winter. She toddled along to the cave, and found a huge bearded sealskin packed full of little auks which had been cooked in their own oily fat, a delicious bonne-bouche which lasted her the winter through, into the spring, when she reappeared and waved down her returning family – returning to burn her frozen body and hut – a customary ritual at that time.

The Nordair plane was late leaving Yellowknife, a heavy mist obscured most of our flight as far as Frobisher Bay, southernmost part of Baffin Island, a land of ice-capped mountains, glaciers and frozen sea-fiords – as large as New Zealand. Population under one thousand, more than half in Frobisher.

Walked for an hour about the busy, untidy streets, faintly green with late summer grass, here and there the yellow Arctic poppy. A supply ship unloading winter stores in the ice-free harbour.

And so on and up again into the cloudy north, first over the mist-wrapped Fox Basin. We touched down at Hall Beach, a tiny Eskimo hamlet with large oil-storage tanks, where three half-caste Inuits left. Then once more aloft on the last leg above dimly-seen muskegs and icefields and lochans of the Melville Peninsula and long Gulf of Boothia, a beautiful, desolate frozen landscape of white hills merged with iceberg and glimpses of pancake ice.

Resolute Bay proved disappointing when at last our pilot, circling for what seemed an hour, found a hole in the low clouds through which, guided by lines of empty painted oil barrels, he landed on a steep metalled airstrip outside an ugly complex of wooden shacks, oil company offices, a Hudson Bay Company stores, and a bitter wind between. But the one Airport Hotel was welcoming with central heating, self-service restaurant and my booked room shared with A. N. Other.

Strictly a business centre, no roads fit for cars, but plenty of planes and 'copters for hire: 'Take you anywhere you like, from Ellesmere Island to Greenland – at $500 an hour,' said my room-mate, an agreeable young oil firm employee. 'I bin here more'n a year. Ye mus' come char-fishing if ye're free weekends. Great sport just now.'

But the sun suddenly emerging from the mist late that afternoon, I walked the track to the Eskimo settlement, three miles south, over rocky barren shale. Not a land-bird in sight, low-growing wild plants crouched behind stones: species of stunted Arctic willow, poppy, buttercup, chickweed, plantain, a purple bittercress, milkwort, gentian, thrift (armeria), stitchwort, moss and grass. These grew beside the track chiefly because of the scattered exuviae of human waste there creating a more fertile terrain.

The village was deserted at that hour. An old half-caste sweeping the porch of a surprisingly neat wooden church explained that everyone was still at work in 'Resolute town'. Inside, the church was oil-heated, with soft carpeting, cushioned pews, and an Eskimo curate, who welcomed me with a warm handshake.

'It's Anglican,' he explained as he donned a long fur coat and walked down to the beach below neat wooden houses, hospitably inviting me to tea in his.

Among the inevitable litter of plastic and tin cans of Eskimo (and white) settlements in the Arctic, six large white bodies lay on the beach, attended by scavenging village dogs. It was my first close-up view of the beluga or white whale. The whaling fraternity called them canaries, because of their habit of singing to each other under water or ice. Alas, these beautiful animals had been slaughtered and their heads cut off.

'A shocking waste,' said the curate. 'They only use the teeth these days, for carving, now that narwhal tusk is so hard to come by. In my father's time not a bit was wasted. After the fresh skin had been stripped off and eaten raw – it has medicinal properties, rich in hormones – all the meat was cut up and frozen for future use. But today the young people prefer to buy tinned food.'

There were several hair-seal skins stretched to dry at the top of the beach: 'Some of the old men still like to eat seal meat, but their women will no longer chew the skin to soften it for making clothes and footwear. Easier to buy everything at the Hudson Bay shop.'

Beyond the open tide-fretted sea-edge, old winter ice still covered the sea. A skidoo (motorised sledge) and its tow-box lay isolated on the ice. 'Typical laisser-faire of my Eskimo brothers,' said my priestly companion, clearly pleased to exercise his good English (he had been to university in Toronto). 'The skidoo has lain there since these belugas were killed at a hole in the ice weeks ago. Now it's beginning to sink in the melting ice. Of course the owner has every intention of recovering it before it's gone to the bottom. But he'll put it off until it disappears, so long as he's earning good beer money at Resolute, he's happy, believing that he can buy another newer, better skidoo.'

The days at Resolute passed all too swiftly. Despite the frequent mists, not a single day elapsed without a flight to a distant island, most of them at no charge to me as guest of a scientist and his company. The first was in a twin-engine Otter to Bathurst Island where, after landing men at a new oil rig site, we flew over the North Magnetic Pole, that movable point on the globe which in 1978 was sited above a remote beach which is a walrus roost. Perhaps 500 tusked pink walruses were fast asleep as we swooped overhead. The Otter then buzzed a family group of muskox grazing willowbush on the tundra above.

Ellesmere, northernmost island of the Canadian archipelago, and as big as the North Island of New Zealand but virtually uninhabited, boasts a record that can never be surpassed – during one cloudless July, 744 hours of sunshine (thirty-one days of twenty-four-hours' sunlight) were registered at a weather station there. Perhaps because the sun circles the sky continuously at midsummer and the soil is fertile it is richer in wildlife than more southerly islands. Muskox and caribou tread flowery summer meadows of dwarf willow and Arctic cranberry. The tall, lean, grey Arctic wolf and Arctic fox hunt the

white hare, lemming and ptarmigan. All these animals turn white before winter.

They seemed to gaze in surprise on seeing that rare visitor, man, as curious as you are to study them. But they soon lost interest. The migratory snow and Lapland buntings and Greenland redpolls flew about in new-fledged family parties.

'As to Nanook,' said the Eskimo guide to our small party (which included three intrepid American widows on an Arctic tour), 'I don't care to meet a polar bear on land in summer. It means she's ill or hungry, and it's awkward if you haven't your gun handy. But if you haven't, and she comes at you, watch carefully which paw she raises first to make that terrible death swipe. She can be either right- or left-handed. She's a bit short-sighted, and slow to turn, so you must run around her blind side, behind that raised paw, and spear her before she can turn on you.'

To see narwhal or beluga at all we had to make swoops in the Otter plane over likely ice in Smith and Lancaster Sounds, with no great success. We did spot a polar bear with two small cubs, but they made off at once into an ice-crack, impossible to photograph.

Scientist Bill Koski told me that he had had to get the best counts of Arctic cetaceans from the air north of Alaska in the shifting icefields of the Beaufort Sea. During this summer he estimates that there were a maximum of 20,000 narwhal (the original unicorn; the male alone has the spiral tusk, an aberrant protruding tooth as much as nine feet long, a sexual adornment rather than a fighting tool) which inhabit breathing holes and leads in the ice, and do not migrate far south. He reckons there were some 12,000 beluga – they migrate in winter south to the Aleutians and the Gulf of St Lawrence; but only 2300 bowhead or Greenland whales.

There is excellent discipline at the Resolute (Air) Hotel, where only men may stay. You must take off your boots and parka when you enter the public rooms, which are spotlessly clean, thanks to abundant Eskimo and vagrant white help. Bar-tenders waltz to and fro dressed in red jackets as they deliver ordered drinks. Some men find this and the lure of the vast emptiness of the Arctic induces them to stay long. One such is 'Scotty', a talkative Dundee-born fiftyish bachelor who has been engineman to Norwegian whaleships in the Antarctic.

In his room Scotty showed me the two huge ear-bones of a right whale, which he had mounted to look like human skulls, front and back view. He drank rum and ginger ale solidly as he displayed other treasures – these included the pair of large fangs (also mounted on wood) which a spėrm whale uses to hook giant squid from the ocean floor several hundred fathoms deep.

'The best char fishing, curiously enough, is on the farthest north loch, Lake Haxen on Ellesmere. Now's the time. I gotta Honda three-wheeler stashed up there at Eureka. We'll flip up on Saturday, Ronald?'

But I had arranged to fly to Bylot Island, where British ornithologist Tim Birkhead, a friend of my Pembrokeshire days, was making counts of sea-bird numbers and ecology.

The Otter descended in perfect sunshine to drop off four barrels of oil and collect empties on a raised pebble beach on Bylot. No sign of Birkhead, away watching puffins on some distant cliff? But near his tent was a polar bear with a cub, which ambled into the green tundra to escape the noisy aircraft.

One had to admire the skill of the pilot in alighting on this rough beach, careful first to touch down with the twin rear wheels before lowering her nose and single front wheel. This wild beach was littered with the bleached leg-bones of walrus, and the moulted feathers of snow-geese.

Pond Inlet, sheltered by Eclipse Sound, is the northernmost village of Baffin, Greenland the nearest east land 500 miles distant across Davis Strait. Five hundred souls live here in well-insulated and heated modern wooden houses built by the Government. Most of the inhabitants are true or half-caste Eskimo, with a substantial sprinkling of white officials. I was directed to the bungalow of Alred Haines, who invited me to stay the night, seconded by his wife. The view from the window was superb – Eskimo parties cruising through the pack ice in small wooden umiaks powered by outboard motors. They carry rifles and take sea-birds as well as jigging for cod and other fish.

The village is less beautiful. The one dirt street from the landing-place to the houses on the hill is littered by modern trash and discarded skidoo, Honda tricycle and much else – revealed by the melting of winter snow.

I take photographs, and so does the young lone journalist and author Lyn Hancock, who lends me her popular book *A Seal in My Sleeping-Bag*. This cheerful, enterprising lady invites me to use her spare tent, and roam other remote islands with her which she intends to visit, photograph and write about. She also shows me a magazine with her interesting first-hand story of a peregrine falcon. But I decline this invitation to freeze by night in a flimsy tent. I explain that I have already accepted the offer of Bill Koski to fly me free towards Frobisher Bay. He will drop me off at a truly Eskimo settlement on the outer coast of Baffin – it has a difficult Eskimo name but is marked on the map as Clyde River.

How delightful is this hospitality – and offer to enjoy free flights! Lyn admits she has done it much of her married life – sometimes with her husband; he is just now studying bald eagles in British Columbia.

It is difficult to go to bed under the midnight sun. At Clyde River two village officials, a Mountie (Royal Canadian Mounted Police) driving a van (a horse could not live in this barren land) and the Eskimo secretary-manager of the newly-created 'hamlet council' kindly house me in the brand-new empty council chamber with central heating, a mattress, loo and other mod cons. Charlo Ariak then invites me to supper in his comfortable, well-appointed house where his pretty young wife is eminently photographable, blushing as she poses with a bonny papoose slung in the hood of her fur-lined burnous.

The Clyde River (white) Wildlife Law Enforcement Officer calls in for a chat – and possibly to size me up as a wandering naturalist. Seeing the camera around my shoulders he politely warns me that I should 'go easy on photographing in the village'.

After he had left, Charlo Ariak explained: 'I'll tell you why. It's not you, but white people in general are unpopular. But chiefly with our younger intellectuals who have been to college in Montreal. They resent the way the white man has marched into their hunting grounds. This land belongs to them, not the white government they were not even invited to vote for, or against. Look at our community. It's just been told it now has achieved "hamlet status" – which means it is legally entitled to have what it has always had, its own council of elected residents – but only to manage local affairs within narrow boundaries arbitrarily decided by some white official far off in Yellowknife!'

After supper of roast muktak (seal meat: Ariak's brother-in-law had lately killed a bearded seal. Its pelt was stretched on a frame to dry outside the house), Mrs Anna Ariak settled to suckle her fine boy on the sofa in the centrally-heated living room. Charlo adjourned to my room in the Council Chamber and we gazed through the windows overlooking the village square. Children and grown youths were playing a species of football, with no boundaries, up and down between the wooden look-alike houses. Tall lamp standards well above winter snow level exhibited lights already, though the sun was still high in the sky. Older couples were strolling down a vista opening upon the icebound harbour, wearing their best anoraks, the ladies with black skirts hiding their boots.

'It's Sunday,' explained Ariak, interpreting my raised eyebrows as a sign I wished for more information. 'It's pathetic what the age of oil has done to our once-proud Eskimo spirit. Only a few of us really care. Most of the old folk are apathetic, wallowing in the slothful ease of the State Handout. The old-age pension and the unemployment dole have been doubled, the politicians are frightened stiff that we shall demand the land back, and the oil and minerals beneath our land.'

I had read a plaque on the Council Chamber wall defining the new parish boundaries, and signed by Stuart M. Hodgson, Commissioner for the Northwest Territories.

'It means that our people, accustomed to roaming free over our ancestral lands, are being caged in one small spot. It implies that our hunting grounds outside are no longer under our control, but bossed by the Mounted Police and this new official, the Wildlife Law-Enforcement Officer.

'My relatives in this village have elected me chairman of the new council because they rightly believe I have no intention of using the chamber for its purpose, which is to supplant the customary gathering of our chiefs in private session.'

As we talked I felt both glad and ashamed that I was enjoying the cosy warmth of this oil-heated building, even as I deplored the ugliness of thousands of empty rusting oil barrels discarded and unwanted around the village and towards the shore, not worth collecting by the annual supply ship; this had not yet been able to break through the winter ice filling the harbour mouth. These barrels and the derelict household rubbish marred the natural beauty of the snow-clad distant mountains and tundra.

Charlo Ariak said he was a pure-blood Baffin Island Inuit, accustomed to strenuous dogsled travel and hunting in winter: 'the best season in the Eskimo year. We used to go visiting from one village to another, sharing our seal and caribou meat with relatives and enjoying fine singing and dancing parties. But the rot set in during the war, when a Royal Canadian Air Force base was set up at Resolute Bay; I worked there as a conscript engineer. But it was closed down after the war, by which time I had become too soft, too fond of Air Force beer and baccy . . .'

Charlo, who had a French-Canadian twang to his good English, said he had met Peter Freuchan, and also Donald Macmillan who brought his training ship *Bowdoin* to Resolute each summer, and both had wintered with his tribe.

'I grew to hate Resolute Bay when the oil bosses moved in, and the Government set up DEW [Direct Early Warning] lines to listen for Russian activity by air and sea, and sub. movements. I went back to my birthplace on Baffin. But it was no good. I was too long in the tooth, like my older hunting companions, to enjoy the tough life. I had grown too fond of the beer.

'Let me tell you a story. One winter night I was boozing in another village fifty miles away from Clyde River. It was blowing a blinding nor'easter, horizontal snow from Davis Strait, and forty degrees below zero. With all that beer and whisky mixed up I got boastful, and said I was going home by moonlight. Actually there was no moon, and I knew that my sled-dogs were a poor undisciplined lot, easily tired.

'Of course we were both tipsy. When I staggered to my feet and started to put my parka on, my friend got up too, and knocked me down, saying he would kill me if I tried to leave. We fought like the mad drunks we were, and in the end he very nearly did kill me!

'His wife tried to separate us, and he nearly killed her for interfering. She crawled away and came back with the local Mountie, just in time. I was dead to the world. The Mountie locked up my friend in the calaboose.

'Fortunately we had a wise magistrate on circuit at the time, a half-caste Inuit – a real old Solomon. He told us it was bad white law that my friend had been put in the cooler, but good Eskimo justice that I should be fined ten bucks for being a drunken idiot. He commended my pal for saving my worthless life, and told me he'd have fined me another ten bucks if I had not already had a ten-dollar thrashing.'

'It's fine for us,' concluded Charlo. 'My wife and I get over $600 a month pension. But the young people don't like it. They hate the white hand that gives and then takes away.'

'Takes away – what?'

'You ask them. With a doubled dole there's no incentive to work. It's so boring to do nothing. You can take up carving, but that means killing narwhal, walrus and beluga, already shot almost to extinction around Baffin. And of course good carvings have become very dear, snapped up by dealers who fly up in the spring and buy them at top prices. By the way, don't waste money on any for sale in the Hudson Bay Store. We dump our rejects there.'

'So the manager told me today,' I agreed, 'when I remarked that I was disappointed with those on display.'

The Hudson Bay Store is the only shop here, developed today as a modern chain store. I told Charlo of how I had observed a young Eskimo mother filling a trolley with one of almost every item on the shelves:

'She didn't seem to be sure what she was buying. I mean she did not look at the price tags. Everything went in, even a small transistor. I'm sure she did know what *that* was! At the pay counter she held out a fistful of $20 notes. The clerk took what was due and gave her the change, filling a plastic sack with her purchases to overflowing. Outside the store the big fat baby in her hood began yelling. She passed up to him the first thing she could take from the top of the plastic bag. It was the transistor. The papoose bit it, howled and threw it to the ground. The mother did not trouble to pick it up, but passed him the next item, fortunately a bar of chocolate. And off they trudged, both satisfied for the moment.'

Next morning I boarded a small oil company freight plane bound for Frobisher Bay, on my way home at last from this harsh, sad, barren and scenically beautiful Baffin Island. My seat-companion revealed himself as a half-caste Eskimo whom I supposed to be returning to university in Montreal.

'I saw you bird-watching the other evening. You passed our Youth Discussion Group up on the hill above the village where we meet on the fine evenings, rather than in the new village hall where you were given a bed. At these seances we talk endlessly about putting things right. But as for me,' he said, lighting another cigarette, 'I've talked myself dry. I've decided to give up college and a city career. At Frobisher I'm picking up my Eskimo wife and baby. Together we are going back with her father to the old camping and hunting life he loves and will teach us. We are taking only a dog team he has trained – no breakdown skidoos and petrol problem for us, thank you. We shall just load up some flour, salt and tea, and perhaps some shag for rolling cigarettes. All this coming winter we shall hunt caribou and muskox for food and skins, and snare the silver foxes. Perhaps that way I shall regain my self-respect.'

He wrote his name in my diary, but with no address. He no longer had a fixed abode.

Jan Mayen

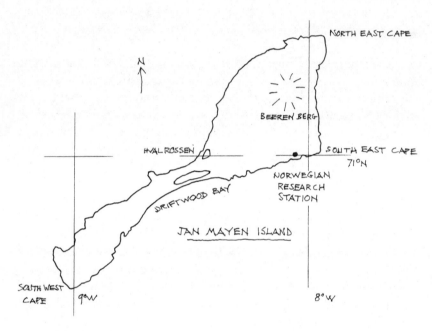

Jan Mayen must be one of the loneliest and least accessible of the islands of the Atlantic Ocean. It lies 965 km southwest of Svalbard (Spitzbergen), 480 km east of Greenland and 560 km north of Iceland. It is utterly hostile to human settlement in its almost perpetual wind and cloud, as well as its volcanic nature with a peak rising to 7500 feet almost perpendicular from a harbourless coast.

Beerenberg has rarely been climbed, though it has attracted some young climbers because of its remote inaccessibility. As a young graduate, my friend W. S. Bristowe, noted later as a world authority on spiders, wrote an account of how his party of biologists were three days in reaching the summit and forced to camp out in ice and snow, which had defeated earlier attempts. At that time Jan Mayen was uninhabited, save for one lone half-crazed trapper of Arctic foxes.

First discovered in 1607 by the explorer Henry Hudson seeking the Northwest Passage, it was named by the Dutchman Jan May in 1614. Two years later it was occupied by the Dutch as an offshoot of their whale-fishery at Spitzbergen, at that time sorely harried by British and French competitors. For a while the hardy Dutch had Jan Mayen to themselves. But in 1632, after they had gone home for the winter, the French, smarting from their bloody defeat over hunting-grounds at Spitzbergen, raided Jan Mayen and looted and burned the Dutch factory.

A grim history of the ancient greed and courage and suffering of man in seeking the vital fat and oil for the lights of cities and the new machine age. The Dutch returned to rebuild their base on Jan Mayen, and in the next winter placed an armed guard there. During the eight months' winter these men all died of scurvy.

To us, landing on that ancient Dutch whaling beach on the island's west coast was made possible by a radio message from the team of Norwegian meteorologists who maintain a station on the east coast. Courteous but hungry for a visiting ship, they advised us that they would stand by to help us land on the only beach where a small boat can come safely ashore. This is Hvalrossen, its black volcanic sand strewn with the immense whitened bones of slaughtered Greenland whales – today extinct, but 300 years ago numerous in this krill-rich stormy latitude.

Well above highwater mark stood a single building housing the modern lifeboat belonging to the meteorological station; its doors were thrown open, and the motorboat poised ready to be launched in case of need. Hard by stood a large Landrover. Our party of *Lindblad* naturalists would be driven across Jan Mayen to reach their quarters under the shadow of ice-capped Beerenberg.

Some of us preferred to walk by the black lava track around the base of the towering mountain, its lower cliffs murmurous with multitudes of cackling fulmar petrels – here the dark blue High Arctic phase; all were feeding well-grown young.

For the birdwatchers there were these noisy but dove-like *Fulmarus glacialis*, but few other birds. Most of the puffins and Arctic guillemots had fledged their young and were away to sea, forming rafts far offshore – their young are feeble on the wing at first, but adept divers.

The botanists had to be content with the few plants capable of surviving in the hostile terrain of loose black lava sand constantly blown about by the wind. Here and there a larger boulder made a microclimate where tiny flowers grew: a pink *Silene acaulis*, the Arctic poppy *Papaver relictum*, dwarf willow *Salix reticulata*, some mosses and the alpine hairgrass *Deschampsis alpina*. The last I had

seen flowering on a high crag in Sutherland, but here it clung close to
the rock, cleverly developing leafy bulbils in place of flowers which
would have blown away in the gales if the parent plant did not
develop new plants viviparously, that is by planting them in the soil
around them; although doubtless some of the bulbils are torn off by
the wind, in which case a few may be blown into crevices suitable to
establish new colonies.

I was pleased to be rescued from my floundering in the seemingly
endless lava desert track across the centre of Jan Mayen by the
Landrover sent by the Norwegians who had warned us that a strong
wind got up every afternoon in summer. We were taken to their cosy
quarters where they dispensed drinks and cakes, and the eager talk of
men long sequestrated from society's hum and discourse of the
world's this and that.

The temptation was to linger in this warm haven, and listen to the
tale of their existence on this desolate island. One attraction for us
was to have our passports stamped with the Royal Arms of Norway
and the words FORVARETS STASJON JAN MAYEN 71°01′N,
8°28′W. They seemed to be very young and reasonably content,
serving only for eighteen months here as part of their training for
work on the 'Mainland' of Norway.

As prophesied, the afternoon gale gathered strength as we drove
back to Hvalrossen, facing the stark middle landscape spitting salty

rain and black lava grit. Here, as we awaited our turn to re-embark in the ship's zodiacs, I lingered to examine the ancient graveyard of the original Dutch whaling settlement. Heaped boulders and the indestructible vertebrae of giant whales marked these, with some wooden crosses still standing, though mostly askew. On fine days, said the Norwegians, it was the custom to tidy up these graves – sometimes the little Arctic foxes would scratch there. 'They are impudent thieves and will carry away everything, even your gloves, and hide and gnaw them when hungry. In summer they fatten on sea-birds and their eggs and young, and devour the afterbirth of the seals at whelping time.'

Away on a little hill was a larger wooden cross with the still-legible letters HOLLANDER HAUCEN. But there was no time to enquire who Haucen was; the last zodiac was leaving, the sea was pounding on the beach. Snatching up a bunch of leaves of a large sorrel beside the boatshed I tumbled into the zodiac, and the helpful Norwegians released the ropes holding her to the beach, stern on and outboard humming.

All was well, if soaked with salt spray before we reached the *Lindblad Explorer* which had already lifted her anchor and was moving into deeper water.

I was curious about the sorrel, obviously not a native of the island. I had seen this large-leaved *Rumex* before, on remote windswept

Hebridean and Icelandic islands, always associated with farm buildings (but there was no farm stock here). On St Kilda formerly the
leaves were fed to cows at milking time, and were believed to have a
sedative effect, helping the cow to 'let down her milk'. I remembered
too that sorrel leaves applied to your skin soothed the pain from
nettle stings.

Farewell, then, to this island of the world's worst climate. Yet, as
the lower mists enveloped her, the tall mountain still held the
sunlight, glittering with snow and ice, proudly erect and austerely
beautiful.

That evening our historian described Jan Mayen, as he chalked her
outline on the board in the ship's lecture theatre, as 'like a graceful
pregnant lady, or perhaps a mermaid rising from the sea with
snow-white hair'.

More prosaically he added that the Norwegian Met. Station was
set up in 1921. During the whole of the Second World War it was
manned with Free Norwegian soldiers, protected by the Allies to
prevent German occupation, Hitler having overrun Norway and
using the coast as a submarine and naval base for raider-ships.
But the Allies needed a weather-forecasting base at the site, the
'maternity ward' of European weather.

It was here, in the comparatively safe stormy sea between Jan
Mayen and Greenland that the Allied leaders secretly conferred
aboard warships when planning the strategy for the invasion and
reoccupation of North Africa and France, as they studied the coded
weather forecasts from the Jan Mayen meteorologists.

Nevertheless, during the war the Germans, landing from submarines, were able to plant their own radio transmitting station
secretly on the Jan Mayen coast. This was not discovered by the
Norwegians for more than six months, when it proved to be auto-
matic, unmanned.

Island of Bears

Björnöya (Bear Island) lies halfway between Svalbard (Spitzbergen) and Norway's North Cape. It was shrouded with heavy mist as usual as we approached. As we drew nearer to the surf crashing upon cliffs the cackling cries of innumerable fulmar petrels reached us punctuated by the deep bass groans of the puffins and Arctic murres. A watery sunlight developed to reveal a horseshoe-shaped anchorage on the south-east shore under a bird-whitened escarpment.

The inflatable zodiacs landed us at Hvalrossbukta (Walrus Haven), so named from the great herds of walrus seen on this beach by Barents when he discovered Bear Island in 1696, the same year in which he discovered Spitzbergen. It became a staging post for the early Arctic whale slaughter.

Only the bleached skeletal evidence of that slaughter lies scattered above the highest storm tide line in the lonely green tundra, amid derelict rusted trypots, winches, boilers and the foundations of whalers' huts. The grim evidence of human pollution under dark sky and mountain mist was agreeably lightened by wild flowers and sparse grass among stones underfoot; we found the nests and pear-shaped eggs of the purple sandpiper under rosettes of the handsome roseroot.

Skuas swooped savagely again and again with stabbing bills upon my protective sheepskin cap as I passed near their nests. But the little sandpipers put on a more cunning distraction display; the parents tumble in front of your boots, wings trailing as if mortally wounded to lure you away from their camouflaged chicks lying as still as the very stones – but when the danger (you) has gone far enough from their brood, when you think you can snatch up a parent, it rises into the sky with a triumphant squeak and vanishes. And by a round-about route it returns to its crouching babies, walking close to the ground and piping a whispered all-clear.

This broken-wing trick is a deceit practised by most wading birds and some small duck species; ornithological authorities believe it is instinctive (inbuilt rather than learned). They are probably right; although the chick has undoubtedly learned, rather than inherited, the distinctive dialect of its parents' calls – expressing joy and encouragement in a low intimate conversation of pips and squeaks as well as sharp cries of warning – even before it emerges from the egg beneath the warm adult breast.

Once more, in this wild windswept wilderness of a remote Arctic isle, as I gazed down upon one of the purple sandpipers' downy chicks crouched as still as death at my feet, I admired the ability of this morsel of life to survive predation by this complete blending of its buff and brown-black velvet dress matching the variegated carpet

of frost-shattered stones and sparse Arctic flora. Its life is a mixture of subconscious instinct, and the maturation of that instinct (learning from example of hearing and seeing its parents). More than that, in the few weeks it takes a human child to survive by instinctive first suckling of its mother's breast, this sandpiper has learned not only the meaning of its parental language, and to respond accordingly, but within two or three brief summer months it will have become independent, finding its own food; and will have flown southwards a couple of thousand miles to wintering grounds on southern European coasts. The purple sandpiper was a regular winter visitor to Skokholm, and some juveniles would remain the ensuing summer feeding along that Welsh island's rocky shore; but older adults, assuming the rich cinnamon-red plumage of courtship, had vanished northwards late in April.

That this flimsy flying machine should be capable of long migrations, the juveniles apparently without the guidance of the experienced adults, remains for me a miracle, an unsolved mystery, despite learned papers by scientists attempting to explain their precocious skill. Instinct, my dictionary informs me, is the 'innate propensity, especially in the lower animals, to certain seemingly rational acts performed without conscious design'.

At that moment the sun appeared, dispersing the mist, raising the ambient temperature, energising man and bird alike. A good hike inland was indicated to explore the now derelict village (formerly a brief mining community) of Austervog amid rugged hills of glacial stones, said to be the moraines of the last Ice Age. The valleys between were gleaming with silver lakes, calm today with only a few glaucous gulls disturbing the surface as they bathed in the ice-cold water.

And this I noticed, everywhere I have been in the Arctic and Antarctic, that even with the water at zero temperature, birds enjoy bathing, generally after feeding activity; nor does it matter that the water is salt sea, which freezes at one or two degrees lower than fresh water does.

Austervog was no more than a levelled site, marked by whitened whale bones and the wooden beams of collapsed mining huts, here and there decorated with pink moss campion and small saxifrages I could not name growing in the humus of ancient human waste. Scattered pairs of Arctic skuas and Arctic terns were nesting here, but as it was now July 30th, their young were well-grown, old enough not to rely on lying doggo, camouflaged. Instead they got up and ran away when we approached; their whereabouts betrayed by the swooping attacks of parent skua and tern.

The sun was now close to the hills of the western horizon – though in this month it does not set at 75°N. I had wandered far from my companions over the desolate ridges towards the appropriately-named Mount Misery, 536 metres above sea-level and only just emerging from the cloud crown of Björnöya. I had been lured farther inland by a path long untrodden by human feet, yet indubitably a path. Could it have been made by the polar bears and foxes which come here in winter?

It was time to return to the ship, to abandon this lonely, fascinating island before those white mists enveloped me. They were beginning to obscure Mt Misery completely. I felt in my pocket; the compass was safe there, ready for consultation if the sun became hidden in the sea-mist.

I love solitude, yet solitude in a thick mist on Arctic island has its unease. Using the compass and guided by the distant cries of the fulmars and kittiwakes on the cliffs above the landing place, I made directly over the snow-streaked hills on a bearing for Walrus Haven, our rendezvous to be picked up by the zodiacs. Suddenly, alarmingly the steep stony hillside began to slide under my feet, carrying me willy-nilly towards the edge of the last steep cliff overhanging Walrus Haven.

'I watched that horrible slide of yours anxiously enough,' said naturalist Dennis Puleston afterwards. 'I was sketching and botanising far below, and saw you rolling and tumbling out of control. Luckily you were able to dig in with hands and feet before you reached the precipice, otherwise I would have had to pick up your remains below that 200 feet drop! I felt exactly like Barents when he watched his men on just such an occasion in 1596!'

Back on the ship, we read in a copy of Barents' 1596 log that going ashore on Björnöya in search of 'sea-mews' eggs' on 11 June, his men

were in great danger of their lives. For that going up a great hill, when they came downe againe, they thought they should all have broken their neckes, it was so steep they sate and slidde downe, which was very dangerous to breake both armes and legges, for that at the foote of the hill there was many rockes . . . Meanetime William Barendsz sate in the boate, and was in greater fear then wee to behold us in that danger. But by God's help we got safely downe again.

On the next day, 12 June 1596, Barents saw

> a great white bear, which was rowed after, thinking to cast a roupe around about her necke; but she was so great wee durst not doe it, but rowed back to the ship to fetch more men, muskets, hargu-bushes, halbertes and hatchets . . . wee fought with her for two hours, one of our men at last strokke into her backe with an axe which stuck fast, and she swomme away with it . . . [Later] Wee cut her head in sunder with an axe, wherewith she died . . . wee found her skinne to be twelve foote [3.6m] long.

In our present knowledge of polar bear life-history, this giant was more likely to have been a male. Females in summer are usually accompanied by their one or two cubs, which remain with their mother for up to two years. The mature male is solitary, roaming all the year on or close to the pack-ice of Arctic coasts, moving south as the pack-ice moves, following it north in summer, feeding chiefly on seals, but mopping-up any young birds or eggs it comes across.

In Barents' time this bear was probably far more numerous than it is today, and adult females may well have denned up for the winter on Björnöya, which is covered then with ice and snow. Polar bears feed heavily all summer and autumn to lay up fat for the winter. Mating takes place from April to June, the male following the scent and tracks of the female, polygamously mating with as many as will accept him; some with very young cubs are not ready and will drive him away.

Polar bear ecology is nicely adapted to the harsh Arctic environment. After mating, the fertilised ovum remains quiescent in the form known as a blastocyst, and does not implant in the womb for several months. The true pregnancy period is believed to be about eight months. Females seek out snowdrifts in October or early November in which to burrow a denning chamber, diameter not larger than her own length. Here, with more snow falling and thickening the roof, the cubs are born in midwinter, tiny objects less than two pounds (one kilogram) in weight but warmly lying in the female's lap as she sleeps a great deal, curled into a ball. She does not hibernate, although her metabolic processes slow down. She lives on her summer fat, the source of her rich milk nourishing her cubs. We have to imagine that she has no lack of water intake – she has only to lick the snow walls of her winter den, which becomes surfaced with the ice due to the condensation and freezing of her warm breath rising therein. However, her winter coat of white fur is dense and resistant to outer cold.

Depending on the ambient temperatures in late winter and spring, the mother bear breaks open her den in late March or April, when the cubs are substantial black-nosed children weighing up to twenty pounds (about nine kg) each. For a few days they revel in the spring sunlight, playful as puppies. They soon acclimatise to outside temperatures and for the whole summer will follow mother in her search for food along the shore and swimming among the ice-floes. It is believed that as long as the female suckles her cubs – for at least a whole year – she will not become pregnant; thus most females do not produce cubs more than every second, and some third, year.

Svalbard: 80° North

Spitzbergen diary

Saturday 31 August 1982 07.00 news on radio; the world still with
brutal murders, besieged Beirut, the Iran–Iraq bombings. On board
Lindblad Explorer utterly peaceful save for banging and crumpling
of ice-floes as Captain Nilsson tried to break through the dense
ice-pack on the south-east coast of Svalbard – in my youth the
archipelago was known as Spitzbergen. The good ship was almost
stopped at times by floes as large as tennis-courts and six feet thick.

We were trying to get to birds and seals and polar bears on Hopen
Island. Arctic fulmars flew derisively around the ship, and Arctic
guillemots and dovekies (little auks) sat placidly on bergs watching
the ship's unsuccess. All this ice is coming from the chill north-
eastern straits which Hasse had planned to pass through to reach the
limit of the fast-ice of the Arctic Ocean above 80°N.

08.30. Announcement on the intercom that a distant polar bear
has been seen, but that the ship can go no further up the east coast,

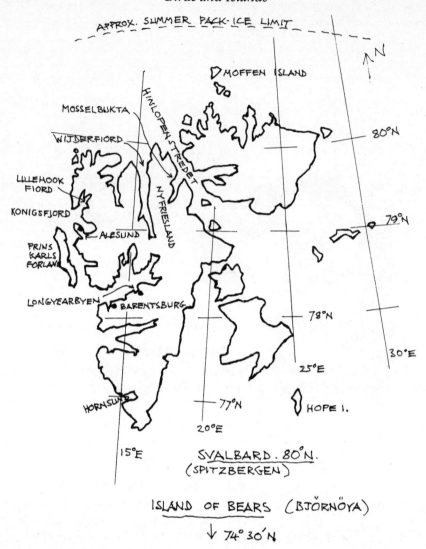

APPROX. SUMMER PACK-ICE LIMIT

MOFFEN ISLAND

MOSSELBUKTA

HINLOPEN STREDET

WIJDERFIORD

80°N

LILLEHOOK FIORD

NY FRIESLAND

KONIGSFJORD

79°N

ALESUND

PRINS KARLS FORLAND

LONGYEARBYEN

BARENTSBURG

78°N

30°E

25°E

77°N

HOPE I.

HORNSUND

20°E

15°E

SVALBARD . 80°N.
(SPITZBERGEN)

ISLAND OF BEARS (BJÖRNÖYA)
↓ 74° 30′N

and will turn to cruise the west coast, always milder and more open from the influence of the West Wind or Gulf Stream Drift from the Gulf of Mexico. Temperature outside bridge is 2°C.

12.00. Running free at last in open sea, with southern tip of Svalbard in view. Expectation of landing in one of the southwestern fiords. But as we try to enter the first, Hornsund, we discover the Norwegian research ship *Polar Björn* immovably beset in the brash ice filling this small haven. Two helicopters are gyrating above the ship and around the cliff walls – rather mysteriously. They do not immediately answer the *Lindblad Explorer* radio courtesy greeting.

Some days later, when the *Lindblad Explorer* entered the long fiord of Longyearbyen, the only town in Svalbard and the main Norwegian administrative and coalmining centre, the mystery was solved for us. By permission of the Norwegian Government, which claims full sovereignty over Svalbard, Poland had established a small research station in Hornsund. The USSR, which disputes the Norwegian sovereignty claim, has long maintained a coalmining base at the entrance to Longyearbyen, which they have named Barentsburg. The *Lindblad Explorer* had planned to land at Barentsburg, but on approaching its wharf, was advised by radio that it was inconvenient, a day on which coal was being exported, or about to be. But there was no ore-carrying ship at the wharf, although a large helicopter flew around, making one low swoop past the *Lindblad Explorer*. There was unfriendly speculation among some of us later that the Barentsburg mine contained more than coal, that it might be a safe hideaway for nuclear warheads. Was not Poland under the thumb of the Kremlin, and the Polish struggle for democracy being suppressed at that very moment?

The subsequent events are summarised in the *Daily Telegraph* of 27 August by Julian Isherwood, reporting from Oslo:

Two scientists working at the Polish research station at Hornsund on Svalbard radioed the Norwegian administration at Longyearbyen on August 10 to submit their request for political asylum. They said they would attempt to cross the open terrain and hills surrounding their camp and submit their request personally. But, according to a spokesman in Longyearbyen, a Russian radio station monitoring traffic in the area, picked up the August 10 message.

As soon as it was known that the men had set off on their long trek of many difficult miles, Russian helicopters were dispatched to prevent the men from reaching the Svalbard capital. Diplomatic sources in Oslo say that the helicopters managed to frighten the men; one returned at once to base, the other hid in the hills and returned to his base a day later. The Norwegian administration now dispatched a Norwegian helicopter to pick up the scientists at their Hornsund base. When this helicopter was forced away by a Russian helicopter, the Norwegian administrator boarded his own helicopter and flew to Hornsund himself. As soon as the

Russian base (at Barentsburg) heard that the administrator was heading for Hornsund, a Russian helicopter was sent to try and reach Hornsund first.

'I have no comment on the case, but the Norwegians won the race,' said a spokesman in Svalbard. 'The two scientists are now in Oslo where their request for asylum will be handled by Norwegian authorities as a case of normal procedure,' a Foreign Office spokesman said. He added that he did not envisage any problems with the requests.

No wonder we on the *Lindblad* had been mystified by the aerial manoeuvring of Eastern European politics in a sky we had believed to be reserved for feathered Arctic birds!

Meanwhile, as the weather was calming down beautifully, Hasse decided it was best to get as far north as possible in such ideal conditions, while the open sea was virtually free of ice. We steamed all night under grey skies along the precipitous coast of the long island of Prins Karls Forland.

Sunday 1 August 07.15 hours, Temp 4.5°C. Near the northern tip of Prins Karls Forland, an immense cliff marked as Fugelhaken, from its loomeries of nesting sea-birds. It has a low forefoot with a light beacon warning of reefs so we could not get near the grassy tundra extending far inland, providing grazing for the indigenous reindeer.

Around the next bluff lay Alesund, a Norwegian Polar Institute research station, which has a shop and post office. Frantic writing and posting of letters by those philatelists who cherish them franked with the unique designs remote islands indulge in for the benefit of tourists and their own pocket.

The background of this little settlement is the magnificent Konigs-fjorden, a glen of many glaciers reaching down to the sea from majestic mountains above 1200 metres tall. The nimbler passengers made for the glaciers, others lingered in the shop and post office. I heard a lady from Chicago ask a local lady (dressed in silver fox-fur coat and very high-heeled shoes) what was the chief amusement here. The answer was that the men played football, women played bridge, you could ski in winter and summer. There are thirty large, comfortable, insulated wooden houses. There is electricity, produced from coal from a local mine, in fact most mod. cons. 'Mail days are when the helicopter comes twice a week, weather permitting, from Longyearbyen City . . .' The Chicago lady carried off the high-heeled Alesund lady for a drink aboard *Lindblad Explorer*. We had been given two and a half hours' leave ashore in this farthest north outpost of Svalbard civilisation.

I kept to the shore and nearby level tundra wet with meltpools, where waders, geese and ducks were feeding. Dunlin, purple sandpiper, turnstone were still guarding chicks, and displaying the broken-wing trick to lure intruders away. Arctic terns nest almost everywhere in the village and, with young crouching in the low herbage or among the stones, viciously attacked the passerby. They repeatedly dive-bombed and struck my head, well-protected by a thick sheepskin cap. A family of barnacle geese – gander, goose and six goslings – were feeding on vegetation in a shallow lake, observed by some idle common eider and long-tailed ducks. All appeared to be moulting.

I have collected so far twenty-four species of plants on Svalbard; that is to say, as it is forbidden to pick them without a special permit, I have listed them in my diary from a guide book, but can't swear to absolute accuracy of identification.

13.30 hours. All aboard for a late lunch as we cruise north, peeping into glaciated fiords. Lillehookfjorden is blocked by a huge glacier flowing from 1000m high peaks. We cruised to within 400 metres of the ice-face where thousands of kittiwake and some glaucous gulls, auks and fulmars were concentrated on plankton and capelin brought to the surface by the upwelling currents at icefoots in summer.

Inland cliffs each side of the glacier rose 500 feet, providing strata on which the sea-birds, especially fulmars, were nesting. The large predatory gull of Svalbard is the scavenging *Larus hyperboreus* – omnivorous devourer of carrion and animal dung.

It was possible to walk or scramble inland at the gravel foot of these cliffs to reach meltwater lakes, a desolate scene of stones, moss and dwarf grass strewn with the feathers of moulting geese and ducks.

A group of harp seals had joined the fish and krill feast at the outfall of the glacier when we re-embarked at 19.00 hours, and presently steamed out into the open sea, moving north all night to round the northern cape. No darkness in this high latitude, save from the shadows of light clouds masking the morning sun.

2 *August* We were roused at 05.50 by shouts of *Walrus ahead!* Sighted from the bridge asleep on ice floes blocking our approach

to the lonely flat island of Moffen, which at 80.3 degrees is the farthest north our ship achieved on this cruise.

Great excitement, and breakfast quite forgotten as Hasse steered towards the brown pod of six large-tusked brutes fast asleep on their ice cradle in bright sunlight. With infinite care to avoid waking them, Hasse nudged the *Lindblad Explorer* past smaller floes until we were stopped alongside the walrus dormitory.

Our skipper had advised absolute silence, his engines shut off, but the clicking of cameras went on from photographers leaning over the bows. The pod woke up one by one, to examine sleepily the red iron hull towering above.

There are no Eskimo or native people to hunt walrus in the Svalbard archipelago where all marine mammals are protected by international agreement. The walrus behaved as if they had no fear of man. When the ship's engines were restarted in order to move forward a few inches and keep the walrus roost tight against the starboard bow, the slight pressure rocked the floe sufficiently to cause those nearest the edge to slide into the sea. Even so they presently returned, and two of them placed their fat foreflippers on the edge of the floe and, comically with whiskered face, gazed up at the admiring human spectators.

At breakfast more sightings of walrus were announced over the

intercom – ten on one floe, and smaller pods on other floes. Plenty of time to study their intensely social behaviour. Males have bigger tusks, we were told, than females. Tusks are rarely used in fighting, although one walrus had only one tusk, and a wound on its tuskless side. The tusks are used to dig out their principal food, clams and other shellfish on the sea-floor. When at rest and sleeping on land or ice the tusks are usually rested upon the broad chest, a necessary habit when several hundred roost together in heaped layers on small, remote rocky islands and beaches in high Arctic latitudes.

Pushing north and east through the pack ice, the ship anchored some distance in shallow water from Moffen Island, a low flat expanse of swampy land, as viewed from the bridge. I was lucky to be in the first zodiac to reach the beach, a moraine of large stones littered with the bleached timber of large and small trees (drifted ashore from Siberian river estuaries hundreds of miles eastwards), and the white bones of whales and walrus slaughtered by the whalers early in the eighteenth century. Scrambling over this barrier to gain the crest of the beach, I came face-to-face with a monstrous polar bear!

Well, that is an exaggeration. The bear was probably an eighth of a mile away, and although ambling in my direction, it was not looking at me. It was fossicking on the ground searching for food, which it presently found – a half-grown gull; this it ground up and swallowed, discarding some feathers, feet and beak. It then continued to march towards me and, by now, others of my zodiac party of ten.

Our leader, Mike McDowell, knew exactly what the procedure was: to retreat quietly if the bear came too close, and get into the zodiacs. On the short-wave to Hasse, Mike was told to re-embark all passengers and lie offshore – a polar bear never attacks a boat at sea.

Which we did, each of four zodiacs keeping station with paddles only, outboats silent.

Still the bear ambled onwards, reached the top of the beach and gazed at the unusual sight of camera-draped men and women in red, blue or yellow Arctic-cold-proof clothes. It did not seem in the least interested in this spectacle. It is known to be short-sighted. It hunts for food with its keen scent, and this it continued to do, disturbing an eider duck which flew from her nest of eggs among the driftwood. The bear ate the eggs and then pursued, caught and devoured a half-grown glaucous gull, tearing it apart with its teeth and long foreclaws and spitting out unpalatable quill feathers, horny beak and feet.

This done, the bear once more held up its great head and sniffed the air above us. The sunlight seemed to blaze down, and all of us felt overheated in our insulated Arctic anoraks, trews and thick fur-lined 'moon' boots.

So evidently did our great white bear. To our astonishment and delight it padded towards a pyramid-shaped iceberg stranded on the beach within a few metres of the floating zodiacs. Taking no notice of us, it gained the flat crest of the berg, and sprawled there, its four feet spread wide and its belly, with its long yellow fur, pressed flat on the ice. It closed its eyes and slept, oblivious to the clicking of cameras for the next half-hour, which flew past all too quickly for the zodiac-confined bear-watchers.

'Of course, the poor thing is overheated in that splendid white winter coat. Can't take it off, as I am going to do mine,' was one comment. 'What a good idea – to cool oneself on a bed of ice.'

But it was presently certain that our bear had cooled down sufficiently or was rested enough to stand up, and yawning towards us, it slithered down the ice and began fossicking for what it could find among the jetsam along the shore. It continued inland, and disappeared towards the farther shore some two or three miles away, splashing through a swampy lake in the centre of Moffen.

We all came ashore and examined the still partly frozen lake. I flushed a red-throated diver from a nest of raised mud containing two chocolate-coloured eggs. The bear had missed this, and a number of moulting ducks and young gulls – but then, a predator must not exterminate its prey, lest it starve itself. In nature most wandering animals are unmethodical, random killers.

Back at the zodiacs several hardy younger and some older fellow-expeditionists were enjoying – they alleged – a quick immersion in the ice-cold sea, their motive to claim that they had swum in the Arctic Ocean close to the fast ice at above 80° North latitude.

19.00 hours. A hot 'glog' (red wine) to celebrate 'farthest north', whether you had bathed or not. The *Explorer*'s health and Hasse's skill in reaching Moffen were toasted as he piloted us through more floe ice, hopeful (he said) of passing clockwise south through the narrow Hinlopen Strait which had been ice-choked a few days earlier.

Polar bears, all supposedly solitary males, were now seen so often that some of the more sophisticated passengers lost interest. The bears were travelling east with us, walking and swimming from floe to floe in a leisurely fashion. One had caught a large fish, which it dragged on to a floe and began eating, gulping down large bites, as seen through binoculars.

More interesting was the bear surprised feeding on a large bearded seal. From the trail of blood on the large floe, it was clear that the bear must have captured the seal as it lay at rest on the edge of the floe, then dragged it to the centre, wounded and pouring blood, leaving the evidence of the victim's struggle in a network of bloody markings on the pure white snow-capped floe. The bear had already reduced the seal to a half-skeleton by rapidly tearing and gulping down the meaty flesh dog-fashion, by the time the ship reached the edge of the floe. When the engrossed bear, looking up, discovered a red monster shoving its dining-room forward, it at once dived and swam away under the nearest floe, leaving the carcase to the scavenging glaucous and ivory gulls.

This evening the ship was anchored in the Bay of Mosselbukta, much used by the first Dutch whalers 300 years ago. Here the intrepid explorer Nordenskjöld wintered in 1872–3.

Tuesday 3 August Mosselbukta is a sad place. Light rain dampened our excursion ashore on this desolate part of North Spitzbergen, made less attractive by our finding its stony beach littered with every sort of ancient and modern trash; bones of slain marine mammals of centuries ago; and the jetsam of modern sea-travel – plastic containers, light-bulbs, broken crates, discarded clothes, scraps of fishing rope, nylon nets and broken buoys. The movement of tides and winds seems to have swept all into this cold north-facing haven, walled-in by cliffs rising 1000 feet high and streaked with ice spilling from the vast icefield above. On my map this has two names, Dutch and Scandinavian, telling of its past occupation – Friesland and Asgardfonna.

Three hundred years ago the Dutch found this region to be the main calving grounds of a gigantic whale, so numerous that it was dubbed the common whale, in French *la baleine*, scientific name *Balaena mysticenus*, the whiskered one, from 300–400 baleen plates up to 4.5 metres long suspended from the upper jaw (described in the chapter on St Lawrence Island). Remarkable tales are told of Dutch, Norwegian, French and British whaleships fighting each other for the privilege of exterminating these slow-moving mountains of blubber weighing up to 100 tons. In the adjacent Wijdefjorden, which is narrow and 100 kilometres long, ending in a glacier, was one of several bottlenecks where this whale was slaughtered. So perished the great Greenland whale. . . .

Very few birds, it seemed to me, no dive-bombing terns, but a pair of red-throated divers on a lochan beside the rivers which bisect the landing beach. But I began to like the place better when I met a fisherman with rod and tweed cap. He was on holiday from Scotland, and said there were 'excellent char trout in many lakes on the tundra, if you follow the streams up the glen. I have a small cabin beside one.'

'But how do you get to this lonely place?'

'Hire a helicopter, but I sometimes sail here in my yacht.' He told me that the stone cairns I pointed out to him crowning the skyline peaks were 'the work of mountaineering fanatics. Been there for centuries. Climbers adore Spitzbergen. Every peak has been climbed dozens of times. Yes sir, you will, if you like room to breathe, come to enjoy this glorious peaceful land. But it's getting a bit overcrowded this summer.'

He glanced meditatively at the *Lindblad Explorer* anchored half a mile off shore – where my lunch awaited me.

Westmann Islands: Isles of Fire

As we sat on lava boulders on the shore opposite the grey-white glaciated horizon of distant Iceland, the old man Magnus said: 'It is written in the *Landnama Book* that the first men to land on these islands were men of Christ who left behind them bells and books. It is believed that they were Irish monks, who had sailed north from St Columb's holy cathedral of Iona in the Hebrides, but that two young Viking brothers, seeking what they could plunder, sailing west from Norway, came upon them peacefully at prayer here. They saw that the land was fair and fertile, with birchwood from fell to foreshore. They named it the Isles of the Westmen, that is, the Isles of the British.'

On a windy midsummer day of 1935 I landed from the Danish Mail steamer at Kaupstadur, the only inhabited island in the Westmann archipelago south of Iceland, a magnificent cliff-bound cluster of sea-worn volcanic cones. The little port was hideous with gaunt

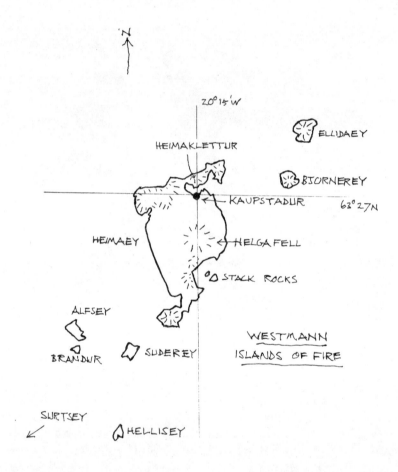

concrete warehouses and the stench of rotting fish. It was the first of several visits I was to pay.

My diary records that I complained to the British Vice-Consul Mr Björnsson that I had read about people here living simply, self-sufficient on fish, sheep, sea-birds, and little farms with cattle.

'Some still do. I shall show you,' said he, 'but with the 1930 Depression over, and new modern diesel craft arriving, we have rebuilt the old harbour with a new breakwater. Population has doubled to 3,700. Foreign trawlers find it convenient to use our shelter and facilities as they sweep for cod in our rich seas – outside the three-mile limit.

'We have our own gunboat now, not altogether unprofitable. It has just brought in another German trawler caught within the limit. Like the last poacher she will be fined £1,000 and her catch confiscated, and sold to our own merchants.'

The worst stink in the port was from tall rows of raw cods' heads awaiting shipment as deck cargo to fertiliser factories in Norway.

'You'll get used to it,' laughed Björnsson. 'To us, it's the reek of prosperity. You'll find them stacked in the back quarters of the town. We call them Lover's Lanes. At night these heads glow with phosphorescence, a dim romantic light, where sweethearts stroll every fine evening.'

He drove me to a dairy farm on the slopes of the long-quiescent volcano of Helgafell, where his friend Thorbeard would welcome my company to practise his English. The little lava-hedged paddocks were sweet-smelling with yellow buttercups, dandelions and silverweed, topped with luxurious stems of the lilac cuckoo-flowers – a mosaic pasture which some men were hand-scything. When withered in the seawind and sun, the hay is gathered into cocks and covered against rain with discarded fishing canvas.

Thorbeard was considered progressive: he used a mechanical haycutter drawn by two ponies – one white and one roan. His dozen cows were milked by his large family twice daily, squatting on old polished skulls of cattle – the horns convenient for carrying from cow to cow.

The effluent from the stalls drained into a covered cesspit, to be enriched periodically with a load of fish offal from the port. Top-dressed with this nutrient, his pastures were the richest in the island, he boasted.

Each morning the rattle of bottles awoke me as Thorbeard's sons packed their carrier bicycles with the town milk supply. Below my window was a neat fenced garden planted with potatoes, red currant, rhubarb, herbs and hardy flowers. Away on the green hillside above the farm buildings snow buntings, white wagtails and pipits sang sweetly. It was a happy place for me, accepted as one of this large friendly family.

Breakfast consisted of wind-dried mutton, eaten raw with *skyr* – curds sweetened with fresh cream and sugar; and the family gathered around to discuss in broken English the plans for entertaining the man from Wales. Difficult passages were translated by ringing-up Mr Björnsson.

Thorbeard's pretty wife Helga put on (for my benefit) the handsome traditional Westmann dress of laced bodice, skull-cap with long tassel, ankle-length sequinned skirt and a silver necklace, heirloom of her mother. The phone rang frequently; Helga used it freely to ring up and exchange gossip with neighbours. Roars of laughter sometimes followed, and from the glances at me it was obvious I was under discussion. Björnsson had mentioned that there was no charge for local calls.

The farmhouse itself was contained within solid concrete walls and roofed with corrugated iron, as almost everywhere in Iceland. But somehow there was enough room for Thorbeard and Helga, their four sons and one daughter, and for Helga's two retired uncles, her father Thorstein, and her mother. Thorstein was a huge patriarchal figure who enjoyed his snuff, and tended the garden. Her mother engaged incessantly in spinning her treadle wheel and knitting garments of wool from their sheep (each farmer had an agreed number on the many off-islets, which I was presently to visit).

By Westmann custom the land is inherited through the female line in this island of many widows. Helga's daughter Unnur would inherit. Her four sons (Engilbert, Leifur, Ingi and Bjorn) would live more dangerously as fishermen, as cragsmen on the sheer birdfowling islets, or in tramp steamers abroad.

My week flew by in the cloudy midsummer days. One was spent on the steep-sided islet of Bjarnerey. Our party was obliged to ascend its 400-foot high cliffs by ropes held by the expert cragsmen climbing first, and wedging themselves in rock-ledges I shudder to remember as I write this.

But once you have achieved the grassy bowl of this extinct caldera it is delightful with wild flowers, sheep, and a comfortable hut with six bunks, used by the cragsmen when collecting sea-birds for food. Today half a dozen laughing Westmann maidens hastened to make coffee while the others spread in a half-circle to drive the sheep into an ancient corral of lava boulders.

The several owners of the sheep proceeded to 'roo' the ripe wool off by tearing it away by hand. But if it was not ripe they hacked it off with tailor's scissors. Then nicked each new lamb in the ear to mark ownership.

No one mentioned to me – I was to read his obituary in the local paper later – that expert cragsman Gigurgeir (37) had a week earlier slipped and fallen to his death on that very cliff up which we had been roped so perilously that day. He had been wildfowling for puffins with the long handnet.

One day Thorbeard took me to the 230-metre crest of Helgafell – a stony waste with few Arctic flowers – stonecrop, bilberry and wild thyme, where golden plover and whimbrel screamed above their growing chicks. On the undeveloped southern slopes men were laboriously removing lava boulders and levelling the surface with iron-tipped wooden spades, as their Viking forebears once did. Björnsson later told me that they were penniless squatters from Iceland come to pioneer little farms and share in the new prosperity of the fishing port.

'What wonderful courage!' my diary records. 'And what a wonderful view from this dead volcano.' It was calm and clear, the sea ultramarine around those bird-whitened stacks I had explored, and climbed some of the easier ones. But not perpendicular Hellisey, crowned with a colony of snow-white gannets.

It was all very beautiful, yet when dark clouds spread swiftly as we returned to the hayfields, there was a sense of utter desolation, almost of foreboding.

When I said goodbye to Björnsson a full gale was raging. Trawlers were seeking shelter in the harbour. The mailboat for Scotland and Denmark had arrived earlier, but it was certain that it would not face the weather that evening.

'It'll blow over, don't worry,' said Björnsson cheerfully. 'Summer gales never last long. You should be here in the sunless night of our four months' winter – we forget the climate then, in many social activities indoors. By the way, Thorbeard and Helga have invited you to stay with them next summer.'

But nearly forty years were to elapse before I set foot in the Westmann Islands again. The newspapers meanwhile had recorded frequent volcanic activity in southwest Iceland – not in the least unusual. A new island had erupted in 1963 from an undersea cataclysm twenty kilometres southwest of Kaupstadur. It had been named Surtsey, and was said to be rising into the sky, reaching 300 metres tall, then slowly subsiding. A scientist was camped there, in an A-frame, measuring its activity, but alert to radio for a helicopter if molten lava flowed too alarmingly.

Ten years later came the news that on a midwinter night of January 1973 old Helgafell had burst open, overwhelming most of the port of

Kaupstadur, including all the land on the harbour side. So that Helga's farm was buried under a seventy-metre mountain of red-hot magma, still moving and giving out clouds of steam.

Fortunately that lava flow moved downhill slowly enough for every human to flee before it; and as it was midnight the island fishing fleet was there, and was able to embark and convey the terrified inhabitants to the nearest Icelandic ports.

A year later, having planned to fly to Greenland via Reykjavik, my plane passed over the Westmanns, low enough for me to see its harbour filled with boats, but looking strangely curtailed in size. I dropped off at Reykjavik and took a day excursion to the West-manns, which now boasted an airport – on the south side where those squatters of 1935 had slaved so diligently. A minibus conveys passengers to the town and port.

A new British Consul could not tell me what had happened to Thorbeard and his family.

'Most older folk never came back. There was not even a cow or hope of a blade of grass to nourish it. Every farm building has disappeared under the still-smoking lava. See for yourself, but you won't get farther than the edge of the town, where you'll see the crushed houses of the suburbs pushed into heaps to the bottom of the hill. But we are rebuilding. Already our population has doubled that of 1973 because of the boom in cod. If you stay a few days I shall be able to trace what happened to the Thorbeard family.'

There was only time to inspect the change in the layout of the harbour caused by the eruption. The red-hot magma had slumped down from Helgafell and been in danger of closing the harbour altogether; but just in time the fishing fleet concentrated on playing their deck-hoses upon the glowing magma, cooling it sufficiently to harden it into solid rock, leaving just enough deep water between it and the sheer cliff, a thousand feet tall, of the Heimaklettur – ancient wall of an older volcano – for medium-sized vessels to enter the harbour, by its new mole of lava safer for ships than ever.

'Yes,' said one fisherman I met in the dock, 'there is money in cod at the moment, simply because we have a greatly extended limit keeping foreign fishermen out – 200 nautical miles – our so-called economic zone. Kaupstadur is crammed with fisherboats from all over Iceland, and every skipper and his family has a flash car to drive home to new condominium suburbs, though we have only about one mile of tarseal! But already this season the cod catches have dwindled alarmingly, through heavy overfishing. But you can't tell these jumped-up young Reykjavik boys anything. Some of them are now turning to tow-netting for shrimps and capelin (sardine-size fish), the food on which the cod and many other edible fish, as well as sea-birds, especially our favourite winter store food the *lundie* (puffin), depended for survival.'

In 1984 I paid my last visit to Kaupstadur, this time in the comfort of the cruise ship *Lindblad Explorer* on its high Arctic excursion. The good ship, still commanded by Hasse Nilsson, passed smoothly through the new narrows. But for most of us it was a sad visit. Everywhere the ship had touched in Arctic lands we saw the results of man's insensitivity to this overkill of the shrimp, capelin and plankton, by ships of many nations, using long bagnets, towing through the upper layers of the ocean where plankton is most abundant.

We were told that about ninety per cent of the tow-net catch is non-edible marine organisms; after the saleable fish have been sorted out the residue is processed for fertiliser or manure, but as this pays no useful return, it is more often dumped.

Meanwhile in that and the following years up to 1986 at least, puffins, which provide a main harvest for the islanders as winter food, have been unable to rear their young. Some may not have laid their egg, but if a pair does hatch a chick it is underfed. In an Icelandic newspaper which I have just read it is recorded that starving young puffins, undersized and hardly able to walk, are leaving their burrows prematurely, falling down from the cliffs into Kaupstadur harbour or the streets, to be eaten by cats and other scavengers, but a 'mercy squad' of island children has been organised to collect the

survivors and feed them, and hopefully to release them in the sea at night.

From my experience of rescuing and trying to feed waif puffins and other sea-birds elsewhere, it is rare for the unfortunate bird to survive this well-intentioned interference with its normal healthy life as an adolescent.

Return to the Faroes

It was in 1936 that I first set foot on the Faroes, half way between Iceland and Scotland. They rise forbiddingly hundreds of metres almost sheer from narrow fiords sliced deep by glacial action. The ice sheet which once covered this oceanic plateau swept away all life, so that not even a hardy plant survived. Ten thousand years ago the first vegetation returned with the returning seabirds. But human settlers did not arrive before about 800 AD.

In 1936 I released at sea, near the capital of Torshavn, two shearwaters which I had brought from my island home of Skokholm, Wales, in those early seabird-orientation trials which were to prove their marvellous long-distance homing ability.

My irresistible curiosity about the people and wildlife of remote islands had drawn me to the Faroes; in particular I was seeking an unsophisticated outer island where I might find the rare Leach's fork-tailed petrel. In Torshavn I found ice-cream, lipstick, radio and cinema available to inhabitants of this wood-and-corrugated-iron

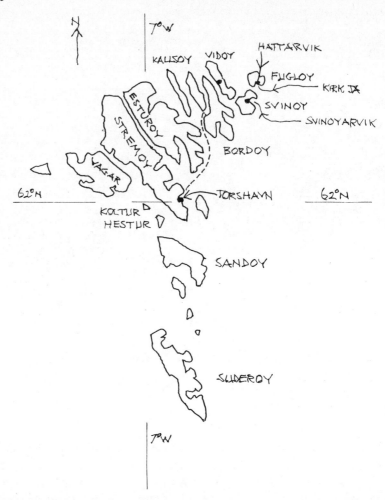

seaport painted in bright colours against the sombre background of green mountain and grey cliff.

But there I met stocky little men on stocky little ponies riding from lonely hamlet and farm hidden in almost inaccessible glens and ravines of the main island of Streymoy. They wore the sprightly, gnome-like national dress of warm homespun wool – close-fitting knee-breeches, decorative waistcoat, silver-buttoned jacket and jaunty tasselled skull-cap. I discovered a richly innocent wisdom in their weather-wrinkled faces, as if they were thinking of their birch-bark and grass-roofed homes, their hardy sheep, milch cows, potato gardens, their wild-fowling, and hopes of a good whale-hunt. In returning home they must cross the stony Fjeldmerken, 600 metres up in the grey mist where whimbrel, golden plover, purple sandpiper and tjaldur (the oystercatcher, national bird of Faroe) were nesting.

I did not find the fork-tailed petrel, but in searching for it I was taken to the 300-metre tall cliff on lonely Koltur Island where the Faroe shearwater (identical to the Welsh bird) nested in burrows with the more abundant puffins. The puffins are the principal quarry of the island fowlers, who sweep them into long-handled nets at the evening fly-past of these clown-like birds. They are dried or salted down for winter use.

I shudder today to remember how I was lowered by rope to join the fowlers on that giddy ledge 250 metres sheer above the Atlantic surf. When my Koltur host, delving into burrows there for plump young puffin fledgelings, drew forth a shearwater and its new-hatched chick, the idea came to me that it would be interesting to take this parent bird back to Wales in a reversed homing experiment. Although he understood virtually no English, and I no Faroese, Niclas Koltri smilingly, unhesitatingly, nodded agreement.

When I tried to explain (what he already well knew, I was to discover later) that the shearwater pair take turns to return to feed their chick only at night, he continued to nod affirmatively; obviously, I thought, out of a natural politeness to a foreigner, not from understanding that he would have to rope down that terrible cliff night after night if he was ever to recover the homing bird.

Koltur, as I dubbed this parent bird, slept several uneasy days in the box which Niclas, a skilled boat-builder, made for me to carry home. The box was under my arm when I at last reached the crowded quay at Torshavn to board the boat for Scotland. Prime Minister Stauning of Denmark had just arrived that evening on an official visit (until 1948 the Faroes were a dependency of the Danish Crown). Lively by night, Koltur poked her head through the bars of her prison to gaze with me at the entertainment provided for the distinguished politician – a typical Faroese chain-dance by people in national dress.

Koltur achieved some notoriety when the Prime Minister, perhaps a little bored by the monotony of this dance, which lasts while a ballad of 200 verses is sung by the performers, spotted Koltur's head, and heard her loud unmusical groans.

He came across to ask me what bird it was, and put out his hand to stroke her sleek black head. This impertinence Koltur repelled, as I feared she would, by a swift snatch and wrench of Stauning's splendid flowing white beard in her sharp hooked beak.

True fame came to this shearwater later. I placed a numbered ring on her leg and released her at sea in sight of Leith (Edinburgh) harbour, 800 km from Niclas Koltri's island. She had been too long confined in the box to risk the further seventeen-hour journey across Britain to my island of Skokholm. She skimmed away vigorously down the Firth of Forth out of sight, and virtually out of my thoughts.

I was sure that Niclas, even if he had understood my proposal, could not reasonably be expected to visit that wild precipice night after night. If he did at first perhaps, I knew he would most likely find only Koltur's unringed mate making the usual nocturnal visit to feed the growing chick in that burrow.

On reaching Skokholm I went out the same night to my marked burrows and recovered both shearwaters I had released near Torshavn nearly a fortnight earlier. They had probably returned many nights earlier – a flight of at least 1160 km.

As for the bird from Koltur, I had almost forgotten about her in the next week or so. Then Niclas wrote – in Faroese – by the Koltur postboat, to say that the shearwater had returned 'with ring on its leg numbered RW7664. I found this bird in the company of its young on August 9.'

On that 1936 visit I had achieved landings at several hard-to-reach Faroe bird-haunted small islands. I had been warned then not to attempt the most isolated group, north-east in the open sea, 600 km distant from Norway. The weather was always bad, there was no harbour; if I managed to land, I might be stranded for weeks by a gale. Which made me all the more determined to get to Fugloy (Bird Island). I write this on the very evening that I have, more than forty years later, arrived to live awhile on Fugloy.

The little steamer brought me from Scrabster in northern Scotland to Torshavn. I enlisted the help of the Faroes newspaper *Dagbladid* in the hope of finding Niclas Koltri, for I wished to ask him a question which had troubled me for nearly half a century: did he really go down that tattered old rope we left on that dreadful cliff on Koltur every night for a whole month until he found the shearwater with the ring on its leg which I had put on in the Firth of Forth?

To my joy the newseditor located Niclas at his new home near Torshavn. In the intervening years he had become famous for his skills in building the double-bowed sea-worthy Faroe fishing boats, traditionally used in the treacherous tide-wracked fiords. At seventy-two years his record is 340 boats entirely hand-built.

Our reunion earned a full-page story in the newspaper next day. A reporter translated Niclas's laughing reply: 'It was nothing. Of course I kept my promise. Each evening I climbed down that place, to take with the net puffins and fulmar petrels on the wing, until they went to bed at dusk. Then I waited till it was quite dark for the shearwaters to come home to feed that chick. Every night I looked down their burrow till at last – about a month after you left the island – my torch showed one wearing the ring you put on its leg when you released near Scotland the bird which bit Stauning's beard.'

To get to Fugloy you must journey from Torshavn by ferries to the nearer islands, crossing mountain roads between until at last you reach the base for the isolated north-east group. Some of the high mountain ridges now have tunnels to ease the road to the remotest islands. Majestic walled-in Hvannsund Fiord is the point of departure for Fugloy.

The genial sandy-haired Viking skipper of the final and smallest postboat ferry, Oli Petersen, was confident I could find a bed at Fugloy – if his little ship *Masin* could put me ashore there.

'You'll stay with Tummas, the island postman. You'll have to – no one else speaks a word of English. I'll warn him on the short-wave radio. You'll find all the same that silence is golden with Tummas. He won't smile at you, but take no notice – he has the heart of a lion, and the thoughts of a godly man. I ought to know. I was at school with him.'

Emerging from the shelter of the fiord we coasted along mountain-crowned cliffs, using the tidal currents skilfully to avoid bucking into wind squalls blasting between each island from the open ocean. There are two tiny hamlets on Fugloy, but no harbours, just a platform of rocks where in fine weather you must jump and be helped ashore.

On the radio Oli jabbered in Faroese, to be told that the ocean swell was bad and increasing. He translated the message to me, saying with a wry smile: 'We'll have a look anyway. Got some cargo to deliver.'

Showers of spray thudded on the windows of the wheelhouse as the little *Masin* bounced towards the first hamlet, Kirkja, a cluster of grass-roofed houses perched well above the highest storm tide. I could not imagine myself landing in that surf on these jagged rocks. But Oli called up his crew – just two (engineer and deckhand) – to load the substantial Viking double-bowed rowboat which we were towing. Baggage and mailbags were thrown in, Oli manoeuvring the *Masin* to keep a leeway as far as possible.

Somehow by skilful handling of the oars, the plunging rowboat reached close to the rock platform, where a dozen islanders, hitherto standing well above the surf-line, now rushed to snatch up the thrown ropes, and with great speed and energy yanked passengers and goods ashore each time the boat was carried near enough on a white wave.

Meanwhile, as a second trip was necessitated by half a dozen long zinc sheets still in the *Masin*'s hold, the skipper and I were fully employed in hauling them on deck and coiling the ropes ready for the returning longboat, Oli darting between the wheel-house controls of the *Masin*'s engine, and helping me – his supernumerary deckie, as he dubbed me.

Oli's perfect command of English had been acquired, I learned later, in ten years aboard a tramp ship in all oceans. Then why, I asked him, had this blue-eyed Viking come back to this tough assignment of a little postboat on this worst-exposed Faroe coast?

'Aboard that merchant ship,' he explained, 'I was nothing, a tiny fish in a huge pond. Good money maybe, but I couldn't stand the heat of Hong Kong, Sydney and Calcutta. Here I am master of my fate, and because I was born and brought up there [pointing to the island of Svinoy close to starboard] the Government has trusted me not to put this little ship on any of the rocks I know so well. So I have a pretty free hand. I'm essential as a ferry service for my many friends on Svinoy and Fugloy. Faroe is really one big family helping each other. We have to be – to survive in this terrible climate!'

All aboard at last and steaming under a massive cliff that separated Kirkja from my destination Hattarvik, nearest Faroe settlement to Norway. Here the same scene was enacted; I was yanked ashore by the strong hands of the postmaster from the *Masin*'s longboat, skilfully managed by the two-man crew.

The postmaster, a robust Viking with grizzled red hair, about forty plus, led the way to a comfortable warm wooden house in the steep hamlet close above the landing rocks. It had three floors, including the basement cowhouse. Here his smiling wife Kathni brought us coffee, her daughter Bergille (six) and baby son (four) clinging to her skirts.

Difficult to communicate at first, save by sign language and pointing at and naming objects. But later, on a fine day, while walking around the tiny village of a dozen houses, Bergille held my hand less shyly, and we named birds and flowers to each other in English and the Faroese equivalent.

Tummas, who signed his name with twirling flourishes in my diary
– Tummas Fritleif Juglo Hattervik – owns four cows, chestnut
coloured with white bellies, grazing the fenced 'inmark', and some
fifty sheep, mostly black or brown, running free on the 'outmark', the
wild and dangerous high cliffs where they were liable to be swept
away in a sudden willicwaw.

Again that wonderful sense of peace, far from mainland cares and
ugly modern urbanisation. To escape the wind and walk about the
sheltered inmark land was heaven. The chief birds were starlings,
rock-pipits and white wagtails with fledged broods. Snipe drumming
in the upper air or crying wickwock from the roofs of hayshed
and house were absurdly tame. Whimbrel (the sub-Arctic curlew)
whistled their love-call on this midsummer day, as they stalked
through wet hollows golden with huge kingcups – the poet's 'orbed
moons of pale yellow' – and purple and spotted orchids. In fact
several flowers familiar in the Welsh spring come into bloom at
midsummer on Fugloy: ragged robin, buttercup, cuckoo flower,
chickweed, lesser stitchwort, daisy, thrift, sheep's sorrel, butterwort
and wild thyme. In small gardens close to each house potatoes grow
uneasily in banked rows; little else save rhubarb.

A stream of Arctic terns, carrying fish in their bills, came from the
sea and flew steadily up the little glen of the inmark. I followed them
to chill barren heights where they viciously struck at my fur-capped
head when I walked through their nesting ground, where downy
chicks crouched low at the signal of their warning cries. I wondered
how these babies could survive the north wind blast – it drove me
back to the shelter (so I thought) of the south cliffs. Thousands of
puffins, fulmar petrels and gulls gyrated here, but even as I crouched
for safety behind a rock, a violent gust swept my cap far out to sea.

Sudden violent salty rain frequently drove me indoors. Kathni fed
me ryebread, liver paté and other tinned delicacies, margarine,
rhubarb jam, fresh milk. She became talkative, possibly as a relief
from her silence-is-golden husband. I had to write down the names of
some of my relatives in return for her entering the names of the island
families in my diary: Gullaksen, Hansan, Kerloch, Klein, Joensen
and Zachariasen, in total only fifty souls.

The little boy liked to sit next to me at the table, gazing wonder-
ingly, silent as his father, at the rare stranger to his island world.
Bergille would invite me to talk to her big talking doll – to stop it
talking you gave it a dummy teat.

But why, I wondered, did these good people continue to live on this

remote stormy island? How did they amuse themselves in the long
dark northern winter? There was a tiny church, and a tinier shop –
where I would walk the children to buy a bag of sweets for forty-five
kroner (about £4); rather expensive – but think of the transport cost.

The answer came when the mailboatman Oli Petersen collected me
a few stormy days later. 'Ah,' said he, as I tumbled aboard the *Masin*,
carrying the sealed mailbag of Hattarvik. 'It's because Faroe would
be nothing without the sea.'

It had been a difficult morning. He had radioed Fugloy that he was
picking up mail and passengers at Svinoy first; but on getting to
shelter at Svinoy, the passengers there – 'mostly my relatives', he
grinned – had flatly refused to go north into the northerly gale to
Fugloy, so he was obliged to service Fugloy first. This meant that we
also had to pick up the passengers dumped at Kirkja, with the same
skilful handling of the longboat through the inshore surf. We got
away from Fugloy before the northerly gale which blew us east-
about under the sheer 345 m high bird-haunted cliffs of Eysterhoodi
(a name I picked out on the chart) where, said Oli, 'as a boy I was
taught to use the *flaygustong* [fowling net]. I still like to take my
summer holiday at Svinoy, harvesting the old birds before the young
birds take wing.'

Oli repeated the convenient Faroe fairy-tale which I had heard in
1936: that it doesn't matter how many adult puffins you take – there
are at least seven old birds to each chick, so there are always some old
birds left to feed the unfledged youngster with a beakful of little
fishes. It did not seem important to tell him that my ringing research
at Skokholm so long ago had proved that the young puffin is far too
fat at this stage to go to sea, and is instinctively abandoned by its own
parents. It remains perhaps for a week until it has slimmed enough to
flutter clumsily down to the sea at night.

Meanwhile the adolescent puffins, born one or more years earlier,
come ashore about midsummer. They are prospecting for a burrow
home, 'sweethearting' in preparation for establishing a burrow for
breeding in the years ahead. These juveniles more than double the
adult population at this season, and are caught in the fowling net –
and, being fairly young, are good eating. Miraculously the fledgeling
puffin, departing alone at night, unguided save by instinct, swims
hundreds of miles into deep ocean where it remains for the next two
years. It thus escapes the fowler's net to survive as the reservoir which
will maintain puffin population levels.

As we lurched around the farther headland into the sheltered inlet of Oli's native village of Svinoyarvik, I was happy to see a substantial landing pier. There was no hurry now; all his passengers, coming or going, were standing around gossiping and snacking. Skipper Oli walked me to the house of an English-speaking couple. It had a sod roof (above birch-bark tiles) colourful as a hayfield, luxurious with long grass starred with ragged robin, buttercups and long-stemmed daisies. Yet the street was tarsealed and lit by tall lamp standards.

Oli's explanation came with talk over tea and biscuits: until the twentieth century the hardy Faroese lived isolated from the world. The wild landscape and weather restricted them to fishing close to home from their seaworthy small double-bowed rowboats, harvesting seafowl from the great cliffs, hunting the gregarious pilot whales by driving them ashore. Their few cows were housed in the basement for the winter, an admirable way of heating the living rooms above – a wooden shaft for the purpose ascended to the roof, which, with its weight of grassy turf, was firm against the gales. When the hay ran out late in the winter the cattle readily ate dried fish.

During the Second World War they welcomed British occupation which prevented a German invasion – just in time. Afterwards these 40,000 Norse-descended islanders secured independence in 1948 as a self-governing nation. From supplying Britain with fish during the war, the enterprising Faroese have modernised their fleet to exploit all seas as far as Greenland, Newfoundland, Spitzbergen, and the Murman coast beyond Norway.

To maintain their traditional superb seamanship the new Government has subsidised its source – the inhabitants of the little islands so hard of access – by grants to pay for improved services: daily postboat, electricity, tarsealed roads and, where possible, tunnels under mountains and bridges over fiords. These advantages have kept people content to dwell in the remoter settlements. The young men crew the new large fishing vessels, and the older men spend more time at home, enjoying their savings from the highly profitable trawling and line-fishing.

Denmark may now belong to the Common Market, but not the Faroes. The Faroe man is a born fisherman, and now, claiming a 200-mile limit around their islands, they fish with their own sophisticated diesel-powered vessels, built with the latest scientific equipment in several shipyards tucked away in the narrow fiords. The average income of these fishermen lately has been around £15,000 from exports of frozen filleted or salted fish of many species.

'You see what I mean?' concluded Skipper Oliver Petersen. 'We are nothing without the sea'.

The Farthest Hebrides

A voice so thrilling ne'er was heard
In spring-time from the Cuckoo-bird,
Breaking the silence of the seas
Among the farthest Hebrides.

Like William Wordsworth in *Memorials of a Tour in Scotland 1803*, we have been roaming the farthest Hebrides – the Long Island of Lewis and Harris, farther than which you cannot safely roam.

The misty midsummer land rings all day with the melodious calls of the male cuckoo, numerous because the open moors are the home of the dainty meadow-pipits, whose nests, although hidden from man in the tufted heather, are carefully studied by the female cuckoo in early morning spying flights.

On sighting with her large red-gold eye a pipit about its nest preparation the pregnant cuckoo makes a mental note of its location. She will visit it regularly, ready to lay just one egg as soon as the pipit has begun to lay her clutch of four to six eggs. She needs to do this before the pipit lays its last egg of the clutch, for the good reason (but how does she know?) that the young cuckoo must hatch at the same time – it usually hatches half a day earlier – as the young pipits hatch. For the naked, blind newborn cuckoo proceeds at once to wriggle beneath each pipit egg or new-hatched chick and, hoisting it upon its hollow shoulders, topples it out of the nest. Another miracle of instinct, you may suppose? The usurper's itch or instinct does not last more than a few days, during which it must remove all competitors for the foster-parental food supply.

The young cuckoo is never fed by its real parents, although it most likely hears and learns the distinct voices of the adults, the incessant cuckoo of the male, and the sibilant bubbling response of the female. She is usually silent except when she wants to call a mate. During the two short summer months of May and June she will lay up to two dozen eggs, at intervals of forty-eight hours. For this purpose she must keep a succession of pipit nests under close surveillance, ready to drop her next egg in the right one.

Patient studies in the field have revealed that the female cuckoo spends her morning finding or watching a suitable nest, sitting

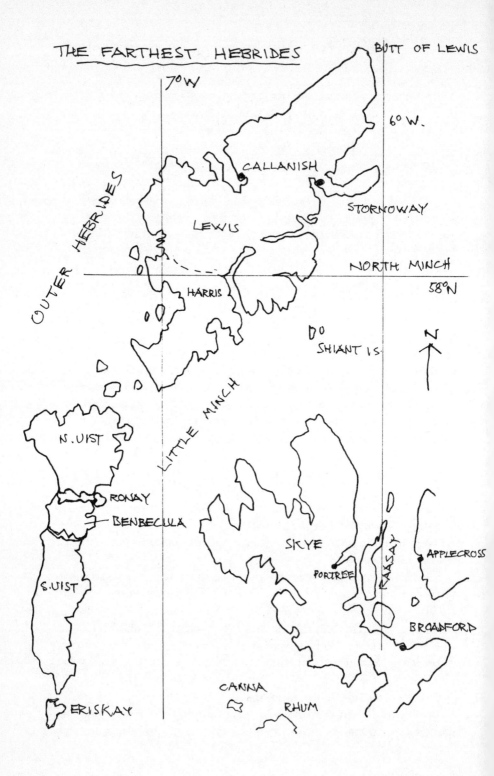

THE FARTHEST HEBRIDES

BUTT OF LEWIS

7°W

6° W.

CALLANISH

STORNOWAY

Outer Hebrides

LEWIS

NORTH MINCH

58°N

HARRIS

SHIANT IS.

N

LITTLE MINCH

N.UIST

RONAY

BENBECULA

SKYE

RAASAY

APPLECROSS

PORTREE

S.UIST

BROADFORD

CANNA

ERISKAY

RHUM

quietly on a fence post or top of a bush or other viewpoint, in which period she will have studied the activity at the nest, remaining so still that the pipit accepts her as part of the background, or she may not even see the hen cuckoo. At this time the role of the male pipit is often to mob the male cuckoo haunting the territorial area where the female cuckoo is operating; it is the male's frequent calling that attracts the pipit to attack him as he flies around.

The cuckoo on the wing, with its long tail, sharp-pointed wings, and black-barred underparts, closely resembles a hawk. The attack by a pipit, however, is feeble: it never strikes the parasite, which generally ignores it. The cock cuckoo takes not the slightest interest in the female's activities at the pipit's nest, except that her presence has lured him to call and indicate his readiness to mate. It is now generally believed that during her month or more of laying her eggs, singly at two-day intervals, she accepts any (perhaps more than one) male that courts her – in other words, her promiscuity ensures that every egg will be fertile.

Perhaps the hen cuckoo delays laying her egg until after midday, when the hen pipit is likely to be out feeding. At any rate her deposition of the egg is a matter of seconds. She invariably flies straight to the selected nest, grabs one of the pipit's eggs in her bill, and almost in the same moment ejects her own egg into the nest.

Observers report that if by chance, in this hasty movement, the egg is ejected so that it rests on the edge of the nest, or falls to the ground, the hen cuckoo never returns to replace it. The computer-biological clock in her brain, which directed her with apparent skill to locate and prepare to lay her egg in the right nest at the right moment, moves on to the next natural action. Which is to swallow the pipit egg in her bill, or she may drop it. Perhaps she is not hungry. If it breaks it becomes – probably – an object she no longer recognises.

It is all very well for the observer to rationalise, or anthropomorphise the seemingly instinctive actions of any animal. One would like to think that such a beautiful bird is not a complete automaton in her seemingly intricate system of duping other birds to rear her young. There are glimmerings of some intelligent thought/action where a hen cuckoo lays an egg in the nest of a suitable foster-parent which is domed over or otherwise too difficult for her to enter. Although she can poke her head in far enough to steal an egg from the nest, does she then lay her egg on the ground and convey it to the nest in her bill? No, that might be too much for her limited mental agility. Instead she flutters towards the nest hole, pressing her tail against it,

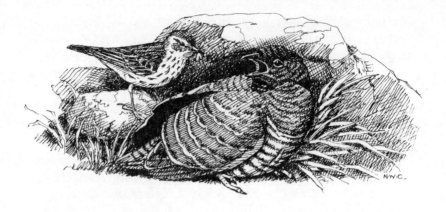

and ejects her precious egg directly into its cosy warmth! The naked blind cuckoo born there, in turn has a slight problem: it must somehow find the right position for the ejection of the nest-owner's eggs or chicks; but being blind, how does it find that place in a domed nest? I do not know, but I imagine the young cuckoo's naked skin is sensitive to the cooler air of the entrance.

In such domed nests, built by a small bird species, the young cuckoo, fed by both foster-parents, soon outgrows the original walls of the nest. It is about half-grown and well-feathered when it climbs out and sits on *top* of the structure, all the better to be fed by its loving foster-parents, which will presently alight on its head or back in order to stuff the monster with insect food.

In my New Zealand garden the beautiful shining cuckoo, *Chalcites lucidus*, hardly larger than a sparrow, barred like the European cuckoo, but with its upper parts an almost iridescent metallic green with gleams of copper and gold, comes each spring, calling with its loud whistling song. It is mainly parasitic on our tiny native grey warbler, which has a cheerful wren-like song resembling a staccato version of its scientific name *Gerygone igata*.

In its life history and migrations it resembles the European cuckoo; and by midsummer I often find the huge fat fledgeling Chalcites sitting on top of the once neatly domed nest of this warbler, insatiable for more grubs and bugs brought by its foster-parents, its huge gape wide open and squawking. At the sight of any other warbler, not necessarily of its foster-parents' species, it will shiver its wings to draw attention to its hunger; and in this way supplements its food at the expense of the young of other small insect-eating native species – whitehead, yellowhead, silvereye, even the introduced dunnock (hedge-sparrow).

Interesting that these two cuckoos, half a world apart, never see their true parents to recognise them, for by the time they have become independent of foster-parental care, the blithe, carefree adults have migrated back to their winter quarters: the European cuckoo south to tropical Africa north of the equator; the shining cuckoo north to tropical islands of the Pacific south of the equator. A few months later when the juvenile cuckoos are strong enough to migrate they find the same winter quarters entirely on their own initiative, nor are they known to travel other than singly. One does not see them much after fledging, but I have watched young fledged cuckoos in their bright first plumage feeding on caterpillars of the hairy species, larvae (of butterflies or moths) which feed on stinging nettles and similar coarse plants, in English waysides and in my New Zealand garden.

What an unusual taste! But then these cuckoos are as unusual as they are handsome – with that wonderful urge or instinct in their pretty heads to gulp down a hairy caterpillar without a whisper of example or encouragement from any other living soul.

There were plenty of these hairy caterpillars browsing the heathy surface of Wordsworth's farthest Hebrides on the day two of us wandered there and to which I must now return, with apologies to the reader for the above dissertation on the thrilling mystery of the cuckoo bird.

For the voice which thrilled Wordsworth was not that of a bird; but of 'yon solitary Highland lass', who sang 'perhaps . . . for old, unhappy, far-off things, and battles long ago: . . . some natural sorrow, loss or pain that has been, and may be again?'

Like Wordsworth, we on the same wandering walk gazed upon that lovely peach-and-rose-white complexion of young Hebridean women induced by the soft island mists; and were pleased, yet felt that same natural sorrow which links the enjoyment of beauty with a consciousness of the fragility of the wild flower and of human emotion.

Even on this rare fine day, as we talked with the tall, blue-eyed, fair-headed crofter woman within the enclosure protecting the 4000-year-old Standing Stones of Callanish we had that feeling of 'old, unhappy, far-off things, and battles long ago'.

In her slow graceful gestures and unhurried answers to our questioning there seemed to be a watchful timelessness, a sense

of remembering or brooding upon or waiting for some perhaps cataclysmic event 'that has been and may be again'.

Climate makes character. To look into the brooding eyes of many a young and old inhabitant of the Hebrides is for me to see those 4000 years of history, of a land once fair made desolate by a changing climate and economy. As she told us of old times I waved an imaginary wand over this Callanish woman and made her the priestess of this late-Neolithic temple of the sun and moon, as remarkable as its contemporary Stonehenge, but much less troubled by tourists.

The cruciform alignment of these fifty-three tall stones suggests a Christian origin which may have saved them when fervent Christian missionaries arrived and began destroying all symbols of paganism.

But they were erected at least 4000 years ago in a millennium of warmer weather and calmer seas, when this now stark land was richly wooded and had attracted colonisation by a people contemporary with Minoan civilisation, who tended their flocks, grew wheat, fished fertile seas, and hunted deer, wild boar, bear and wolf in primeval forests. Only such a wealth of production could have supported a priesthood of learned astronomers who so long ago aligned great stones to make a compass and calendar marking the exact positions of sunset and sunrise, moonset and moonrise, at midsummer and midwinter solstices and the seasons between.

Until some 130 years ago the Callanish Stones stood half-buried in peat as deep as a man is tall, deposited during subsequent water-logged centuries of cold wet weather which inhibited corn production and delayed the decay of vegetation – a time of battles long ago, when hungry people strove for possession of a now-sodden landscape and stormy coast in order to win a meagre subsistence.

The Vikings came, but respected the site. They thought the stones were trolls – men turned to stone by an enchanter. In 1695 one Martin, gentleman and itinerant tacksman (rent-collector) for the Macleods of Skye, wrote of Callanish: 'The inhabitants told me that it was a Place appointed for worship in the time of Heathenism, and that the chief Druid or Priest stood near the big stone [nearly five metres tall] in the centre, from whence he addressed himself to the People that surrounded him.'

Our Callanish lady guide informed us that when in 1857 the peat was removed entirely from the stones by the lord proprietor of Lewis, Sir James Matheson, workmen found at the base of the great stone a chambered tomb containing the fragmented bones of a cremated person, no doubt a priest.

As she talked soberly, learnedly, a male cuckoo alighted singing on the centre stone as if to mock her with his cuckoo, cuckoo. The day was June 4th, close to midsummer. Presently a distant bubbling trill invited him to fly in search of the triller. Appropriately, but perhaps inadvertently, our local historian told us that until as recently as the last century the arena of the Stones was visited at midsummer sunrise by sweethearts betrothing. Some engaged couples still do – something of a fertility cult, perhaps? But it was considered a bad or evil thing if a single man or woman appeared there at the midsummer solstice sunrise. It caused gossip as to his or her morals. But today, if you come here at dawn on midsummer day you will find quite a crowd – it's become a tourist attraction.

We walked the length and breadth of the ancient temple, in the form of a rough cross 405 feet from south to north – this long axis points due north – a double parallel line of ten stones each, as we counted them. There is a centre circle of a diameter of forty-two feet with thirteen stones eight to twelve feet tall. Two further stones lie, marking approximately the east and west points of the compass. A quite remarkable sundial, or calendar, crematorium, planetarium, and scientifically accurate observatory for the study of the celestial bodies – probably all these things to the megalithic priests and their acolytes who erected them. Preserved by the superstitious dread of the common people for the priest's power to divine the movements of, and consult with, the life-giving Sun God . . .

The stones are well-preserved, still remarkably upright, sunk deep into the bedrock, and rough-hewn – cleaved but not dressed – from the Lewisian gneiss.

At the local inn that evening, some fine tales were circulated with the nips of whisky, and warm welcome extended to fellow Gaels. A Welsh-born Celt with the name of Lockley was accepted as a Scots clansman. Said one crofter:

'For I have heard Wales is full of these ancient standing stones, each one a sundial, and marking the grave of a Druid priest. And now the custom is revived in the making of the stone circle of your Gorsedd at your annual Eisteddfod. You should stay in Lewis for the midsummer festival, and be up betimes before the sun rises. For then it is that a mysterious glittering beam of light will be glancing down the avenues of stones, indicating the visit of the Shining One.'

'What is the significance of the cuckoo which alights and calls so often on the great tall centre stone?' I ventured, in a slight lull in the talk.

'The same as motivates the dratted cuckoo which cuckoos from the chimbly of me house,' answered another man, as he lit his pipe from a peat ember on the hearth. 'Them cuckoos go on all night just now, for the wee pipit birds are laying their eggs in their nests in my machair hay ready for the convenience of the foreign parasite to supply the means of fostering the great lump of Master Cuckoo. As to the Standing Stones, there's a load of rubbish about them being a temple of the Druids. Nothing of the sort. They were built by the early Pictish kings thousands of years earlier, when Scotland emerged from the last Ice Age, and the land was open and free, and the sun melted the ice. Did ye not see that whole story depicted on the telly last month, man?'

So the argument went on, for the Lewisman loves a debate. We were in no hurry, having secured a bed for ourselves in the loft above the taproom. The crofters left one by one as a misty twilight floated up from the sea across the rich, salt-fertilised machair fields, ankle-deep in white clover and midsummer daisies. There is no darkness in the Hebridean night in June.

A late visitor – a sea-fisherman from the dry, prosperous, sunny east coast of Scotland (he told us he was at present fishing in the Minch off Stornoway, but sailed home once a month via the Caledonian Canal to his base at Inverness) was scornful of 'these dissembling two-faced lazy crofters, and their layabout habits. Man, ye'll never see a grown Lewis crofter here but he is slouching about his home on a fine day, with his hands in his pockets, when he ought to be at the 'taties he is too lazy to weed, or even grow, or at the peat-digging. He leaves the croft work to his wimmun . . . why, he can't even find time to clean the mess around his own front door. Just observe how every croft has a derelict car or tractor or two spoiling the grand scenery for the visitor!'

We felt obliged to agree with this criticism. But it was later explained to us by the landlord of the tavern, a Lewis man lately retired from skippering an ocean liner.

'It all goes back to the bad old days of the Clearances, way back early in this century. My folk had nothing to eat save what they could toil from the sea and the machair. There was no money to buy sugar or salt. The poverty was so bad and a world-wide depression setting in, a Highlands and Islands Board was set up, to lend us money to survive. Along comes a second world war in 1939, and suddenly we became important again – as bases for naval and army training. Those men who were too old to fight, or did not want to, were granted all sorts of help, in the form of subsidies, to keep them producing food for increasingly hungry Britain – the German submarines were sinking hundreds of food ships from America. I ought to know, I was in a destroyer convoy. But my brother at home could now get a full grant for a tractor, for repairing his croft, for a new boat for inshore fishing, even a new car to do the shopping in Stornoway. Naturally we won't throw away any machinery when it dies. 'Tis needed every bit for spare parts, and only safe outside his front door . . .'

'Aye,' chipped in his brother, who had just called in. 'There's still a subsidy for each sheep or beast you keep, though I doubt if many crofters bother to count 'em, and maybe a few have been dead these several years.'

'Then there's the dole for every day it rains . . .'

'And the whisky up at the still on the mountain. Man! 'Tis a grand life I'm thinking the Long Island people do be having!"

'Aye, you need some consolation for living in the terrible weather we do have in this wild island, when there's nowt to do but work the Harris tweed looms alongside the old woman, God bless 'em. 'Tis lonesome then, for the childer will be gone to the cities – till they shake the wanderlust from them, and come home to roost.'

Summer in the Falklands

John Strong, commander of the privateer *Welfare* (270 tons, thirty-eight guns), sailing the southern ocean in 1689–90 with Letters of Marque to seize as prizes any French ships, was first to record a landing on the remote, galeswept, treeless, uninhabited Falkland Isles.

'The designe of our Voyage being Discovereyes,' wrote Strong, 'oblidged us to remain some time in this place. The Islands are parted by a great Sound, which we past through . . .'

He named it Falkland Sound, and 'sent our boats on Shoar for fresh water, and did kill abundance of Geese and Duck. The Penguins, being mustered in infinet number, seemed to salute us with a greate many Graceful bows, expressing their Curiosity and good Breeding . . .'

But it was the French scholar and entrepreneur Louis de Bougainville of Brittany who landed the first colonists – two large families – in 1764, well-equipped with stores, farm seeds and cattle, on East Falkland. Eleven months later John Byron in HMS *Dolphin* established a British fort, which he called Fort Egmont, on the north coast of West Falkland, unaware of the French settlement at Port St Louis, 100 miles away on the extreme east coast of East Falkland.

The Spanish Crown strenuously objected to these 'invasions' of the Malvinas, as they called the islands from the name *Malouines* bestowed by the Breton colonists from their home town of St Malo; the Spanish claimed that by a Papal Bull of 1494 the Spanish Crown had been granted all land in South America. Protestant Britain ignored this claim; but Catholic Bougainville agreed to cede his colony to Spain 'on sufficient compensation of Hard Dollars'. Taking with him those of his compatriots who preferred not to live under the Spanish flag, Bougainville sailed for St Malo in 1767, 'with a profitable cargo of sealskins and whale-oil'.

In the next hundred years the whales and seals, and even the penguins, were slaughtered almost to extinction by the crews (many were escaped convicts, debauched seamen and press-ganged youths) of European and American whaling and sealing vessels. The Falklands become a no-man's-land, the Spanish governor intermittently

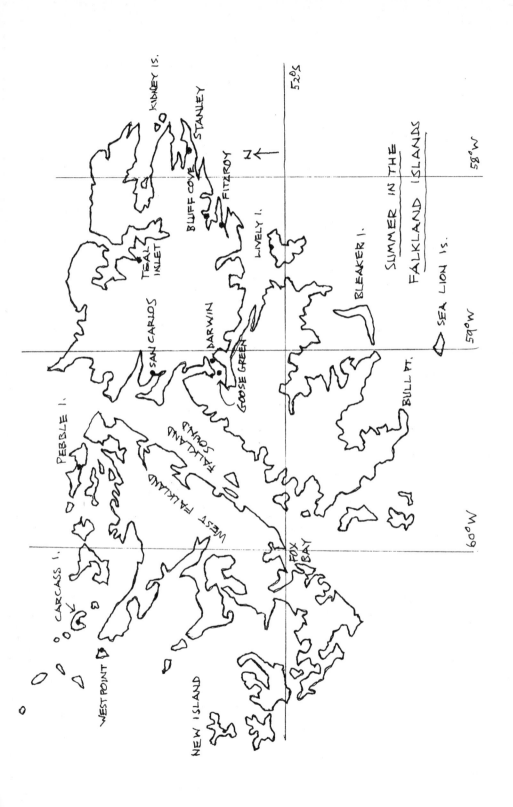

SUMMER IN THE
FALKLAND ISLANDS

resident at Port St Louis but helpless to keep order outside the bay there. Soon all America was a ferment of wars of independence, in which Spain lost all her American colonies.

In 1834 Britain, claiming the Falklands by right of discovery, appointed Lieutenant Henry Smith, RN, as Governor. He took up residence unopposed at Port St Louis, renamed it Port Stanley, and within four years established the Falkland Islands Association of British Settlers. It has survived in modified form to this day.

It would be hard to find a more loyal British (one should perhaps say Scottish) colony so well adapted to the cool climate who pioneered so successfully, making use of their skills in shepherding and fishing taught in Highland and upland British pastures and sea-coasts.

Such was the historical background of my visit to the islands, barely two years after the sudden attack by Argentina upon the Falklands and South Georgia, the failure of which we were to discuss in detail with the islanders.

My first visit to the Antarctic had been in 1981 with Richard Adams, meeting him and the *Lindblad Explorer* party in Buenos Aires, before flying south to Ushuaia to embark at this most southern port of Argentina. Here we had to listen to the port officer complaining of the rude behaviour of the Chilean gunboat patrolling the channel southwards to Cape Horn. It was an old rivalry between the sister nations, beginning when both secured independence from Spain, when Argentina, larger and more powerful, tried to seize from Chile all Tierra del Fuego and the Beagle Channel. But since the military defeat of Argentina in the Falklands and South Georgia, Chile had become the aggressor, determined to win back the bleak island and seaway Argentina had seized. But more about this hatred of politicians later.

For this reason the *Lindblad Explorer* in 1984 was, to the delight of Chile, using the Chilean port of Punta Arenas.

Diary. 6 January 1984 Punta Arenas, Chile. Expedition members assemble from northward world-wide, most flying in from Santiago. Walked about the town. It has 100,000 inhabitants, and growing rapidly, a mixed community of dark Indian (Fuegian), but much European, stock. There are schools for all – British from the Falklands and Patagonia, Germans (strong in Chile), and even Yugoslavs lately emigrated to work in the newly-discovered oilfields. So said our bus tour guide. Chief export is wool and cattle from estancias, and oil from rigs along the shore. The centre is full of impressive stone and bronze monuments; churchyards have massive family mausoleums of ornate appearance – too grandiose as they peer down at humbler graves. Long rows of Chilean cedars form symmetrical avenues carefully clipped by some topiary expert, probably employed by the hereditary owners of the long-established sheep farms.

The best of the monuments was a memorial of bronze figures on an open hill, depicting the humble shepherds, their dogs and sheep, which had brought wealth to Punta Arenas (Sandy Point). In a public park was a museum of early transport – fine four-wheel carriages, two-wheel sulkies, victorias, a stage coach, traction engines, Model T Fords, etc., as well as old farm implements, whaling and sealing trypots and harpoon gear. Less attractive was an exhibition of local wild animals in too small cages; a puma, condors and foxes, looking unhappy, moulting and smelling rankly.

It was Saturday and most of the well-dressed inhabitants were strolling through a huge modern chain-store of two decks. By contrast the pavements sprouted grass, dandelions and sheep's sorrel, from seeds probably shed from the baggy trousers and ragged skin shoes of the Patagonian Indian peasants. Typical of Latin American countries, where the air of riches contrasts so vividly with the stench of poverty.

The *Lindblad Explorer* was berthed next to a smart-looking Chilean gunboat, the skipper of which said he would be escorting the *Lindblad Explorer* through the Straits of Magellan, *Estre de Magellanes*, which is an entirely Chilean waterway 'though the Argentine gringos disputed and tried to drive us out during the Falklands War. You will recollect we helped you British to land by night behind the Argy base of Rio Gallegos and blow it up? They launched from the helipad on my little ship . . .'

Aboard our ship many friends of previous voyages. Delighted to meet again Swedish skipper Hasse Nilsson – as passionately fond of remote islands as I am.

My cabin-mate is Donald Bradshaw, a big bearded fellow, expert photographer and naturalist. He tells me he is head of Burroughs Wellcome in Japan, and happily married to a charming Japanese lady much engaged just now with small children. There was a get-together early dinner of Patagonian delicacies – abalone, steak, wine, etc., and a brief floor-show in the Penguin (theatre) Room by Chilean and Indian belles, before we sailed around seven pm.

Handsome blue-eyed (Antarctic) cormorants, crops bulging with fish as they perched on the spars of a broken-down wharf, seemed to wave us goodbye with wings rigidly extended. Out in the Magellan Strait, which varies from one to twenty miles wide, there were sea-swallows fishing in the calm tideway. They were the South American tern *Striata hirundinacea*, and the Antarctic species *S. vittata*, agreed Donald and Ronald, poring over bird guides, but too sleepy with good food, sweet air and marvellous views of the mountains each side of the strait which Ferdinand Magellan was first to navigate, in 1521. He went on to be first to sail across the Pacific to Asia.

7 January At sea. A following wind blew us clear of the strait, escorted by leaping piebald dolphins, not two metres in length but with the long name *Cephalorhynchus commersoni*. Everyone dashes to the bridge or bows at the shout of 'Whales!' over the intercom – and the experts agree as to the species. Novices write down the scientific names, cameras click. Luckily the bridge spans the whole width of the ship, with port and starboard wings in the open air. You are even permitted to study charts, depth-finder and radar screen, and there is a little alcove where self-help tea and coffee and biscuits are available.

In the open sea the long-winged wandering albatrosses glided around us, joined by hundreds of the smaller mollymawk, the black-browed albatross. The surface swarmed with lesser petrels, and the diving sort called prions.

Two illustrated lectures in the Penguin Room sensibly prepared the uninitiated for tomorrow. Historian-yachtsman Alan Gurney, who lives on the Hebridean island of Islay, expounded on the past and recent history of the Falklands. Dennis Puleston, doyen of years of sea-travel to remote islands, expatiated on the identification of the sea-birds we should see this trip. He is a darling smiling man, and has given me a copy of his first adventures at sea – he writes and illustrates exquisitely.

As a teenage youth, Dennis sailed round the world 1930–36, with like-age companions in second-hand half-open lifeboats, starting from home in England. Using the north-east tradewinds they reached the Canaries, thence across to the West Indies, living on caught fish, then picking up the odd job in Central America. They reached China on the Pacific tradewinds, only to find the Japs were invading, so

Dennis escaped home to England via the Trans-Siberian Railway. He must be seventy, but looks half that age.

8 January New Island. A sunlit dawn and a strong following wind brought the *Lindblad Explorer* to anchor at 07.30 hours in the shelter east of the most westerly inhabited of the several hundred isles of the Falklands.

Led by Dennis we hurried the half-mile of grazed grassland to the west cliffs in a forty-knot gale. A spectacular sight are the rookeries of rockhopper penguins at the top of almost sheer 200-foot-high and sometimes overhanging rock walls. Some of these handsome, tubby tuft-crested two-foot-tall birds were landing on low rock-shelves from the huge ocean swell, but many others were riding in on a wave directly upon the 200-foot-tall cliff.

Somehow, using their narrow flippers, long bill and clawed web-bed feet, each grabs the cliff as the wave subsides, and immediately begins to hop – yes, *hop* – upwards, from one invisible (to us) crack to the next. Thus they ascend the rock wall, more easily than a human climber could. In centuries of this crag-climbing they have worn an almost vertical rock-ladder, to reach the broken plateau far above. Here they congregate in thousands in a grand rookery shared with blue-eyed cormorants and black-browed albatrosses.

At this season all have well-grown young, which all three species feed by regurgitation. The cormorant and albatross fly in easily, though the blue-eyed beauty is a bit clumsy in landing on its untidy seaweed-cum-guano nest. But the penguin must hop all the way from the sea. Like the common sparrow the rockhopper penguin seldom walks – its habit is to hop to reach its nest of little stones collected in a depression in the gale-blasted terrain.

They are very tame and curious, staring at you, even making a gesture of approach, forever waving their long flippers and neck-craning. The youngest chicks were still being guarded and fed at intervals from stomach-loaded adults, who have the ability to dole out just so much as each baby needs as it gropes for nourishment with its head submerged down the parental throat. A nice provision of nature, enabling the parent to enjoy long periods at the nest after its long spell of fishing at sea and then that wearisome climb up the sheer cliffs.

Rockhoppers, like some other crested penguins, lay two eggs, but seldom rear two chicks; one egg is smaller than the other, and almost invariably neglected – unless one of the two is lost – a form of

insurance, one may suppose; and perhaps this penguin is evolving to become a one-egg layer? Or is it on the way to laying two eggs of the same size?

Older chicks, still warmly clad in down, were huddled in mobs (creches) – safety and warmth in numbers – guarded by one or two adults defying the attempts of predatory gulls, skuas and the hawk-like caracaras which were flying about, ever ready to pounce upon the unguarded egg or chick. The splendid dark-browed albatross on its neat cup nest rears only one chick, just now in pale grey down, and pugnaciously able to repulse any predator (including a human) by ejecting a stream of foul-smelling stomach oil directly at the intruder.

The blue-eyed cormorants stood on guard near their untidy guano-mucked nests containing two or three scrawny-necked black-garbed children. Here and there were small groups of the dark red-wattled king shags. Inland, as I strolled (almost blown) down the hill over sheep-grazed turf there were other, larger penguins in a totally different nesting terrain.

These live in burrows, from which they peep shyly at you – until assured you are harmless by your good behaviour of squatting on the turf and outstaring them. They are one of four *Spheniscus* species which occupy the cool sub-Antarctic lands bordering the southern coasts of both South America and South Africa. They evolved, it is believed, from cooler Antarctic shores, but were swept northwards by the upwelling east-going currents (so rich in their fish and krill food) of the Humboldt Stream. Three species settled here: the large

S. magellanicus of the Falklands, and Patagonian coast; a smaller one, *S. humboldti*, on the west side from Valparaiso to Peru, and the smallest and rarest, *S. mendiculus*, ended up at the Equator, and is found only on the Galapagos Isles. The fourth was carried past South America as far as South Africa, to nest on the Roaring Forties Benguela Current coast.

But more was to come. Over a hill we came across a scattering of gentoo penguins guarding their well-grown young on a wide beach, somewhat at risk of being devoured by the sea-lions. These penguins are well aware of the risk, and huddle by the edge of the sea awaiting the chance to paddle furiously, with beating flippers, into the water (or out of it) when there is a lull in predator activity. Wild Falkland Island geese and the flightless Falkland Island duck frequent this beach.

There are other creatures on New Island: rabbits and rats, and a human family. New Island is a sheep-station run by young Chris McCallum and his pretty wife Elaine, who rescued me from watching two little birds feeding in the farm garden, absurdly tame. They were new to me – the Falkland thrush and a starling-sized bird they call their robin redbreast.

As a once self-sufficient islander on a remote Welsh island, I enjoyed their hospitality at a table laden with Falkland delicacies – dairy produce, succulent lamb, fish from the sea, home-baked bread and cake, and luscious strawberries. Soft fruit thrives well in summer in this snug dimple of their island, protected by a hedge of gorse, native hebe and wind-bent macrocarpa. Potatoes grow enormously, and they raise tomatoes in a plastic greenhouse.

'No enemy but rough weather,' said rosy-cheeked Elaine. 'Which has its advantages. In gales you catch up with your reading and wool-spinning. We make most of our clothes from our own wool. Never seems to be much spare time. Neighbours are forever gossiping on the short-wave radio, so we get all the inter-island news as well as the international stuff, which Chris listens to. I prefer the local info. Just heard that Mary at Fox Bay has successfully risen from the straw, that is, has given birth to her third – a bonny wee boy.'

I listened in a daze, relaxed and tired from so much tramping, botanising and bird-watching. I complimented them on their wealth of bird life as I hungrily accepted another slice of that gorgeous home-made dough cake.

As the sun set it began to rain. The McCallums drove me on their tractor-trailer to the little harbour below their farmhouse. The trailer was loaded with two or three dressed carcases of their sheep, a gift to the *Lindblad Explorer*, whose zodiacs were re-embarking our expedition members.

We were a merry party at dinner aboard the *Lindblad Explorer*, and afterwards, over coffee and cigarillos in the saloon with the Falklands pilot and customs officer, the ship's officers, the McCallums and everyone else who could crowd into the saloon, including Mr and Mrs Rod Napier, owners of our port of call tomorrow (West Point Island). It was inevitable that much of the talk would be about the recent 'Argy-bargy Affair', as the islanders call the invasion . . .

'A surprise – never thought the Argies would really invade – all a political gamble by the military dictators trying to divert the common citizen from the misery of unemployment and inflation. . . . Never yet met an Argy soldier who wanted to fight . . . most of 'em were conscripts, hadn't an idea what it was all about. . . . Their officers were too well-bred – Spanish aristocrats. . . . Bloody bastards most of them, they despised their conscripts. Saw one shoot a conscript dead in the street for failing to salute when he walked past the poor bugger. . . . Worst thing was for the sons and grandsons of ex-British Patagonian farmers to be conscripted to fight their Falkland relations. I heard many refused – or their parents bought off the recruiting Argy when he called. . . . One thing I'll say – General Menendez was a decent man, he was all for saving civilian lives . . . but ordered Spanish to be taught in the schools.'

But all agreed that Maggie Thatcher had been the Joan of Arc of the seven weeks' war. 'Nobbut a woman Prime Minister would've loaded the two largest passenger ships in the world – the *Canberra* and *Q.E.2* – with thousands of troops and sent them across the length of the Atlantic Ocean!'

9 January West Point and Carcass Islands. 08.45 hours. I scribble this in the shelter of the farm settlement on West Point (Napier's Island) waiting for the gale to subside. A nicely dilapidated dwelling protected by macrocarpas of great wind-twisted age in which new small birds flit and feed, as tame as a bird-lover could wish.

A plain-breasted flycatcher proves to be the tyrant bird, and the robin is called the meadow-lark, according to Nel Jennings, the genial chief shepherd at West Point, who carried me off in a shower of hail to the comfort of his wooden house close by. Here coffee and a large glass of gin-and-orange whiled away part of the morning agreeably. His wife Mary, preparing the barbecue, told me how, during the Argy War, she was shut up by the enemy with some eighty non-combatant islanders in the schoolhouse at Goose Green. She showed me the diary which she had kept, and hoped might one day be published.

The hero of this Goose Green episode was of course Lt-Colonel Herbert Jones, CO of the Second Battalion of the Parachute Regiment. He had been on a skiing holiday when the Argentine army invaded the Falklands and South Georgia on 2 April 1982. Next day the United Nations Security Council ordered Argentina to withdraw its forces. But it was too late. Although the tiny British garrison fought courageously, it was outnumbered more than a thousand to one. No one thought that Britain had a hope of driving out the invaders – except Margaret Thatcher, plus every man of the elite commando and parachute trained regiments, who were determined to enjoy a testing battle anywhere in the world.

'Colonel Jones was a beautiful man,' said Mary Jennings. 'He hated being called Herbert, so his devoted troops lovingly referred to him as Colonel H. or just 'H'. It was his brilliant determination always to attack, and he in the forefront, that hastened victory. When at last we were released from the Goose Green Hall we were told 'H' had just been killed driving the Argies out of the hill above. Utmost gallantry was the citation he got with the Victoria Cross he was awarded posthumously.'

It was clear to us in our conversations with the Falklanders that not only were they proud of the courage and support of British troops and air and naval forces, but the campaign greatly strengthened their loyalty towards Britain.

The day improved as we enjoyed the barbecue of lamb steaks and chicken outside the Napiers' house, with the *Lindblad Explorer* anchored in the Sound below, wine supplied therefrom; and we invited each to contribute a modest £8 towards the upkeep of both West and Carcass Islands as nature reserves.

We re-embarked at 14.00 hours and moved the short distance to Carcass Island, one of the finest wildlife sanctuaries in these isles. First, the sea-pies (oyster-catchers) on the landing beach, though black and white, had pale yellow legs, and a thin wailing whistle unlike our pink-legged European bird with its loud repeated wickering cry. The long bull kelp piled high on the shore was being exploited by a very tame small brown tussock bird. The hinterland of grassy dune provided three species of geese – kelp, ruddy-headed and

upland – while steamer and crested ducks, cormorants, caracara
hawks and skuas all seemed to be feeding young. There were native
snipe and a handsome black-throated finch. A so-called house-wren
was quite at home far from houses. And an abundance of burrowing
magellan and rock-hopper penguins in suitable terrain, plus a gaggle
of gentoo penguins, loitering in very small groups on easy ground, a
fine upstanding creature with a white triangle behind the eye.
Nesting in comparative seclusion it has space to rear two chicks in a
nest generally protected by a few rocks or vegetation. One gentoo
was feeding its chick in the centre of a tall clump of tussock-
grass.

It was hard to tear oneself from the ornithological riches of
Carcass, but we were warned to be ready to sail for Port Stanley that
evening. Then a remarkable coincidence occurred. I was busily trying
to identify yet another new bird, when a man's voice behind my left
ear boomed:

'You are looking at our local rufous-chested dotterel, Ronald
Lockley! But I doubt if you'll identify me, with my beard. You'll
doubtless recognise my wife Janet . . .'

Rodney and Janet Hutchings! The young couple who wrote to me
many years ago seeking advice on how to find, and live alone on, a
remote island, as I had done as a young man in order to study
sea-birds. It came back to me, as we shook hands, that I had advised
him to search the Hebrides, Orkneys and Shetlands until he found his
heart's desire. And a few years later he wrote that he had found the

large island of Stroma in the Pentland Firth. It was completely deserted by its former population of laird and tenants, with a sound kirk and fertile small farms, but all empty. He had taken a lease of Stroma, he wrote, but not a word had I heard from him since!

But as he explained there, on that Falkland Island beach, with thousands of birds wheeling, walking, feeding, swimming and diving about us:

'Stroma is magnificent, but like its owner we found it just a bit too isolated, in the middle of the worst tide-race in the world – the Pentland Firth. Our little son needed school friends. After the Argy war, I was very curious to see the Falklands' reputed splendid wildlife, and we'd read that the Falklanders were the happiest and kindest people in the world, with plenty of the simplest food just for the gathering. So Janet and I gave it a go, and here we are, and here we intend to stay. The people are absolutely wonderful, always helping each other, and glad of my few skills – you'll remember I first wrote to you from my job in a Midlands engineering factory, where I was dying of consumption, and had gone on the dole. Well, there's no dole in the Falklands, and no unemployment, and I have full health again. We have a little house here on Carcass, where I do machinery repairs – pumps, tractors, boat engines, more or less in return for a home, food, and a garden of vegetables, fruit and flowers.'

10 January Port Stanley. Steaming all night northward, the *Lindblad Explorer* cruised into Port Stanley at 08.00 hours. It was sunny, but a strong westerly gale was blowing as we passed through the Narrows, and had to be piloted to an anchorage crowded with ships of all kinds, including many wrecks, chiefly of the bad old whaling days – a few of the Argy war. A number of the modern ships are barracks for the 4–5000 British army, navy and air forces, chiefly engaged in building a new grand airfield. Planes whizzed and 'copters hovered all day on this business. No place at the dilapidated wharves for the *Lindblad Explorer* to tie up; we were put ashore by tender, even so spray showered over the ancient wooden craft.

And so we set foot in Stanley, with its historic associations back to the first settlements of French, Spanish and mostly Scottish stock. The town is largely a collection of wooden shacks, modest cottages and a few pretentious-looking villas. All streets pot-holed and dilapidated by heavy tank and lorry traffic. But the British Government is providing the means of macadamising them, with local labour and army personnel. Meanwhile Landrovers and tractors with trailers are the principal means of transport for the residents – with here and there a beach-buggy or jeep. There isn't far to go on East Falkland before you have to get off and take the ferry to reach the settlements on West Falkland and its many farmed islands.

At this midsummer season the large gardens to every cottage are bright with typical wind-resistant lupins, marigolds, fuchsia, marguerites, nasturtiums, hebe, etc., with low windbreaks of gorse, elder and the inevitable tall wind-battered macrocarpa. Chris McCallum had asked me to see his parents in Drury Street. They were enjoying elevenses with neighbours, coffee and cakes served by his mother Kay. Women with babies wandered in, and out . . .

'No, it's not true,' said Kay, 'that our girls are being enticed by Brit soldiers and sailors to marry and live in Britain. Quite the reverse – the Brits are returning here with their Falklands brides because life is so much happier than in England's crowded suburbs where you can get as lonely as hell and frightened into the bargain by the terrible crimes . . .'

Her husband Jack McCallum, a handsome curly-haired fair Scots type, like so many islanders, went off to collect some dressed sheep carcases from New Island which Chris had sent aboard the *Lindblad Explorer*. He soon returned without them – the ship was isolated from boarding on account of the increasing gale in the harbour where she had been forced to anchor. But the sun was shining, and I dutifully photographed Jack and Kay sitting among the flowers in what their son had assured me was a famous garden. Certainly extremely colourful, for it was adorned with dozens of gnomes, leprechauns and penguins, made of concrete and suitably painted by jack-of-all-trades Jack McCallum.

'You have to be jack-of-all-trades here,' chuckled he. 'It's part of the joy of living in Port Stanley. There's no unemployment or dole, but we do get the British old-age pension. It keeps us in cigarillos, and for the rest we have unlimited free meat, fish, veg and fruit at no cost but for the trouble of growing or collecting them. As for firing, come and see my peat store.'

This was a large lumber shed – attached to most homes in the little town – and filled to the roof with dried peat, free except for the labour of cutting and carting from the abundant peat swamps. 'Burns all night to keep the house warm in winter gales. Never get much frost here, only terrible winds.'

Despite the present gale, the little town, normally housing 800 residents, seemed delightfully cosy, homely, honest to me. Jack McCallum took me to see the cathedral, a tall spired building fortunately little damaged during the hostilities. A gigantic jawbone of a whale stands tall in its graveyard, memorial to the slaughter which helped to make the islands prosperous a century ago. All cetacea are protected here today.

The Globe Hotel, the only hostelry in the town, was jam-packed with beer-swilling army, air force and naval personnel, their local male and lady friends, and a large consignment of *Lindblad Explorer* members, just now denied return access to our ship – and wondering where they would be able to sleep tonight. But reassured by a 'city' councillor coming in at that moment to announce: 'Bags of room for everyone. If it's too rough to return aboard the *Lindblad*, we've made up a list of addresses offering free hospitality to all. Just stroll down to the post office to get transport to your host and hostess allotted for the night if this gale continues.'

The post office was thronged with people buying 'first-day 1883–1983 Commemoration stamps' in envelopes at ten dollars US (for the benefit of American tourists – the Falklands currency is officially the pound sterling).

The GPO houses the offices of the Falklands Chief Secretary, with whom and his staff I became involved, and presently a small party walked the short distance to the Residency – ostensibly to see its very fine garden. Neither the Residency nor its walled gardens were damaged during the war, thanks to the interest in their preservation during their occupation by the Argentine CO, General Menendez.

The whole front of the Residency, a solid colonial-style stone mansion, is one large glasshouse, unheated save by the sun, and at that moment full of sweet-scented flowers – roses, sweet peas, geraniums, etc. Here Lady Hunt received us hospitably, and dispensed gin and vermouth in the grand drawing-room.

'No, Menendez did not abuse our furniture. I think he loved the place, and was sorry to have to leave, very suddenly, after the Goose Green surrender. The only thing we miss is our silver. It was flogged before we got back.'

Lady Hunt described her adventures during the Argentine invasion, the brave resistance of the normal peace-time garrison – a handful of British Marines soon stopped by her husband Sir Rex in order to save lives; how they were repatriated, but in the same year returned to resume life and duty here.

The uniformed butler entered with the latest dispatches, but Sir

Rex at that moment was visiting RNHQ in the harbour. 'He's signalled he's marooned there. Too rough to use helicopters, and he's supposed to dine with your Captain Hasse Nilsson, an old friend,' apologised Lady Hunt. 'I daresay the wind will drop at dusk. Let's have a peep at the veg garden – it's been a wonderful summer for my strawberries.'

Aide-de-camp Michael Gaiger and his charming wife Joyce (mother of five) insisted that I should dine at their house. Joyce wanted me to look at some paintings by her twelve-year-old son. Great promise there, but Joyce, having provided a light meal of salad, Stilton cheese, home-made brown bread and pâté, with white wine, next hurried me to meet the local Port Stanley ornithologists.

Joyce left me at the house of Mr Bennet, a noted collector of bird skins. As I don't greatly care for museum skins, I was almost glad to hear that most of his collection had been burned by a direct hit during the war.

Presently Mr Bennet directed his ten-year-old daughter to take my hand and guide me to the house of Ian Strange, who is co-owner of one-half of New Island. Ian, dedicated artist and conservationist, introduced his Argentinian wife, a bewildering beauty with a three-year-old daughter just as lovely – Georgina by name. A most agreeable evening ensued, looking at Ian's bird portraits and sipping home-made wine.

I was invited to sleep on their couch, and other stranded *Lindblad Explorer*s presently dispersed to sleep at hospitable homes in the town.

South Georgia

The shadow of the dome of pleasure
Floated midway on the waves . . .
It was a miracle of rare device,
A sunny pleasure-dome with caves of ice.
Samuel T. Coleridge (1772–1834)

Coleridge's miraculous, merciless Xanadu seemed to rise on our eastern horizon as, after two stormy days running before the gales since leaving the Falklands, we first sighted the 3000-metre tall glaciated peaks of South Georgia. All around us glided the majestic wandering albatrosses which, happiest in the gales, nest on stormy South Georgia.

Coleridge was an avid reader of the log-books of explorers, and his sonorous rhymes were inspired by adventures such as Captain James Cook's *A Voyage towards the South Pole and round the World*, published in 1777, when Samuel Taylor Coleridge was five years old.

Ernest Shackleton was in our thoughts too at that moment, another visionary who wrote poetry. For our approach was by the same route as Cook in the *Resolution* in 1775, and that of Shackleton following the crushing of his ship *Endurance* in the Weddell Sea ice, in his remarkable sail in an open boat across more than 1200 kilometres of the world's stormiest seas from Elephant Island in Antarctica to South Georgia in 1916.

Shackleton records the agony of icy winds, freezing spray and hunger on that voyage of seventeen days which seemed like seventeen months. 'We might have shot an albatross,' wrote Shackleton, 'but the wandering king of the ocean aroused in us something of the feeling that inspired, too late, the Ancient Mariner.'

But, we argued in the after-dinner discussion aboard the *Lindblad*, the albatross the Ancient Mariner shot with his cross-bow could not have been the wandering species *Diomedea exulans*. With its twelve-foot expanse of wings, and heavy weight, heaviest of all such birds, it would have broken the neck of the mariner forced to wear it as a penance. Coleridge based his story on records of voyages by Spanish and British explorers and buccaneers back to Elizabeth I of England, and tales of ill-luck following the shooting of any bird which, like

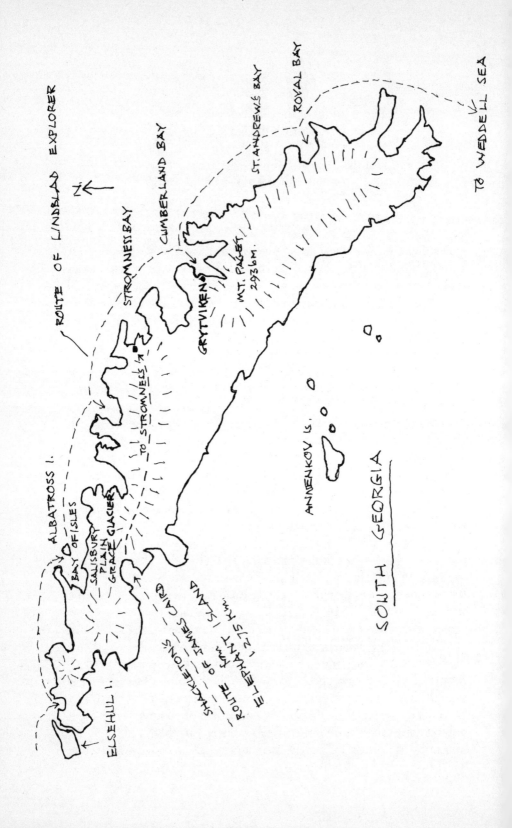

ROUTE OF LINDBLAD EXPLORER

TO WEDDELL SEA

ROYAL BAY

ST. ANDREWS BAY

CUMBERLAND BAY

STROMNESS BAY

MT. PAGET
2936 M.

GRYTVIKEN

TO STROMNESS

ALBATROSS I.

BAY OF ISLES

SALISBURY PLAIN
GRACE GLACIER

SHACKLETON'S CAIRD

ROUTE OF JAMES ISLAND

ELEPHANT 1,275 KM

ELSEHUL I.

ANNENKOV IS.

SOUTH GEORGIA

albatross or storm petrel, haunted a ship 'for food and play'. The superstition still persists that such birds, attaching themselves to a ship day after day, are the reincarnation of humans drowned at sea. As for the 'slimy things did crawl with legs', Coleridge is simply using old records of ships becalmed for weeks in the Doldrums, the vessel attacked by the long-stalked barnacles and wood-boring worms which are numerous in tropical seas, where they attach first as free-swimming larvae, then settle down to feed on plankton by way of their fine cilia. In particular the ship worm *Teredo* can destroy the hull of a wooden ship.

We looked forward to following as far as possible Shackleton's (and Cook's) route, which would include an exploration of the rarely-visited Weddell Sea. Cook's log recorded that he discovered and charted the island and found it '31 leagues long and the greatest breadth is about 10 leagues. I landed at three different places, displayed our colours and took possession of the country, which I named Georgia, in honour of His Britannic Majesty and his heirs forever, 17 January, 1775.'

After giving the main bays and headlands their present names, Cook sailed on south, convinced that Georgia and its southern outliers were 'doomed to perpetual frigidness, whose horrible and savage aspect I have not the words to describe.'

Nevertheless, we in our several landings, from the comfort of our cruise ship, enjoyed comparing the fauna and flora with the record made by Cook and his scientists and artists. We found the same few species of plants which Cook and his gentlemen listed, growing on low tundra near the sea. These were an abundant tussock grass, a flowering burnet, a tiny Antarctic buttercup and dwarf ferns. Of land birds, we saw only three. They spend most of the year on or near the beach: the little Antarctic pipit, a hardy version of the New Zealand *Anthus*; the unique but rather shy South Georgia duck, small as a teal, which we flushed from thick tussock; and the extraordinary pure white sheathbill, extremely tame, a beach and penguin colony scavenger, eating filmy seaweed at one moment, and next running to snatch up fish dropped by incoming penguins or peck at a sickly dying chick. About the size of a large pigeon, it swims well, though it has no webs to its feet. Sheathbills are rather sad-looking, almost sinister, with cold staring eyes, and 'seem to prefer to stand around on one leg and do nothing interesting', said my cabin-mate Donald.

My friend Leo Harrison Matthews (late director of the London Zoo) as a young man was biologist on the *Discovery* expedition to

South Georgia during 1925–7, and wrote-up the first scientific study
of the birds, noting that 'the presence of several whaling stations on
the island attracts great numbers of sea-birds, which come to feed on
the refuse from the working up of the whales. In winter, when
whaling ceases, large numbers die of starvation.' Leo also wrote a
most entertaining book of his personal experiences (*The Wandering
Albatross*) at these shore stations where he and other young col-
leagues kept records of the whale species, their ages and breeding
biology as each whale was delivered and cut up on the flensing 'plan'.
At that time the British Government, alarmed at the wholesale
slaughter of whales in the Antarctic, had placed a resident magistrate
at each factory, charging a fee for each whale processed. Most of
the whales were brought in by experienced Norwegian hunters
employed by Argentine and other non-British firms.

   At least much new information was published on the histology and
breeding of whales, but little could be done to slow down their

extermination. However it was to become uneconomic to tow whales from the increasingly distant feeding grounds, and the larger whaling firms began pelagic whaling, processing their catches at sea and storing the oil in large tanks aboard specially-designed factory ships. These ranged the ocean in search of the last concentrations of their migratory prey. Each factory ship had a fleet of fast small chasers, armed with the latest invention in harpoon guns. Mounted on the bow the gun fired a barbed harpoon containing a delayed-action explosive charge which, accurately aimed by an experienced gunner, destroyed the victim's vitals as soon as the whale plunged and thereby ignited the fuse in the charge triggered to explode the moment the whale surged away and tightened the harpoon line.

Diary. 12 January 1984 At sea, crossing the Antarctic Convergence. At four pm we came up with the extraordinary pinnacles of the isolated Shag Rocks – five peaks up to 75 metres tall, almost sheer, some 242 km west of South Georgia. They looked dull muddy yellow; as we cruised closer we saw that they were occupied by thousands of roosting and nesting blue-eyed shags. Air and sea too were thronged with these Antarctic birds, with black-browed albatrosses and ever-soaring wandering ones. The air was fetid with the stench of guano.

But who could exploit such riches of fat birds and guano in this harbourless spot? Probably, on a rare calm day, some lost ancient mariner or starving whaling or sealing gang in a boat parted from its mother ship, drifting in a fog – a common fate in the days of Moby Dick. Such were our thoughts, as fog presently blotted out the Shag Rocks.

13 January Friday 07.00 hours. With the Chief Officer at the wheel, we cautiously radared and sonared our way towards the misty outline of Willis Island, but doubled our speed when the experienced skipper Nilsson directed the helm through a calming sea over which thousands of the little dove prions were heading westwards. It was the dawn exodus of an estimated twenty-two million pairs of this bird, nocturnal in visiting its burrows in the steep screes of South Georgia.

The high cliffs of Elsehul Bay form a splendid amphitheatre fringed with those screes, with tidal rocks and black grit beaches below. On these were groups of idle moulting elephant and fur seals, and a mixed company of macaroni, gentoo and king penguins. The zodiacs quietly came ashore over the immense long tresses of the durvillea or bull kelp. The mixed assembly took little notice of our motley gang wearing – it was raining – waterproof anoraks and trews, as well-fed and fat-looking as most of the wild inhabitants. Except for some emaciated starving fur seal pups which were wailing piteously. A dozen or more Antarctic skuas and sheathbills were attending to the demise of these hapless weaklings.

It seems clear that, with the great increase of seals in the Antarctic since they were protected about fifty years ago, they are now suffering from overpopulation, resulting in overcrowding at their communal nesting beaches. Master bulls, which fight each other over territory on which to amass a harem of cows, trample willy-nilly upon new-born calves, crushing many. There is also a natural loss of lactating cows during their absence on feeding excursions at sea. The cows are less than a quarter the size of a mature bull, and are more easily preyed upon at sea by orca (killer whale) and leopard seal. Perhaps twenty per cent of new-born pups become motherless in this way.

Yet those pups which had survived and gone to sea with their dams a year earlier were – some of them – back where they had been born, looking sleek, well-fed and in great spirits. They were playing the young lamb's game of king-of-the-castle on the rocks exposed by the falling tide, snarling at each other as they tumbled and were tumbled from the top by their companions; and diving thence into the shallow water and the bull kelp, they leaped and splashed in exuberant good health.

Rafts of Cape pigeons (a medium-sized petrel) paddled about in the exposed bull kelp, picking up planktonic organisms, watched by a few sinister-looking skuas and giant petrels awaiting a chance to pounce when one momentarily dipped its head under the water or weed.

Above us the grey-white rainwashed crags were dotted with the white forms of wandering albatrosses sitting solemnly asleep on their pedestal nests.

During lunch the ship was moved down the wild coast to the Bay of Isles, where it is possible to walk for miles over the tussocky tundra, known as Salisbury Plain. Our main objective was to get on friendly terms with the immense congregation of king penguins.

Of the seventeen species of penguins known to exist, the king is the most remarkable for its shapely beauty, combined with its fearless attitude, amounting to impudence, towards the human visitor who invades its shore base. Of all wild birds which man likes to anthropomorphise, it could be said that the king penguin reciprocates by attributing to humans penguin-like behaviour. Cindy Buxton, who has spent a year studying this penguin in South Georgia (*Survival; South Atlantic*, 1983) describes how the local kings visited her hut in St Andrew's Bay, investigating her little house and studying its contents and her movements with no other apparent inducement than an idle curiosity.

On Salisbury Plain, these penguins were gathered in separate pods of several hundred, perhaps half of them paired adults, most handsome with their glossy black head, neck ruff of golden yellow, velvet grey overcoat, satin white shirt and belly, and a stiff black tail which it uses to prop up its metre-tall body on small, short webbed feet.

They move ponderously, slowly, and you should approach them in the same unhurried manner – for this is their property, the time-honoured nesting ground. They will contemplate you calmly as they go about their business, mostly of being perfectly idle and thinking their penguin thoughts.

It was quickly clear why so many of the adults were idle, dozing or shuffling a few inches in one direction or another. Those least active were incubating their large single egg beneath a belly flap of feathered skin hiding the egg altogether as it rested *on top of the feet.* An admirable insulation in a climate with an average night temperature below zero.

We watched some adults waddle up from the sea, somewhat clumsily on their small feet, staggering ('not looking where you're

going') and stumbling over stones at intervals, but never in a hurry. These were the mates of the incubating individuals on site. Recognition was obviously by voice, judging by the shrill calls and the responses in these look-alike giants (the male is slightly larger than his mate). The adult call sounded like 'Ho – ho – hullo!'

14 January Saturday. This day in January 1775 James Cook first sighted and named South Georgia. A calm and sunlit dawn at 06.30 hours. Everyone eager to go ashore and re-acquaint with the kings of Salisbury Plain, under the splendid snowy heights of the Grace Glacier. Plenty of time all morning to study and photograph; especially attractive were the well-grown princes and princesses wearing the long brown 'woolly-bear' down of immaturity. In this stage the old whalers and sealers knew them as the Oakum Boys*; and like Captain Cook, who 'found them very welcome fresh meat', they were relished for their tenderness and fat.

Like the wandering albatross the king penguin takes two years in which to rear its single offspring. Today we were admiring the result of this phenomenon. Normally the mature kings come ashore in mid-October in order to moult, having fattened up at sea for this period of inaction and fasting. It is early spring when they return to sea to grow fat again feeding on fry and krill, and once more waddle laboriously ashore to meet and mate with an eligible partner who has no immediate family cares. They will however encounter, as we did, the Oakum Boys hatched from eggs laid one year earlier. The newcomers push through the groups of woolly immatures to gain a suitable space in which to make love and, after a period of days of picturesque ceremonial, displaying their sleek spring plumage to each other, the female will lay the single white egg. As it emerges from beneath her flap of belly skin, the devoted father, who has been anxiously observing his mate, and listening to her cackles of anxiety, immediately rolls the egg up over his feet to the warm safety of the bare skin under his belly pouch.

Incubation is shared in shifts of about five days (the off-duty bird goes to sea to recuperate) and lasts two months. Thus it was that in mid-January some pairs were incubating new-laid eggs, and other pairs were feeding their huge brown Oakum chick. Actually few were being fed; in the later stages of rearing the large king chick, the

---

* Presumably because their rough brown coats resembled the prison uniforms of those days. Picking oakum, or old rope, was a traditional labour for convicts in Victorian jails.

parents feed it at longer intervals, spending several days, even weeks, at sea between visits ashore. However, the Oakum Boys, protected by their long brown coat of warm down, are able to fast for long periods through the dark sub-Antarctic winter; they huddle together for warmth in creches during blizzards and chill gales.

Most of the Oakum Boys – about twenty per cent of the group of 10,000 king penguins we studied on Salisbury Plain – were showing signs of moult. In a few more weeks they would assume their first adult plumage, and walk to the sea independently.

Contrast this protracted spring and summer breeding of the kings with the highly efficient winter breeding of the emperor penguin. The emperor is the largest of all penguins, nearly four feet tall and weighing up to forty-five kg, of the same genus as the king (*Apteno-dytes*) and almost identical in markings and colour. Little was known of its biology since it bred in mid-winter on the fast ice of the Antarctic continent. But recent studies have revealed an almost unbelievable life-history.

Temperatures have already fallen to −40° in March when the plump breeding emperors return from the sea (no one knows exactly from where, but they are in fat condition). They assemble at favourite fast-ice sites, marching in columns over miles of pack ice to reach these. The single egg is laid in May, after a prolonged courtship and arrangement of partners (by voice recognition) in the growing seasonal darkness. The male immediately beaks the new-laid egg from her pouch into his pouch, and the female, exhausted by her long

fast during the courtship, and in producing the egg, at once proceeds towards the ocean. By now the open sea, where she can obtain fish, is many, perhaps a hundred, miles distant. But as egg-laying in the emperor colonies is invariably synchronous, the females are able to walk in company, occasionally tobogganing down the declivities. Unerringly, probably guided by the stars (there is no sun visible), they reach the sea.

Meanwhile the males must suffer a further long fast, lasting at least another month, each incubating the precious egg in his belly pouch. During the frequent blizzard, gales sweeping across the fast ice, the colony of male emperors huddle tightly together forming a 'testudo' or compacted circle under the snow. Periodically the outer individuals push into the central mass for a warm-up. In calm weather the birds spread out loosely. All movement is shuffling, to ensure that the egg is not dislodged by undue activity. Snow is the only available nourishment – it prevents thirst!

The female usually remains absent for the whole of the incubation period of sixty-four days. She has a much longer march on her return, the sea-ice shelf having extended still further north during the intense cold of the late Antarctic winter. Should the chick hatch and call for food before mother arrives back, the emaciated male is said to be able to regurgitate and nourish it with some bile or stomach juice.

On arrival at the colony the female never feeds her starving mate. She coaxes her mate to release the egg or new-born chick during a brief voice-recognition ceremony (exchange of gossip?) and away he goes, joining the hungry husband queue on the long trek to the ocean feeding-grounds.

By some process at present unexplained the returned mother is able to retain and dole out the krill contents of her stomach in small doses at first to match the small capacity of her chick to absorb them. This rationing of nourishing food ensures the steady growth of the chick – at first an attractive black downy creature with a white face as it peeps from beneath the parental skirt. However, it is getting hungrier by the time, perhaps a month later, when father returns, loaded with its next meal, and takes on nursery duty while mother waddles back to feed at sea.

It is now summer and the sea much closer to the emperor penguin colonies. Soon both parents will go foraging, leaving the quarter-grown chick to huddle with the other young, forming creches for warmth and the safety of numbers. But there are very few predatory visitors, and none daring to nest, in this chill fast-ice environment.

By the end of March both adult and young emperors have marched to the sea, to spend the brief polar autumn growing a new winter coat, above a thick layer of fat.

In the late afternoon we crossed to a hilly island appropriately named Albatross. Three or four species of these large sailplaning sea-birds nest here, occupying different breeding sites. Tamest and gentlest is the Wanderer, *Diomedea exulans*, so tame it did not budge when I put out my hand slowly to stroke its substantial back first, then its breast. No attempt to grab my hand in that formidable hooked bill, just a calm stare as much as to say, 'I know I am a handsome bird, and so long as you behave politely I shall ignore you.'

Almost certainly the sitting bird's main thoughts are to sit tight and await the return of its mate and so conceal and protect the egg (or new-born chick) from the predatory gulls, giant petrels and even a sheath bill, quick to feast on an unguarded egg. Besides, taking off for this long-winged bird involves a considerable effort of running into the wind.

The majority of the Wanderers were sitting tight upon bulky nests built up perhaps a metre tall with tussock grass, and used year after year. But in a few guano-splashed nests sat a lone, nearly-fledged, well-feathered juvenile in brown-black plumage, hardly any down visible, illustrating that this largest of all albatrosses takes more than a year in which to rear one chick. To be exact, a mated pair on average spends one month in courtship and nest preparation, seventy-nine days in incubation, and the chick remains 178 days in the nest before flying – a total of 387 days of strenuous activity for the adults. No wonder they need a sabbatical interval every other year, which they enjoy by sailplaning around the world on the winds of the Roaring Forties – as ring-marking has proved.

For dusky beauty it would be hard to out-do the odd pairs of light-mantled sooty albatrosses at nests partly concealed in the cliffside tussock, the off-duty bird manoeuvring so gracefully with its tail longer than that of the larger albatrosses. Pairs of grey-headed *Diomedea* mollymawks, distinct by their yellow-striped black bills, zoomed above the same cliffs.

Here and there, in hollows between the Wanderer nests (these were about fifty yards apart), I stumbled on the nests of the giant (stinker) petrel, yet another small albatross or mollymawk. We had been warned about this filthy scavenger which has vulturine habits, and will congregate upon the carcasses of slaughtered whales and

seals, covering their heads and necks with blood as they delve deep
after juicy viscera. We were advised to steer clear of a nesting stinker
– it could squirt its skunk-like vomit directly at you.

They were nesting singly on the flatter ground, but I encountered
one group of four nests close together, with sitting birds which made
no threatening gestures. I paused to admire their sinister beauty as
one pair conducted gentle courtship movements, the heavy bill with
its long tubular nostrils caressing its partner's glossy head and neck
in mutual preening. A calm moment in which to observe love
according to the stinker giant petrel, warmed by the afternoon sun.

The island was positively alive with birds. A South Georgia pipit
ran over bare ground near the stinkers, picking up tiny insects,
fearless of and ignored by the giants. From burrows hidden under
tufts of tussock weird muffled cries arose almost continuously from
the unseen shoemaker shearwaters which, with numbers of Wilson's
storm-petrels, nest here, but rarely appear above ground before
midnight.

It was hard to leave Albatross Island when the ship's siren recalled
us, and a flight of South Georgia pintail ducks flew overhead. Here
and there on a mossy outcrop the Antarctic gull *Larus dominicanus*
cackled us farewell, the black-and-white adults shoulder to shoulder
with their all-brown fledgelings. A pure-white stinker petrel swam
near the zodiac as we embarked.

15 January Grytviken, Cumberland Bay. At dusk yesterday the *Lindblad Explorer* entered this calm sheltered bay while we were at dinner, and tied-up to the dilapidated and shaky wooden wharf below the deserted whaling station. To starboard as you enter Grytviken is a low plateau containing the former research station, now occupied by the British garrison which fought, unsuccessfully at first, the sudden invasion of Argentine troops in April 1982.

As soon as the ship's gangway was lowered, the lounge was invaded by British army and naval personnel. The whole history of the Argentine attack and defeat was the principal subject of a very convivial evening.

Cabin-mate Donald, early to bed at night, was early to rise on this calm Sunday. He was away at 04.30 hours to photograph the sunrise touching the highest peak, snow-capped Mt Paget. Everyone was gleeful to spend such a perfect day in this sheltered inlet.

I had been re-reading with the deepest interest F. D. Ommanney's *South Latitude* in which this scientist gives a racy personal account of the operation of whaling and sealing from Grytviken base in the years immediately succeeding the departure of Leo Harrison Matthews in 1928. There is a post office here at the barracks on the peninsula known as King George's Point, where formerly Matthews and Ommanney had served as biologists. The thing was to have your letters franked with the South Georgia seal to prove you had visited there. The postmaster was also the customs officer, and would clinch the matter by stamping your passport too.

What grim tales Matthews and Ommanney had told, as young observers fresh from college! They had been thrown into the rough company of Norwegian whaling and sealing men accustomed to butcher the leviathans of the oceans. At heart these men are revealed in the main as gentle and compassionate comrades, physically tough and fearless, yet underneath ashamed of their inner tenderness towards living creatures – man or animal – and hiding that tenderness in boisterous laughter as they slashed open the whales brought to the 'plan', or hunted down and stunned the massive elephant seals sleeping on the beaches, and cut off their blubber in long strips to be loaded and delivered to the factory.

Four hundred of these men had lived close to the huge factory, still standing, almost intact, but their wooden bunkhouse and eating saloon, billiards and recreation hall, including a cinema, had all disappeared. Only the little church, built in 1913 and described by

Ommanney as the 'most southerly in the world with a cross upon it' remained. It was a delight to find it had been lately restored by the British garrison, and its exterior walls painted white. Inside, the pews were polished and shining, and the original prayer-books, in Norwegian, rested in front of each seat.

As I sat in the pew near the altar, writing a description of this little sacred Lord's House, a bible in Norwegian beside me, the army padre strolled in with some of the *Lindblad* passengers, and gave us a talk on the history of Grytviken, ending with a brief prayer of benediction.

Outside the church odd parties of moulting royal penguins and the occasional seal rested peacefully on the grass, enjoying the warm sunlight.

'There will be a football match here,' concluded the padre, waving his hand towards a rough pitch of cleared ground inland, with netted goalposts in view. 'The Russian factory ship in the bay will be playing a team made up from my regiment the Royal Fusiliers and some of the naval lads from the destroyer *Fife*.'

Last evening we had passed HMS *Fife* anchored off King George Point, together with the auxiliary *Olna*. They had recently been engaged in removing the Argentine submarine which, attacked and holed by British forces in the recapture of Grytviken in April less than two years ago, had been run ashore towards the old wharf.

The last thing we, or at least I, desired to see at that moment was a football match. The Russians might be fine friendly fellows but their ships, engaged in processing krill taken in immense tow-nets – these also took larger forms of marine life, up to dolphin and seal pup size – were decidedly unwelcome in South Georgian waters. Britain had not yet declared these to be marine reserves. That evening aboard our ship everyone agreed that South Georgia and at least fifty miles of inshore sea around the islands must be preserved exclusively for the regeneration of its wildlife.

It was wonderful to study how that wildlife was already taking possession of Grytviken itself. The enormous high-decked store and machinery shed, which Argentine scrap-merchants had begun to dismantle until stopped by British forces, was still packed with crates full of harpoon heads, flensing knives and other whaling and sealing gear. Some of this had been stolen or vandalised by casual visitors from Russian, Polish and other ships calling on the way to or from other Antarctic fishing grounds. Penguins sat in front of the door to the great shed and elephant seals slept, gustily snoring, mucus dribbling from their ugly nostrils, on the sunwarmed boards of the open flensing plan.

Walking eastwards around the shore you come upon the graveyard, deliberately secluded from the former stench and noise of the factory, which those who worked there had complained was horrific, until they got used to it.

The garrison had tidied this up, too, placing a strong rail fence around its perimeter to keep out the penguins and seals, and also the wild reindeer – long imported for food by the Norwegians.

As a result of excluding grazing animals, the flora within the graveyard was flourishing, especially luxuriant (Norwegian) dandelions, endemic burnet, and I found what appeared to be an annual *Poa* grass, evidently well-nourished by the faeces of penguins and seals roosting here before the burial ground was refenced. Most of the thirty or forty graves were marked by simple stone crosses on which I read Norwegian names of youngish men who had died or been accidentally killed during the seventy or so years of the factory's existence. One imposing marble headstone commemorated the demise of a British magistrate. A freshly-dug grave with a simple wooden cross marked RIP was that of the Argentine soldier killed when his sinking submarine was beached at Grytviken.

Dominating the remote, yet somehow romantically beautiful burial ground is the substantial rugged block of stone inscribed:

Sir Ernest Shackleton
Explorer
Died here January 5th 1922
Erected
by his comrades

Above, firmly cemented in the rock, is a tall, broad white cross.

Before this last expedition to Antarctica it had been planned to explore the Canadian Arctic but, inadequately funded, Shackleton switched to the south having raised enough funds to obtain an ill-founded ship *Goshawk*, which his wife Emily renamed *Quest*, but with some foreboding, for Ernest had developed a weak heart. He was forty-seven years old, yet unchanged in his cheerful romanticism for sea adventure mixed with his practical skill. But after a stormy voyage with many engine failures, he died of a final heart attack almost the moment he landed at Grytviken.

Last port of call in South Georgia was a landing at Royal Bay. Windsqualls were tearing down from inland glaciers when the zodiacs went ashore, weaving their way through somnolent, and some fighting, elephant seals. There was a little hut here which the Argentine invaders never discovered, and which was used by scientists of the British Antarctic Survey, as well as Cindy Buxton, to hide in and transmit code messages to British Intelligence on the movements of the Argentine ships and troops.

Dennis Puleston led an upvalley walk to a grazing ground of reindeer – hitherto unseen by our party. As we struggled towards the glacial screes we took a breather to watch a colony of about a hundred gentoo penguins half a mile inland, with a procession of adults returning from the sea with loaded crops to feed well-grown chicks. Two chicks amused us by chasing the same adult, squeaking and beating their young flippers. At last one chick gave up but the other doggedly pursued its parent, even into the valley stream, chill from the melting glacier, where it was obliged to swim vigorously to reach the farther shore and the adult. At last the parent turned towards the chick, ankle-deep in water, and granted a feed. But having enjoyed a substantial helping from the adult crop, it still harried the parent to yield up another, and presently continued to stuff itself until its belly was bulging.

The moral of all this, if there is one, was suggested by Dennis: 'It teaches the youngsters to exercise themselves and grow up healthy and wise in knowledge of their future nesting site. How else can they learn?'

Some filmed this interesting sequence. We moved on past groups of royal penguins. Skuas and pintail ducks flew overhead, mobbed by many Antarctic terns. There were small herds of reindeer in a grassy valley, too shy to get close to.

I climbed about a bare scree of frost-shattered stones, searching in vain for burrows which might contain prions or storm-petrels. Someone saw a rat drinking water in a stream, alongside a king penguin doing the same.

There are hardy brown rats as well as mice on South Georgia, camp-followers of the early whaling and sealing fraternity.

The Weddell Sea

16 January 1984 A fierce headwind battered the ship as she plunged south from Georgia, on her planned course to as far south as the frozen Weddell Sea would permit. Already the sea temperature had dropped to 2°C and on the next day more large tabular icebergs appeared on the horizon. Many blue petrels now appeared – they are low-flying, graceful, beautiful, very like the numerous prions, but larger, bluer and with a distinct white tip to the tail.

These were the 'blue *peterels*' recorded by Captain James Weddell in his effort to reach farthest south towards the Pole by way of the Weddell Sea, in his sealing brig *Jane of Leith*. Like James Cook, whom he much admired, Weddell had come from a humble home, and worked up to be master of a vessel which made trading voyages to the West Indies. Cook's account of the whales and seals at South Georgia and the South Sandwich Isles spurred him to search for land in the vast bay now named the Weddell Sea. There he was the first to reach 74°.15′ S, to be stopped by heavy ice: 22 February 1822, 'being 214 geographical miles further south than Captain Cook or any preceding navigator reached', Weddell recorded in his diary.

The persistent head gale today, and a heavy lollop in the sea, decided for us a change of course westwards for the South Orkney Islands after an uneasy night strapped and thrown to and fro in our bunks.

17 January Still a fresh cold wind, but calmer sea when we reached the easternmost of the South Orkney group. At 16.00 hours we hove-to off Signy Island, the British research base first manned by scientists during that period dating from 1908 when the United Kingdom officially laid claim to an Antarctic sector covering South Georgia, the South Sandwich and South Orkney Islands, all the Weddell Sea and the Antarctic peninsula and its islands. But as we were soon to find, other nations have laid claim to parts or all of this Atlantic quadrant of Antarctica. To reinforce such claims at present Britain, Chile, Argentina, Poland, and the USA maintain bases in this sector.

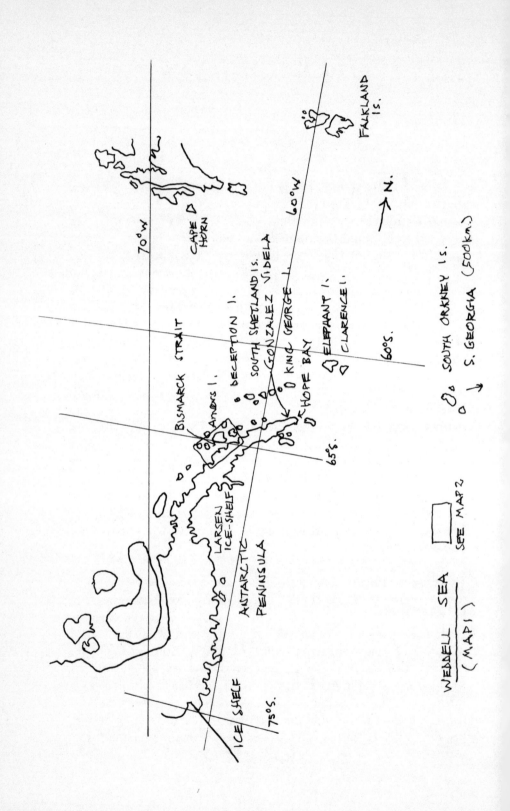

WEDDELL SEA
(MAPS)

SEE MAP 2

Some of the thirty British scientists and their maintenance support on Signy were collected in the zodiacs, happy to be our guides to the seabird colonies on other nearby islands. Weddell Sea weather had shifted masses of loose (brash) ice to jostle around us and fill the channels between some of these. Iceberg Bay on lofty Coronation Isle was choked with lumpy little bergs, but Half Moon Bay proved accessible.

Rafts of chinstrap penguins greeted the zodiacs, and Cape pigeons and giant petrels floated tamely around as we scrambled ashore. Coronation Island is occupied almost exclusively by an immense rookery of the little Adélie penguin, smallest, yet most Antarctic (southerly) of all except the emperor. At this season the chicks were gathered in creches scattered over the flats and high crags of this majestically grim terrain of frost-shattered stones. In centuries of occupation the Adélies had worn zig-zag paths to reach nests high on the rock walls, so that you had the impression, from below, of being in the arena of a gigantic theatre, with thousands of spectator penguins gazing down and yelling like overexcited football fans. On this chill January day, it was still blowing hard, with flurries of snow drifting horizontally, I climbed 200 feet up the crowded slope, attacked by the plucky little Adélies disputing my right of way with flailing flippers and screams of defiance. High above, the pure white snow petrel glided to and from its nest on the snow-laden ledges of the vertical cliff, the velvet dark eye staring at me tranquilly. A perfect camouflage when it settled; most of them nest far inland in Antarctica. One colony has been found more than eighty kilometres from the sea in King Edward VII Land, the mountainous peninsula south beyond the Weddell Sea.

A deeply exciting island. As I squatted below the snow petrel ledge, I was happy to discover small groups of another petrel we had seen frequently following our ship since we had left the Falklands. This was the dainty swallow-like Wilson's storm-petrel, black with a white rump and long dangling black legs with yellow webs. It was flitting above a mossy scree of small stones long fallen from the cliff. Now and then one suddenly disappeared into an unsuspected crevice. When this happened I delved my arm as far as I could squeeze it along the narrow burrow. I knew a lot about this remarkable petrel from studies published by several scientists – Brian Roberts in Graham Land 1934–7, Beck and Brown on Signy Island 1966–9, and the French at their research station at Terre Adélie on the mainland of Antarctica between 136° and 132°E longitude. For

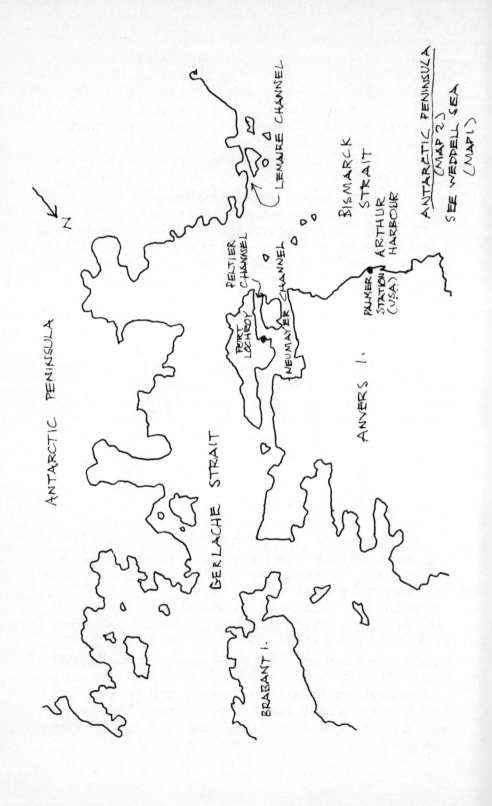

N

ANTARCTIC PENINSULA

LEMAIRE CHANNEL

BISMARCK STRAIT

ANTARCTIC PENINSULA
(MAP 2)
SEE WEDDELL SEA
(MAP1)

ARTHUR HARBOUR

PALMER STATION (USA)

PELTIER CHANNEL

NEUMAYER CHANNEL

PORT LOCHROY

ANVERS I.

GERLACHE STRAIT

BRABANT I.

despite the many hazards of nesting largely in these hostile, often snow-covered sites, Wilson's storm-petrel is one of the most abundant and far-travelling of seabirds in the world.

Interestingly, it was first sketched by Sidney Parkinson, the artist on Captain Cook's first voyage in the *Endeavour*, from a specimen collected off the River Plate, December 1768, in a warm latitude of 35°S. That specimen is still in the British Museum of Natural History, and if any thought had been given at that time as to where the species nested, it would have been supposed that this petrel was wintering in the South Atlantic, from breeding grounds in the *northern* hemisphere. For it was exceedingly numerous and well-known to the whaling, sealing and fishing fleets off the Newfoundland Banks in summer.

We now know that this small petrel, under eight inches from bill to tail, is strictly an Antarctic breeder, nesting on nearly all mainland headlands and screes within an easy flight of the sea. But because spring is late there, the single egg is not laid before late December. There is a risk that the adults may find the entrances to their burrows in the earthy screes completely blocked by late winter snow. Experienced breeders will try to clear the snow with the hooked bill and shovel it away with their feet. As in most petrels the mature male arrives first at the well-remembered site – his duty is to prepare the burrow for the female arriving perhaps a week later. Mating takes place in the burrow, or outside if snow still blocks the entry. Having mated, the hen flies to feed at sea while the single egg is developing in her ovary. Generally the mated male remains on guard inside the nest, keeping open and cleaning the burrow. Forty days' incubation is shared in short spells of up to a week, the off-duty partner feeding at sea, the sitting bird fasting in the burrow.

Brave little bird, that you should dare to nest in such an inhospitable place! For even in December new snowdrifts may entomb the sitting bird, or egg, for several days. When this happens the bird returning from feeding at sea tries, sometimes in vain, to reach the entombed egg or mate. Footprints in the snow at the burrow's blocked entrance prove how persistent the attempt has been, but hard frozen snow under sunless summer skies not infrequently results in a fatal interruption in the incubation of the egg. In a number of cases recorded at Signy Island drift snow has prevented the female from entering the burrow and laying her egg, and it was dropped outside, to be devoured by the first predator – gull, skua, sheathbird or giant petrel – to see it.

However, normally Wilson's storm-petrel is able to dig through soft snow. Forty days' incubation means that the egg will not hatch before February, later if the start of incubation has been delayed by snow blocking access to the burrow in the temporary absence of both adults feeding at sea. But given an uninterrupted incubation, the egg hatches after forty days. Complete emergence of the chick from the egg, and the drying of the thick down it is born with, involves a further twenty-four to forty-eight hours' nursing warmly under the parental breast. It is born blind, and does not open its eyes until about the tenth day. In the darkness of the burrow it will never see its parents clearly, but will know them by their comforting individual voices, and tender movements as they feel for its groping hungry beak searching for food. This is pumped up from the adult crop in the form of an oily soup of predigested krill, and doled out in controlled amounts according to the nestling's appetite, the young beak held firmly, crosswise, in that of the parent.

On this nourishing food the young storm-petrel grows fast and fattens visibly. By the twentieth day it is able to maintain normal body heat without brooding by the adults. The parents are thus free to forage all day to bring home food in larger quantities to meet the growing appetite of their chick. From a birth weight of seven grams, the average weight of a healthy chick increases to seventeen grams at fifty-two days of age, and in fact it is then heavier than the parent, which has lost weight in strenuous food-collecting at sea.

At this stage, late April to early May, the tired adults cease to feed the fledgeling. In any case it needs a period of fast to thin down as it completes the shedding of the natal down and grows its first warm winter coat of feathers. It is now active inside the burrow, emerging at night to exercise its wings; the nights are now longer and dark enough to discourage attacks by the diurnal gulls and other predators.

It was still windy and clouding over blackly as we left Coronation Island. Some of us were tiring of the stench of the guano and the bedlam of calls of Adélie penguins. It was time to dine aboard the *Lindblad Explorer* where the Signy Island biologists were our guests; and afterwards they showed us slides of their life and activities at that station. In summer they wet-suit dive to study Weddell marine life, in winter skiing is a chief joy, and inevitably there is a football season. Few of them shave, most have immense beards (cleaned-up for today's special occasion). The engineer had a cockatoo haircut. The cook had brought some Weddell seal steaks, which he recommended as 'tender as a young bifstek'. A seemingly joyous lot of mostly young men who volunteer for eighteen months' work on Signy Island Antarctic Survey Research projects, which include many subjects, from birds to botany and microbiology.

A good deal of mistnetting of storm-petrels on Signy has established that, coupled with measurements of ice-free areas where these nest on the island, the total population of Wilson's petrel on Signy cannot be less than 200,000 pairs, of which about one half must be young pre-breeders. Thus, in spite of the hazards of untimely snow in summer, and of the abundance of predatory gulls, sheathbills, skuas and stinker petrels, this fragile-looking storm-petrel is flourishing. Ringing of hundreds of the species in Antarctica – and some taken at sea off the Newfoundland Banks – indicates that it must be long-lived, since about half the recoveries are of petrels ringed as nestlings, which do not return to breed where they were born until they are fully mature at around three to five years of age.

Other discoveries as a result of marking these petrels at the nest indicate that pairs are faithful to each other, divorce is rare, and that if one of a pair fails to return the survivor may not obtain a new partner in the season of his or her bereavement. 'He or she will mope around the empty burrow over the critical period of the pairing time . . . the widowed bird cannot incubate or rear a chick successfully alone.'

18 January 'Whales to starboard!'

Thus Skipper Hasse Nilsson on the intercom as I lay reading Wally Herbert's *A World of Men* in my bunk pre-breakfast. Immediately Donald and Ronald dived into warm clothes and rushed to the bow with others who know this is the best place from which to photograph cetaceans – Hasse always alters course to follow marine beasts for our benefit. A school of thirty-odd minke whales were cavorting there, but you needed a quick eye and a high-speed telephoto lens to snap them as they breached briefly, snorting sleek black leaping shapes.

The minke or piked whale *Balaenoptera acutorostrata* is only one-third as large as the blue whale (the largest living animal today) which otherwise it closely resembles in colour, stream-lined shape and world-wide distribution. It is a fast swimmer, easily overtaking the average power-driven ship. Since the blue whale has been hunted close to extinction, the minke, less hunted because of its smaller size, is said to have increased, especially in cold Antarctic waters where its krill food is abundant all summer long.

Apart from its smaller size, the minke exhibits a white panel centrally on its short flipper – if you are fortunate to see this distinctive mark when it rises and rolls sportively to one side as it lunges with gaping jaws to engulf a whirling mass of pink krill.

This is the month when these tiny shrimps fill the upper levels of the Antarctic water close to floe and berg ice, water constantly upwelling with nutrient minerals from the ocean floor, from dissolving rock particles and the rain of the dead bodies and guano of sea animals, from great whales to little fishes, nutrients which are the base of the food chain on which the microscopic plankton of diatoms and algae live, and in turn are eaten by the shrimps and amphipods. (That evening Dennis Puleston lectured on this basic food chain of the Weddell Sea, displaying a glass box full of the tiny animals and algae he had taken in a tow-net earlier.)

We had hardly eaten breakfast before another cry of 'Whalespout' sent us scurrying to the bows. This time it was a lone bull sperm whale ploughing a choppy sea ahead, easily identified by its immense square head and single spout of vapour directed forward from its single blow-hole asymmetrically on the left of its snout.

'He's a solitary bull, outcast from the family pod, probably driven from his harem of cows and their calves, which never come near the ice – they live in warmer sub-tropical seas permanently,' said the much-voyaged Hasse. 'Quite harmless, despite Herman Melville's

Moby Dick yarn. The only time they are dangerous is when they take a deep sleep at the surface, after devouring their giant cuttlefish prey at great depths below. Diving so deep tires an old bull, so he must pant and blow at the surface for a long time. Then like an old man after a heavy meal, he will sleep, cradled at the surface, always on his right side, so as to keep his blow-hole above water on the left of his snout. It's these lone sleepy old bulls which are the danger to sailing-ships at night, when they collide with a mountain of unconscious blubber. The collision can crack open or sink a ship. Many a round-the-world racing yacht has suffered from such a collision, and had to limp into the nearest port for repairs. But you hear nothing of the damage to the unfortunate whale so rudely wakened from his peaceful dreams . . .'

So many large and small icebergs and brash ice were drifting down upon the *Lindblad Explorer* from the great Larsen ice-shelf – their calving source along the eastern coast of the Antarctic Peninsula (which forms the western coast of the Weddell Sea) that, fearing our ship would be trapped, Hasse steered northwest all night towards Elephant Island and the open sea.

'We'll come back and explore the Weddell later,' apologised Hasse. 'Pray for a northerly breeze to drive the ice back to the Larsen shelf.'

(On an earlier expedition the *Explorer* had been holed by an iceberg, and although she had not been sunk, all the passengers had been taken off in a Chilean patrol ship and landed in Punta Arenas.)

19 January King George Island. A brilliant sunlit calm day, as we steamed into Admiralty Bay. The zodiacs weaved a way through brash ice to land on Martel Beach. I am writing this on Bearpole Hill, looking down upon this long beach. As far as eye can see the bones of hundreds of blue, fin, and other large whales testify to the immense slaughter of the giants in the boom years at the beginning of the present century. Frost has preserved and whitened these skeletons. One of a blue whale has been painstakingly gathered and laid out, well above the tide-line, by – we were told – Cousteau and his *Calypso* team, as a kind of memorial to the leviathans ruthlessly slaughtered by the whaling fleets of half a dozen nations, and brought ashore here for wasteful processing in the summer.

Donald and I took measurement by pacing its length and breadth in our rubber boots, but arrived at different figures. Mine gave a length of seventy feet from tip of jaw to the tip of the last vertebra of the tail.

I was interested to discover that Wilson's storm-petrels had dug nesting burrows in the mossy flat on which the blue whale skeleton rested, apparently untouched since I had first seen it in March 1981, with Richard Adams on my first cruise aboard the *Explorer*. And there too was the ancient waterboat used in those bygone whaling days, a solidly-built timber-box a few metres long, aslant upon the beach where it had been abandoned more than half a century ago, yet preserved from decay by zero temperatures ever since. And the same pair of skuas dive-bombing our heads, so we had to pull down our fur caps to make sure of an unbloodied skull.

On the rocky knoll above the derelict shacks of the former whaling station a number of huge Weddell seals (*Leptonychotes weddelli*) lie slumbering in the sun. As we drew closer each opened one eye to examine that rare phenomenon, a human intruder. They are totally unafraid, no longer killed for their pelt and flesh by hungry whalers and sealers, who considered them too stupid to realise their danger. But in fact they are remarkable for their deep-diving under the ice, even in the black night of the Antarctic winter. Dr G. L. Kooyman has studied them at their ice breathing holes. These are kept open by each seal chewing the ice as fast as it builds up. By attaching depth gauges to individuals Kooyman recorded descents to 500 feet (152 m). These seals find their fish and squid prey in total darkness under the ice by sonar clicks, as whales and dolphins do.

Suddenly a distant roar reverberated across the sheltered bay, from the enormous glacier flowing from the skirts of a peak some 2300 metres high in the centre of this sixty-mile-long island. It was calving under the summer sun, as it slid by inches down to the sea each day, the ice wall cracking with a sound like a cannon shot and crashing into the water, making concentric waves towards where the *Explorer* was anchored.

Lunch-time aboard ship. As the zodiacs collected us more calvings took place, the wash from the tumbling mass of ice rocking the glittering ice-floes, on which dozens of Adélie and chinstrap penguins were tranquilly sunning themselves. On one floe four seals were resting; they raised sleek pale heads to stare at our party as if in astonishment. We were certainly an odd lot, dressed in anoraks of assorted colours, gliding along on rubber saucers.

These sleeker seals, with pointed noses, were the so-called crab-eaters, *Lobodon carcinophagus*, which probably do not eat crabs.

They are pack-ice haunters, living principally on krill, with specially lobed teeth for the purpose of sifting water from each gulp of shrimps.

Like the true seals, they and the Weddell, Ross, and elephant seals have short foreflippers and streamlined tails, and can only drag themselves along on land or ice by hunching forward awkwardly; unlike the Antarctic and sub-Antarctic fur seals we encountered, which can almost gallop, having leg-like front and rear flippers.

A grand barbecue at noon on the foredeck. Red wine, hot steak, sausage and sunlight stimulated the hardier passengers to dive into the small swimming-pool, temperature close to zero – so they could claim to have swum in salt water inside the Antarctic Circle.

The ship now moved south through the entrance to Admiralty Bay and the Polish station. We were first put ashore on a long low beach which appeared to be the loitering ground of all the local birds and seals, breeders and immatures alike. Hundreds of Adélie, chinstrap and gentoo penguins, some beginning to moult, but all enjoying the calm sunshine. I climbed a little way inland, in my usual search for nesting storm-petrels in mossy screes. Photographed a group of six nests of the giant petrel containing downy white chicks, guarded by one perfectly white adult – typical of the southernmost form of the stinker. Encountered two US scientists studying the ecology of what they called the Stifftails – the said Adélie, chinstrap and gentoo penguins which use their tails to prop themselves upright and confront mate or rival, avian or human.

At the Polish base the few scientists were welcoming, but explained that its derelict appearance was due to lack of funds. Looking

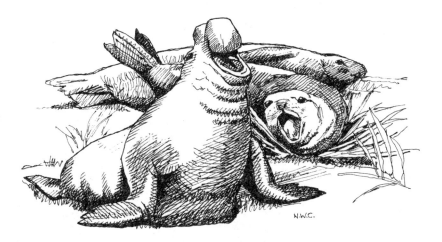

all the more derelict because of the litter of whale-bones of the bad old days. Here and there, where streams of meltwater trickled seawards from the glaciated heights, were clumps of moulting elephant seals wallowing in the fresh water as they sloughed off their entire skin in ragged peeling strips. Doubtless the water is cooling to bodies sun-heated and in such close contact. A somewhat disgusting and smelly spectacle as these fasting but fat giants snore and belch, dribble and fart, elephant-seal fashion.

A dozen Polish and American scientists came aboard for convivial talk before we sailed this evening.

20 January Port Lochroy. A completely grey sky and strong north gale, with snow falling, as we ate breakfast and gazed at small bergs ahead and astern. On deck a blinding snowstorm drove the *Lindblad Explorer* to seek shelter in the fiords of Gerlache Strait. At 10.00 hours we crept up to a small berg on which lay sleeping a young leopard seal. We could see a bloody wound on its head, possibly the left eye was blind. Its only enemy in Antarctica would be the killer whale. The ship's bow, nudging its icy throne, roused it, and after a one-eyed stare at the photographers in the bows, it slithered silently into the sea, demonstrating how this seal approaches its chief prey, stalking penguins by a stealthy approach under water.

The immense mountainous mass of Anvers Island lay ahead, snow-shrouded. Presently we entered the shelter of narrow, twisting Neumayer Channel, a fairyland of ice walls under drifting snow. But it was calmer now as we moved into the narrower passage of the Peltier Channel, and anchored in mountain-walled Port Lochroy.

We went ashore at an abandoned whaling station taken over by nesting gentoo penguins and blue-eyed cormorants, a rocky foul-smelling terrain. It was here that in 1981 the *Lindblad Explorer* had put on a midnight barbecue for us, to see the sun touch the horizon and rise immediately on a new day. On that 1981 occasion my cabin-mate Richard Adams recorded (I quote from our book *Voyage Through the Antarctic* in his words): 'That barbecue was not a very pleasant occasion, standing up to the ankles in penguin shit (pretty strong), in a sharp cutting wind, trying to eat tough lukewarm steak either with fingers or fragile plastic knives and forks, while skuas hovered attentively nearby (skuas can turn nasty, especially when they're sharp-set and can smell meat). I packed it in early and came back in a returning zodiac to play chess with the doctor . . .'

At midnight, continued Richard in his travelogue (which he

cunningly failed to send me proof of before our book was published), he was worried about Ronald but going to the gangway found the last zodiac arriving back with him aboard.

'"Marv'llsh party on rocksh! All shinging shongs to piano accordion. You sh've been there, shtupid fellow!" What a man! He'd also been walking for two hours alone, far over the high ground, searching for nests of his beloved storm petrels.'

I cannot resist here the chance to riposte with the truth, which dear old Richard shan't see until this book is published. For the truth is (I quote from my own diary of that day):

'The barbecue began at 9 pm, the ship's galley had brought ashore a charcoal cooker and turned out unlimited nicely undercooked steaks and hot potatoes (in foil). And all the claret we could drink. Richard and Eric Hosking retreated soon after, shivering with cold (they said), but most of us hung on, singing the songs of our several nations accompanied by a Swiss accordionist, and I hopeful of seeing the storm petrels which Dennis Puleston declared would appear before midnight. To lubricate the songs more drink was sent for, and came in the form of a crate of champagne. Meanwhile, seeing a broken cliff full of likely crevices above us I climbed to the top, disturbing a few Wilson storm petrels flitting to and fro like house-martins nesting in eaves at home in UK. The sun was still warmly bathing the top of the cliff at about 200 feet, where I was surprised to find creches of fat fledged gentoo penguins stationary in the snow, moulting in separate (family?) groups. A very few were still being fed from the bulging crops of adults laboriously climbing up a steep circuitous path from the sea. As each adult arrived it was rushed upon by the nearest immatures, but it would only feed its own chick (one or a pair), and pecked away the others.

'The last sun touched the 9,500 ft peak of Anvers Island in calm beauty as I returned to the song party. More champagne was handed round. It was all most enjoyable. We sang or hummed each other's national song. I led them into *Land of My Fathers* – in Welsh. Even the penguins seemed to listen. Twenty of us survived to see the non-sunset in a flaming red sky. By this time everyone was used to and did not notice any longer the stink of guano. But most of us were stiff with standing in the slush. Some had to be helped to the zodiacs. I have a distinct recollection of four of us carrying the doctor's wife over the hummocky nests of penguin and blue-eyed cormorant, with brief stops to deposit her in a clean cormorant nest. She declared she was not drunk, only a bit stiff, very happy and still singing a Swedish love-song.'

21 January Naming the unnamed island. We were up at 06.00 hours to watch our good ship steam through the very narrow rock- and ice-walled Peltier Channel on an overcast day. The sea and ice-floes were alive with penguins, gulls, skuas and blue-eyed shags. Gradually the day improved as we crossed the open Bismarck Strait, on our furthest south day. It was one of scenic beauty and photography, as *Lindblad Explorer* coasted along to inspect large icebergs of fantastic shapes, with grottoes and caves, and see-through tunnels with dripping stalactites, and veins of blue strata – formed under pressure of glacier ice possibly centuries old. Most of these imitation castles of ice start their sea-voyages when they break free from the huge Ross Barrier glacier shelf, which is larger than France and extends southward to within about 200 miles of the true South Pole. Wind and current carry these clockwise around the Antarctic continent, at first in tabular form. They are drifted north by the projection of the Antarctic Peninsula, and debouch, much reduced by higher temperatures, and dissolve at last in the South Atlantic, Pacific and Indian Oceans.

And so on through yet another ice- and snow-walled fiord, the Lemaire Channel, of even more surpassing beauty, if that is possible. Beyond lay numerous small islands, some low and covered with Adélie penguins, and here and there a fat big-headed sleeping Weddell seal. One group, the Argentine Islands, had been the winter home of the early French explorer Charcot in his *Pourquoi Pas*, that same sailing vessel in which he is alleged to have reached and climbed Rockall. And here too half a century ago had camped my friend Dr Brian Roberts of the Scott Polar Institute and made the first study of the life-cycle of Wilson's storm-petrel, published by the British Museum of Natural History. In this I am honourably mentioned as being the inventor of a simple method of checking the visits of small petrels to their underground nesting burrows. 'Lockley (1930) used a light lattice (of matchsticks) set up across the entrance of the burrows, which was easily brushed aside by birds entering or departing.' Roberts on the Argentine Islands used 'a light lattice of stiff feathery lichen (*Usnes* sp.) for the purpose'. The interesting fact about both studies was that these two storm-petrel species, nesting half a world apart, prove to have almost identical incubation periods (forty days), and the nestling, growing much fatter and heavier than the adult, is abandoned in the burrow by its exhausted parents in late autumn, when these need to moult at sea and recuperate by a long journey across the Equator – the British storm-petrel to winter in the summer off South Africa, the Wilson's petrel to winter in the northern summer off Canada's Newfoundland Banks; the seas of both are rich in plankton then.

On our way to an unnamed island, which by common consent we named Nilsson in honour of our Captain, we came upon two hump-backed whales, mother and child, so engrossed in feeding on the abundant krill that they ignored our red ship dodging through the large and small bergs. Could there have been such an uniquely happy day, wandering about this calm inshore sea in perfect sunshine, landing on Nilsson Island, which is just one vast Adélie penguin metropolis? And I was permitted to set foot briefly on Brian Roberts' Galindez islet, where I could examine the bank of petrel burrows which he studied in 1935–7, in the mossy turf, with patches of snow here and there. No time to do more than examine the burrow entrances, cackle down one or two of these, and receive a squeaking protest from deep inside. And all around, the glorious backdrop of massive snow-covered mountains of Anvers Island and the mainland of the Antarctic Peninsula.

But the day was not half over yet. After hot glog on the bridge, to celebrate the naming of Nilsson Island, and admiring its pink glow – due to the vast quantity of red krill staining the rocks from the faeces of the Adélies – the ship glided across Bismarck Strait (more minke whales) to Arthur Harbour, site of the USA Palmer Station.

It was too good a day to spend long inside this immaculately maintained research station, where a dozen scientists study everything from the meteorology and geology to the life-cycles of bird, beast and bug. As an icebreaker was due to call in tomorrow, some of us and the base staff intended to write letters home.

Towards sunset Donald and Ronald joined a small zodiac party to cross to nearby Torgeson Island, to watch the homecoming of its chief inhabitants – Wilson's petrels and Adélie penguins. From the low rocky crown of this island we could admire the white breasts of a thousand Adélies waddling back to their creches of well-grown downy chicks, their long shadows thrown eastwards by the westering sun.

Both male and female Adélie marched in pair formation to reach what must have been their own territorial niches in the rocks below us. It was amusing to study how the pair billed face to face there, discussing the triumph of achieving their bedroom for the night, where they were joined by their twin children, which had left the daytime creche to sleep with their parents, invited to do so by voice-recognition of their family chatter.

What were the soot-brown children saying to Mum and Dad? All seemed tired with the day's adventures. But they must have felt satisfied that they were safer on dry land than sleeping at sea. Their dread enemy the leopard seal was still patrolling the island shore. One had also landed and gone to sleep in a little bay below us; on land it cannot move fast enough to catch a penguin; it does not try, it comes ashore to sleep and dry its fur.

A number of lone Adélies were also coming ashore, looking around hesitatingly, before moving into vacant spaces on the rocky platforms below us. This timidity suggests they were the 'unemployed' Adélies (failed or more certainly pre-breeders not above two years old). They too seemed sleepy, and presently squatted down, eyes half-closed; and finally lay prone on their bellies, necks stretched out as if dead.

Thus do Adélies sleep, away from family cares.

Researcher scientist Dr Obst at Palmer Station had said that no Wilson's petrels nested on Torgeson, they only visited. In the hush after sunset, and some darkness falling, these little storm-petrels, abundant at sea all day, came flitting like moths about the topmost rocks on which we were perched. One or two kept disappearing from sight among jumbled rocks where the boxes and trashcans of tins and other rubbish from Palmer Station had been dumped.

Curious about the rubbish, which today a reputable scientific station in Antarctica is forbidden to dump on land or at sea, but is supposed to take back home, I wondered if the Palmer Station lads, in suggesting Torgeson was not a Wilson's petrel breeding island, had been ashamed of their dump on the island. For delving in the rock debris and rubbish I found three Wilson's petrel's burrows, each with a single egg. One of these was actually beneath a heavy wooden crate full of used beer cans, at least providing a weatherproof cover for the little birds which had burrowed beneath it.

So fascinating was this midnight scene of sleeping groups of silent Adélies and the flighting of the storm-petrels around the rocky throne of the island that Donald and Ronald were reluctant to obey the shouting call of the zodiac-driver waiting impatiently by the edge of the sea.

And so to bed by 01.00 hours, and another instalment of *War and Peace* (my fifth reading) to woo sleep, as the engines of the *Lindblad Explorer* and the rattling of her anchor home to the hawse-pipe indicated that we were steaming north.

Rounding Cape Horn

22 *January* The intention was to re-enter the Weddell Sea, but a head gale was blowing down the Gerlache Strait under black clouds, and Skipper Nilsson sought shelter in Paradise Bay under the ice-clad cliffs of the mainland. Here it was calm enough, apart from some small avalanches descending from the mountains, to go ashore at two semi-derelict whaling stations.

Although the Chilean station had been abandoned many years

ago, three men had been sent from Chile to try to revive it, 'to keep up a presence' – evidently a political manoeuvre against the Argentines, who occupy the other station known as Almirante Brown (founder of the Argentine navy: with such a name he ought to have been, and probably was, British).

The Chilean base of Gonzalez Videla was occupied by a splendid colony of gentoo penguins scattered around the moribund installations, some with their two chicks inside a doorless engine shed – it was stinking besides with a recumbent moulting cow elephant seal. One Chilean scientist I met said there had been heavy snowfalls and several avalanches lately. Cold-eyed, yellow-wattled scavenger sheathbills sat on the roof of one empty hut, silently disapproving of intruding humans taking photographs.

The Argentine base was little better than a shed perched on a sheer cliff, with enough water at high tide for the *Lindblad Explorer* to berth against a rickety wharf there. It was manned by fourteen men, unshaven and rough-looking, but hospitable enough to invite us to sign our names in a book, and have our passports rubber-stamped with the logo ESTACION CIENTIFICA ALMIRANTE BROWN – ANTARCTICA ARGENTINA, circling an inset map of a quadrant of the polar continent identical in extent with the British claim. Once again we had the feeling that these men, speaking pidgin English, none of them identifiable as scientists, were political pawns of their country, possibly army conscripts. For which reason few of us signed their visitors' book.

But we enjoyed scrambling up the adjacent cliff to photograph a Cape pigeon sitting tight on her downy chick in a crevice in the rocks, and afterwards cruised around this beautiful mainland bay with its tidal caves, and drifting bergs and floes of all shapes and sizes, the more tabular ones packed with Adélie penguins, blue-eyed cormorants, a few gentoos and chinstraps, and Weddell seals, all idle and content to bask in the afternoon sunlight.

The drifting icebergs were now filling Paradise Bay on the flood tide. The zodiacs were recalled and hoisted aboard, lest we be trapped in the bay. It was time for tea, and an announcement that there was to be a fancy-dress parade after dinner, everyone requested to appear disguised as an Antarctic animal.

The weather was easing, and maybe we should land on Paulet Island in the Weddell Sea tomorrow.

Monday, 23 January Grey seas and black skies, lifting slightly as we

steamed towards Hope Bay at the northern tip of the Antarctic
Peninsula, off which we anchored at 09.30. That is to say, we
intended to, but found the whole bay inshore blocked by large floes
of pack-ice.

Hasse made several vain attempts to push through, so that we
could at least get near enough to photograph the settlement of some
twenty small buildings housing an Argentine 'presence' on what was
once a British whaling base.

Weddell seals, many penguins and one stinker petrel gazed at us
quizzically from the floes jammed around us, and we had to be
content with scanning the Hope Bay settlement through binoculars.

It has an interesting story. Under the provisions of the Antarctic
Treaty which came into force in 1961 between Britain, Argentina,
Chile and a dozen other signatory nations, existing territorial claims
were frozen for thirty years, and no military activities were to take
place in existing bases. Antarctica by this agreement was 'reserved
for peaceful purposes only'.

Argentina suddenly broke this agreement by occupying Hope Bay,
in the temporary absence of its small team of British scientists, and
made a great public display of establishing there a whole village,
complete with families and children 'to determine whether Antarctica is suitable for family life, and to reinforce the inalienable rights of
Argentina in those far-off lands'. It was re-named Esperanza.

By 1978 the settlement consisted of eighteen men (five were
soldiers), eight women and nineteen children. Commenting on the
first human birth in Antarctica the *New York Times* reported: 'Silvia
Morello de Palma, mother of the child, says she hopes her infant son
Emil will love Antarctica. By the year 2000 there will be better ways
of making life comfortable here.' But for the sun-loving Argentine
women, at that moment of our inspection through binoculars, Hope
Bay looked unrelievedly miserable under a black sky, snow-drifted
and ice-bound, not a soul in sight, just a few dim lights from a street
lamp and some buildings.

At the outbreak of the Argentine attack on the Falklands and
South Georgia in April 1982 the Argentine garrison at Hope Bay was
reinforced and for a while resisted the small force of British Commandos which attacked it. 'A waste of time, better to let the enemy
stew in its own juice for the winter in that frozen prison village,' was
a general comment we had heard in the Falklands. (There would be
plenty of seals and penguins to save them from starvation.) But
Dennis Puleston reports that on a visit earlier this year he found the

village in a sad mess; children are allowed to molest the penguin colonies, seals are freely slaughtered for food and skins, and rubbish dumps accumulate in unsightly heaps with hundreds of rusting empty forty-gallon fuel drums.

Our ship had to weave through flotillas of large and small icebergs as we entered the Weddell Sea, and aimed for Paulet Island, fortunately at that moment almost free of brash ice. At noon we zodiaced upon a low promontory, ignored by the usual crowd of Adélies and a dozen slumbering seals staring idly at us. For the sun had re-appeared and the wind died down.

Inland, Paulet is a rough plateau below a 500-ft crag. Uninhabited now, it was a refuge for the Nordenskjöld Expedition after his ship *Antarctica* was crushed and sunk in the Weddell Sea in 1903. The hut in which the twenty-two survivors lived for seven months still stands, well-built of stones, but today occupied by a pair of Adélies in a nest atop one wall, with a substantial chick looking very king-of-the-castle. Also preserved under a heap of large stones nearer the landing beach is the grave of a crew member who failed to survive.

There must be at least one million pairs of Adélies nesting on Paulet, and a fair sprinkling of blue-eyed shag colonies. For three hours of warm sunshine we were free to roam the island, climbing to a higher plateau snow-free at 200 feet and equally crammed with Adélies.

There is a yellow crater lake in the hollow of Paulet, which the to-ing-and-fro-ing Adélies made use of as a short cut, either to swim across or to toboggan over the frozen portion. It was good fun to join the Adélies in both exercises, made hilarious to us if not to the uncaring penguins, by the antics of some of the heavier men of our expedition trying to maintain an upright position when the lake ice began to wobble under their weight. But the ice was at least a metre thick, as I found on warily crossing it hand-in-hand, so to speak, with lines and files of penguins, following their tracks of pink krill and guano, easier-going than on land, to reach their inland nests and creches.

It was yet another glorious day sandwiched between storms. Back at the landing beach even the penguins were enjoying the beautiful afternoon weather, basking on ice-floes or porpoising exuberantly in the sea.

But a southerly wind was bringing large bergs rapidly north, threatening to hem *Lindblad Explorer* into the island shore. That evening the ship was several times stopped, and obliged to reverse and find the best open leads to gain the Drake Passage and our course for Cape Horn.

24 January Deception Island (again). Dawn was breaking as our ship approached the mist-crowned South Shetland Isles, and the volcano which is known as Deception Island – from its harbour hidden within the caldera itself. It had been planned to land on the outer coast at Bailey Head, the site of a vast chinstrap colony, but a heavy onshore swell and a grey sky decided Hasse to make for the hidden entrance appropriately dubbed Neptune's Bellows. In just the same weather, or worse, had my cabin-mate Richard Adams and I passed through these sheer cliff narrows on the *Lindblad Explorer* on 5 February 1981, that is, pre-Falklands War, on my first Antarctic voyage – to Scott Base. What should we find today?

I quote from my diary: 'A cloudy morning with rain and a Force 4 wind made the crater uninviting to some who decided not to go forth in the zodiacs. Richard and I and our photographer Peter (Hirst-Smith) were first to get ashore on the beach at Whalers' Bay, the site of a derelict whaling station, the remains of its huts and storage tanks toppled and upheaved, and hundreds of empty barrels scattered over the black lava beach. As described by Alistair Hardy (in *Great Waters*, 1967), a thriving whaling settlement in this harbour had been destroyed by the eruption of December 1924; this occurred at midsummer when the factory ships were tied together and their fires out during the whaling close season. Suddenly there was violent earth movement and the sea actually boiled, the sulphurous steam blistering the paint of the moored ships. Fortunately the scalding lasted a relatively short time. But there have been intermittent smaller volcanic disturbances in this harbour since. Hasse promised us that, weather improving, we should move across the caldera lagoon and enjoy an afternoon picnic and swim in the warm natural sauna off Telephon Bay. But it was not to be.

'Meanwhile our trio made the best of the unpleasant wind and rain. Well-protected by our thermal underwear and waterproof anoraks and moonboots, we puffed our way through the tottering remains of the British Magistrate's quarters and the former Norwegian whaling complex. Both had been burned-out to skeletal ironwork. The whole area of black sand was now occupied by moulting groups of penguins, mostly gentoos. A moulting penguin dislikes any activity which will compel it to move an inch from the dry spot in which it stands surrounded by the warm jacket of its moulting feathers. We found them dispersed among the rusting barrels; with here and there a party of male Antarctic fur seals (identical with the New Zealand species, I thought) also moulting but fiercely aggressive and ready to attack if we moved close to their barking, fanged faces. These eared seals have ugly pointed snouts and the males quarrel among themselves, except when moulting.

'It was a considerable effort in our own unmoulted Antarctic clothes to toil up the steep slope to Neptune's Window, a big split in the caldera wall giving a view of the outer sea and colonies of Cape pigeons and Antarctic fulmars at nests on the hanging ledges. The piebald Cape pigeons, squatting beside their single black chick, looked charming, but photographer Hirst-Smith, approaching the nearest by crawling along a ledge on his tummy, was rewarded by a sudden shot of the stomach contents of the adult consisting of a stinking oil of predigested pink krill (reserved for its child), staining Peter's face and frontal approach.

'"Bloody beast of a bird!" exclaimed Peter, with further (unmentionable) expletives as he mopped the mess away, but the stink was to last many days on his anorak. "I did warn you!" I said. "The only way to get rid of the stink is to boil your clothes – and yourself – in cow urine. At least, that is the official antidote in the Faroe Islands when a cragsman is hit by stomach oil ejected by a fulmar petrel, when collecting these charming birds or their eggs for winter food. Of course it is a protective device meant to deter its natural enemies – gull, eagle or other avian predator. The fat chicks of these tube-nosed birds are quite delicious eating."

'Toots on the *Lindblad Explorer*'s siren far below indicated a recall. Our skipper had decided to abandon the sauna picnic. A storm of rain and wind indicated an early lunch and departure from the crazy cauldron of Deception. Yet as soon as we entered the Bransfield Channel, the sun flooded out, the wind eased, and in the distance we spotted a Japanese whale-catcher. Most of the passengers were indignant and tried to persuade Hasse to intercept her and complain at what they supposed must be a violation of international law.

'"Quite useless," answered Hasse as we clustered around him on the bridge. "I have already been on the radio, and the Jap skipper says he is only on reconnaissance or whale-counting. From experience of trying to embarrass such a ship at sea, the best I can do is to say that we are also counting whales in Antarctic waters, and our passengers will be signing a petition to the United Nations demanding a complete moratorium on killing whales in the foreseeable future. Anyway, my ship is far too slow ever to catch up with those fast Jap whale-chasers!"'

On this January 1984 day, the weather gradually improved as Ronald and Donald roamed the same dilapidated whaling village. We were surprised to see a Chilean flag fluttering above a small hut freshly-planted outside the former British station. On one of the huge damaged oil tanks close by the Chileans have also painted signed notices claiming that Alcacar (Deception Island) belongs to Chile. But a parallel notice insists that the island is Argentine territory – both notices are painted in English! And above both some wag has painted in large capitals (he must have used a ladder) 'GO HOME!'

After lunch aboard Hasse said it was calm enough to cross the lagoon to enjoy that sauna in Telephon Bay. Immediately on landing there Dennis took us inland on a long hike to view a series of lava craters, some still warm and grumbling beneath the barren black gravel. Here and there lay a large scoria boulder. The area was desolate of birds, save for a few Antarctic terns flying and calling overhead – evidently on the way to or from nesting colonies we had no time to search for. Everyone was now anxious to take a dip in the hot springs at the edge of this bay.

The ship's steward had laid on hot glog wine as a reward for the bathers. Ronald and Donald and others were coached in the safe procedure of immersion in the near-freezing water of the lagoon and the near-boiling springs issuing from the laval sand. The thing to do was to leap from the dry, warm black sand a yard up the sloping beach, and land exactly in the tepid zone between the very hot water and the cold outer sea.

Quite exhilarating, and those who did not bathe took photographs of those who did, amid much undressing and laughter, and some hiding of clothes by miscreant spectators. The spiced wine and biscuits warmed Ronald and Donald up nicely.

Among those who did not bathe was an attractive French woman passenger, a Parisienne who seemed to have few friends on board except one zodiac driver Colin M., a young scientist who, like most of these young zodiac drivers, was given a free passage on the *Explorer*, in return for his services, including lectures he was expected to give at sea.

When we returned from the amusing sauna picnic and all were aboard the ship by six pm, the time scheduled for our departure from Deception, it was discovered that Mademoiselle the Parisienne was missing. A search of the ship proved this.

Hasse ordered two zodiacs to be relaunched and a search of Telephon Bay carried out. I joined one zodiac, not to do more than go ashore and hold the painter ready for re-embarking.

Half an hour passed, and at last the missing Frenchwoman was found, crouching behind one of the larger brown scoria boulders half a mile inland. She was brought weeping and protesting to the zodiac by its driver Colin M. Our zodiac followed Colin's back to the ship. Suddenly there was a commotion ahead of us. The protesting lady had leaped into the sea, and begun to swim – in that freezing water – back to the bathing beach! She was quickly intercepted and dragged half-drowned and nigh frozen aboard Colin's zodiac. The rest of this adventure and the reason behind her behaviour I was to learn later from Colin.

Meanwhile he had applied life-saving drill to revive the seeming corpse, and on the walkie-talkie had informed Hasse of the mis-adventure. Hasse at once ordered the gangway and all passages to her cabin to be cleared of spectators – so as not to embarrass the lady. She remained in her cabin all next day when the ship rolled rather heavily in crossing the Drake Passage, but on the 26th emerged to gaze at Cape Horn under a tranquil sea, and looking herself as tranquil and normal as if nothing had happened to her.

'Mademoiselle told me it was a mental aberration,' Colin confided to me, before we parted at Punta Arenas four days later. 'Her excuse was that she had applied to join a French expedition to Antarctica but had been turned down at the moment of flying south to Santiago. She had joined instead the *Lindblad Explorer*, securing a vacant berth at Punta Arenas. While the ship was berthed in Whalers' Bay in Deception Harbour she had met two Chilean scientists (we had just missed seeing them) in their hut at Alcacar, who told her they were genuine scientists studying marine biology and the tidal data, but were badly funded and needed assistants. As she was partly trained in marine ecosystems, she offered to stay and work with them. They agreed, and she hurried back to the *Lindblad Explorer* to collect her suitcase. But at that moment the ship upanchored and steamed to Telephon Bay. Still, as she had packed her bag, she determined that she would jump ship (not a word to anyone aboard) and walk around the caldera to reach the Chileans' hut.

'A good thing she didn't start out, for the distance to that hut must be more than fifteen miles, with impassable snow-covered mountains between!' exclaimed Colin. 'She realised this in a discreet conver-sation with one of the zodiac drivers, but all the same decided she would hide and make the attempt after the ship had left, perhaps somehow signal the Chileans to fetch her in their dinghy. In the end she was glad that I had found her, for I happen to know some of the French scientists who might help her at their Adélie Land Station.'

A very remarkable New Zealander is Colin; among his early achievements when working as an apprentice scientist at Scott Base was to be the first to descend into the deep crater of Mount Erebus, of which he told me: 'Just a long drop on a rope to the edge of the fumarole at the moment when it was more or less quiescent.'

When Ernest Shackleton's party was the first to climb this highest mountain in Antarctica (13,500 ft) they were nearly a week struggling through snow and gales to arrive at the top on 10 March 1909: 'Looking down into the crater far below, they saw clouds of steam rising from large holes, with periodical booms from the bowels of the mountain.'

26 *January*   Cape Horn. 07.00 hours. The notorious Cape grew even larger but more smiling as we approached over a quiet sea, normally one of the stormiest in the world. The weather was unusually calm. Hasse announced that we would make an early landing – on Cape Horn Island itself. But as the ship was still a little east of the Horn, we should cruise a mile or so to the west, close inshore, so that we could claim, like the clipper ships of old, to have 'rounded the Horn'. Having done so and glimpsed a calm Pacific Ocean, we turned eastwards and entered a sheltered cove on the east side.

A small Chilean patrol boat was anchored here. The sailors and soldiers on board welcomed us and helped us to climb up a steep bushy cliff to their encampment in a little glen at the top. There is a radio station and a small chapel.

How the Chileans and Argentinians hate each other! At least, their politicians do. The Commanding Officer of the Chileans, speaking perfect English, explained that they were obliged to maintain a strong presence at Cape Horn because of the aggressiveness of the Argentinians, who claim sovereignty of the Cape and its scattered islands.

The view from the little chapel on the brow of the Cape was magnificent today; a smooth deep blue sea above rocks scarred by storm waves, and yellow with golden and grey lichens, long tresses of kelp floating in the sea, and everywhere handsome penguins, gulls, terns, shags and black oyster-catchers feeding or resting peacefully in

the sun. There are no grazing animals on Cape Horn, which is a bush-covered nature reserve. We could go where we liked, provided we did not photograph the radio installations; Argentine commandos had tried to blow these up one dark night during the late Falklands War, and the land approaches had been mined by the Chileans – and still were. But not the cliff terrain; we could climb about where paths had been made to reach the colonies of burrowing Magellan penguins, and the beach where terns screamed at us, anxious about their well-grown chicks. Most of the small land-living birds were of the same species we had seen on the Falklands. The beauty of wild flowers and the greenness of the grass was a healing sight for eyes tired of the desolate ice and rock of the Antarctic islands we had lived among so long.

A Chilean pilot had just landed and brought with him an itinerant priest to give Mass at the little chapel. We were invited to attend. To reach this we trudged uphill through thick tussock and hebe shrubs, the ground soggy with the tracks of the nesting penguins. Each pair normally raises two chicks, now nearly fledged and peeping suspiciously at us from the mouth of holes dug in the peaty soil.

We flushed native snipe, dotterel, upland geese, lark, pipit, tussock-bird, tyrant-bird and others hard to identify, but very tame as we struggled through the exuberant summer vegetation.

At the door of the tiny log chapel stood a plump macaroni penguin deep in moult and quite oblivious to anyone – you could pat its sleepy head. Obviously it was a pet to be patted or given a flipper hand-shake.

The service was timed for twelve noon. We had been told to be there ten minutes earlier if we wished for a seat on the seven benches, holding only four each at a squeeze. Ten of us were in place at 12.15 while the white-robed padre was still chatting to the Chilean CO outside in Spanish, with asides to the uncomprehending macaroni bird standing in disrobed feathers.

It was too boring to be idle or scribbling-up our diaries while the Chileans still gossiped outside, and Donald and Ronald presently crept out and returned down the hill to the little peninsula of nesting seabirds, sheltered and positively hot in the sun. Plenty of nooks in the rocks for us to disrobe and take a dip in icy Cape Horn water – in our scanties – there were lady *Lindblad Explorer* passengers with binoculars paddling in the tide hard by.

All aboard by 13.30 hours for lunch, as we steamed towards the Beagle Channel. It was early evening and still miraculously calm and sunlit as we entered this boundary waterway between Chile and Argentina. Suddenly a gunboat raced up from the east (Argentine) side to intercept the *Lindblad Explorer*, which was being piloted by two Chileans picked up at Cape Horn. On the bridge with Hasse we heard him speaking in Swedish to his radio officer, the gist of which

seemed to be that the gunboat desired the *Lindblad Explorer* to heave-to.

But our Chilean pilots argued that it was all a puerile show of force by the Argies, the channel was Chilean, and as they were piloting our ship, no notice should be taken of the gunboat. But even as this conversation continued a helicopter suddenly swooped from the Argentine side and buzzed us, within a few feet of the ship's foremast. Then, as Hasse had taken no action to advise the senior Chilean pilot at the ship's telegraph to slow down, the gunboat fired a shot dangerously close above the *Lindblad Explorer*'s bows!

With some choice Swedish expletives Hasse took over the controls and put the engines at Stop.

Quite an entertainment for us, as we crowded in the wings of the bridge – until Hasse tersely requested us to leave, when he permitted two Argentine naval officers to climb aboard. A little later, as the ship moved slowly forward, we learned that our visitors considered Hasse had insulted them by failing to fly the Argentine flag in passing through the Beagle Channel. The Chilean flag had been hoisted and was still flying, ever since we entered Chilean waters at Cape Horn.

All the same the senior Argentine officer insisted that his country's flag be hoisted, and the ship conned by his pilot through the narrows as far west 'as Argentine sovereignty extended' (which we judged was to the land boundary some twenty-five kilometres west of Ushuaia). Ushuaia had been the Argentine Fuegian port the *Lindblad Explorer* had sailed from on our 1981 cruise to McMurdo Sound and Scott Base. Quite truly this little port, then little more than an overgrown village, is considered to be the southernmost in the world. But opposite it, across the Beagle Channel narrows, is Navarino Island, maintained as an active base by the Chilean Navy. The enmity between the two nations goes back a long way into history, to the unequal carve-up of South America after the collapse of the Spanish conquest. But more recently the discovery and exploitation of oil in the region has renewed the political struggle.

Meeting on the *Lindblad Explorer*'s bridge the Argentinian officers studiously avoided speaking to the Chilean pilots, but directed their complaints at Hasse, and his first officer, in English, as together they briefly studied the charts brought to the bridge. It seemed clear to us, after the Argentinians had left, that all land and islands south of the Beagle Channel belong to Chile, by right of occupation since Chile became independent – thanks to the assistance of the British Navy – a century or longer ago.

Of course Hasse tried diplomatically to soothe the three pilots, apologising to the senior Argentine officer for 'absent-mindedness in forgetting to fly your flag'. So the uniformed and braided gentlemen could do nothing but fidget and smoke until at last they were picked up by their pilot boat from Ushuaia. Our Chilean pilot had ignored their repeated voluble requests that they give the helm orders when, as they asserted, the ship was closer to the Argentine than to the Chilean coast.

Friday 27 January Up at dawn to watch the ship cruising through the western narrows of the Beagle Channel, a wondrous sea and landscape of ice and snow-clad mountains, split by glaciers descending steeply to the sea, through valleys with silver waterfalls spilling on pebble beaches. The lower slopes are covered with thick wind-blown southern beech *Notofagus betuloides*. This fiord is now virtually uninhabited – we saw only the odd crayfishing workboat at first. The *Lindblad Explorer* slowed to a stop briefly to answer an SOS radioed from the Swedish yacht *Anagada*, which had run out of lubricant oil. It was a chance for Hasse to exercise his native tongue when their zodiac came alongside and was given a gallon canful.

We lingered in the western narrows of the Beagle Channel on such a lovely day. We nosed into Cockburn Sound, and anchored off Brecknock Island. Dennis led the way by a steep climb to a boggy and bare rock area which reminded me of typical Scottish Highland terrain, his object to show us the rare rufous-crested dotterel, a handsome wader we had sought in the Falklands.

A family group was spotted, and while our more avid photographers pursued them rather relentlessly, Ronald and Donald retreated towards the shore, and its vivid display of wild flowers of the Notofagus zone, most of them white, as they are in New Zealand's alpine beech zone: saxifrages, anemones, mountain daisies, pearlworts, berberis, and tiny orchids.

Climbing through the tangled Notofagus along the rocky shore I came upon the camp of two local fishermen, raggedly dressed, dark-skinned Fuegian Indians; obviously, I considered, descendants of the oldest Amerindians, the first humans who, it is believed, arrived on the American continent from Asia by way of the land-bridge which joined Siberia to Alaska unknown centuries ago in the Stone Age. Magellan himself in discovering the Strait in the year 1520 was nearly wrecked here. He named the large island on the south side of the Strait (north of the Beagle Channel) Tierra del Fuego

(Fire Land) from the campfires of the primitive native inhabitants who carried smouldering peat (so precious was the living flame in that rainy climate, hard-won with wooden-drill and dry grass) in their canoes or under the cloak of animal skins.

In the same century Francis Drake's chaplain found these Indians 'a comely race who built canoes of such grace and beauty, the sight and use whereof princes might seem to be delighted'.

Later they were described by the buccaneering John Davis – forced to winter in Magellan Strait in 1592, where he raided seal and penguin colonies – as naked savages who killed nine of his crew.

Darwin, from the comfort of the *Beagle* 150 years ago, saw and despised the natives: 'They can't count above five, and are the colour of Devonshire cattle, the most abject and miserable creatures.'

This was hardly surprising; by then the Fuegians had been hunted and shot as vermin by the Spanish conquerors of South America, by land-hungry settlers, by whale- and seal-hunters, and trigger-happy miners.

No wonder the once-proud Magellanic Fuegian Indians hated the white invaders with death-dealing guns. They survived into the present century in small numbers only by hiding among the cold desolate islands and sounds, living nomadically as they have always done, on seals, fish and sea-birds, making hit-and-run surprise raids on the sailing ships which in increasing numbers passed through those sounds to avoid the stormy Cape Horn passage.

Captain Slocum on his single-handed voyage around the world in the sloop *Spray* in 1896, demurred when the Chilean officer Samblich at Fort Punta Arenas warned him not to proceed further into the westward straits without an armed guard against the Fuegians, who had lately massacred a schooner's crew. Slocum, as he loaded provisions for the long passage, found no one willing to accompany him but accepted the officer's parting gift of a bag of carpet tacks, though 'I protested that I had no use for carpet tacks on board,' he wrote in his diary.

The sagacious Samblich replied: 'You must use them with discretion . . . that is to say, don't step on them yourself.'

Sure enough, when *Spray* passed through narrow Thieves' Bay, two canoes put out from the shore and followed in her wake. 'I now began to feel jaded and worn, but a hot meal of venison stew soon put me right so that I could sleep,' Slocum recorded. 'As drowsiness came on, I sprinkled the deck with tacks . . . I saw to it that not a few stood business-end up . . . Now, it is well-known that one cannot step on a

tack without saying something about it. A good Christian will
whistle when he steps on the commercial end of a carpet tack; a
savage will howl and claw the air, and that was just what happened
that night at about twelve o'clock while I was asleep in the cabin,
where the savages thought they "had" me, sloop and all, but changed
their minds when they stepped on deck . . . they howled like a pack of
hounds [and] jumped pell-mell, some into their canoes and some into
the sea . . .'

Slocum completed their rout by firing a volley of gunshot into the
air 'to let the rascals know that I was home'.

All is changed today. Treated as human beings, with equal rights
of full citizenship and modern education, these proud Fuegian
'savages' prove to be a gentle and peace-loving race – what is left of
them.

Rarotonga

'We must live as if every moment were precious except the final one. We should go down with our preferences and prejudices nailed to the masthead.'

Cyril Connolly

Drowsing in the fragrant shade of the frangipani trees beside the coral reef of Rarotonga I looked up to admire the sight of half-naked islanders wading barefoot in the clear water of the lagoon, snorkel-ling in deeper places, some for pleasure, some with handnets in search of fish. Leisurely and timeless is this Rarotongan existence fit for poets and lazy writers like myself. Day and night the temperature is never below 22°C. Hours to stand and stare and exchange news and philosophy with these happy islanders.

Exham Wichman is a splendid example. He told us his name was derived from the trader Exham, who in 1888 was invited by Queen Victoria to become Resident Agent for the Crown when the Cook Islands were declared a British Protectorate. He is a tall broad Polynesian with a paler than usual golden skin.

'Some white blood in me,' he said, 'from the Pakeha (European) traders and whale-hunters visiting these islands in the old sailing days. I can tell you the whole history of the Cook Islands, so named by Captain James Cook when in 1777 he landed here, and found my forebears speaking the same dialect as the Maori people of New Zealand, from which Cook had just arrived in his famous *Resolution*.'

In his battered farm wagon Wichman drove us in the next few days around every good road, and many a barely-negotiable lane of Rarotonga's length and breadth. Greatest length is only about 12 km, breadth 6 km.

'The first thing I tell people is not to confuse Rarotonga with Tonga. We in the Cook Islands are in the same latitude but a date-line day away, and much nearer Tahiti. The Tonga Isles are quite independent and noted for their hereditary autocratic monarchy with absolute rule. Remember Queen Salote, who believed she was equally royal with Queen Elizabeth – when she attended our Queen's wedding? Or was it coronation? But we are 1500 kilometres east-wards. All the same we are New Zealand citizens, free to live in that

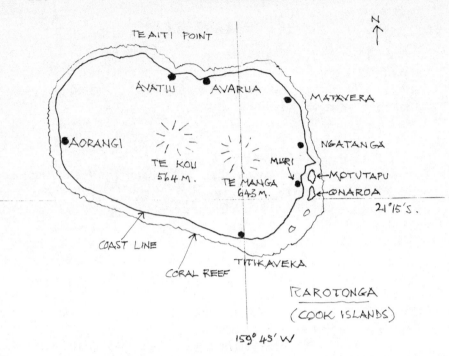

TE AITI POINT

N

AVATIU   AVARUA

MATAVERA

AORANGI

NGATANGA

TE KOU
564 M.

MURI

MOTUTAPU

TE MANGA
643 M.

ONAROA

21°15'S.

COAST LINE

CORAL REEF

TITIKAVEKA

RAROTONGA

(COOK ISLANDS)

159° 45' W

cool country – it belongs to us. We Rarotongans were the first settlers there, setting out in our fine long double canoes hundreds of years ago, perhaps a thousand years. We called it *Aotearoa* – Land of the Long White Cloud . . .'

Much more did Exham tell us, as we dawdled through the rich cultivated plain around the base of the 630 m high central mountains, the collapsed ragged caldera of volcanoes which have made most of the Polynesian islands what they are today – the emergent denuded tops of submarine islands upthrust from the deep mid-ocean abyss, where the thin hot crust of Earth's mantle is squeezed together by the drifting of the continental mass of the Americas towards Australasia . . . 'Just a lesson in tectonics,' said our loquacious host of the encyclopaedic brain.

Exham was proud that his ancestors had been explorers of the whole Polynesian triangle, occupying islands from Hawaii (which Cook dubbed the Sandwich Isles after Lord Sandwich of the Admiralty) in the north, to Easter Island due east, and to New Zealand in the far south-west. All these Cook visited, puzzled that at each extremity the inhabitants were typically Polynesian in appearance and language.

'There are more Cook Island Rarotongans living in New Zealand today than the 20,000 who still inhabit our fifteen habitable Cook Islands. But always these come home in old age, tired of the stressful Pakeha way of existence. In any case they have sent their savings earned in New Zealand to their parents at home. That is the custom, a good rule – in fact a religion here.'

Ten thousand dwell on Rarotonga, the largest island, and seem idyllically happy, ever smiling. And the reason?

'For one thing the land belongs to the people, not individuals. You can inherit, or lease, land; but never buy or sell it. Which prevents overseas exploiters moving in.

'And for another, if you can be content with your home plot of an acre more or less, you can easily grow your own food, and sell enough to buy a few luxuries. Money in Rarotonga is not important, personal health and happiness is.'

Exham strolled with us around his inherited plot, planted with every imaginable tropical and sub-tropical food, including coffee and cacao (producing cocoa and chocolate, enough for each household). Basics are banana, taro, arrowroot, kumara (sweet potato), paw-paw, mango, coconut, maize, citrus, etc. The surplus is exported to New Zealand, the overripe fruit and waste fed to the small plump Polynesian pigs. Avocado pear grows enormously, its huge fruit regarded mainly as food for pigs.

To keep pigs under control they are tethered by one leg under

fruiting trees. They are friendly and tame, and put to bed at night in fenced enclosures. Their dung is a principal fertiliser for the crops, the volcanic soil already rich in essential trace minerals. Some produce two litters a year, the sucklings much prized for the *hangi* – the ground-oven feast, Polynesian style.

A trench is dug in the ground, within which large stones are heated by wood waste; green palm leaves are placed on top of the hot stones, then the dressed pig or other meat – often a whole fish with root and other vegetables, covered up with more green vegetation, and the whole mounded and made as airtight as possible with earth. In three hours a perfect meal is turned out, tender, melting in the mouth; the steaming moisture produced by this method retains the full flavour lost in modern metal oven cooking.

Chickens run free underfoot, domesticated descendants of the wild jungle fowl of south-east Asia, the original home of the Polynesian people. These fowl sleep in the orchard trees, but some have escaped to breed wild in the forest mantle of the volcanic centre.

'Cattle and sheep are a luxury,' said Exham. 'Few of us have enough grass to graze them. You could say they are a status symbol with some wealthier landholders. Most of us drink fresh coconut milk, not cow's milk. Horses are scarce, but much loved, principally for racing, bare-back without saddle. Great fun when I was younger.

'The national game is cricket, with home-made bats and wickets. It's a spectacle you must see, especially when our large matrons play – they love it, shake like jellies with running and laughter. The rules seem to be made up as the game proceeds, with many stops and starts, for lost balls, and half-times for drink and food.'

Exham took us to his parents' home by the sea in the hamlet of Aorangi ('Dawn-sky' – it can also mean 'Beautiful Weather'). The house was empty, although a truckle bed and mattress lay on the open veranda.

'My parents are dead,' he explained. 'According to island custom no one will ever live in that house again. But their hospitality remains. Hence the bed outside, open to the passerby, perhaps a visitor like you who would fancy a rest, even a night's sleep. So we've left the facilities – a bed, electricity, water on tap.

'When in old age your parents die – always in the house they built when they married – you won't wish to disturb the home you were brought up in. Anyway you will have built a home of your own somewhere near on the inherited property or on your bride's in-herited land. Your parents' old home will be allowed to moulder into dust – it's sacred to their memory, and your own happy memory of childhood days, and the love of your father and mother. They are there in spirit for as long as their children remember them. Moreover, here in Rarotonga everyone wishes to be buried under the very ancestral soil where he and she toiled and were happily independent, growing their own food.

'There is a wise law in the island that a corpse must be buried not less than six feet deep and within twenty-four hours of death. The whole manpower of the village – neighbours and relations – assemble to make the coffin and dig the grave. The women meanwhile collect contributions of money or in kind to pay for the cost of materials, the pastor's fee, and so on; and of course prepare the *hangi* – the feast to honour the departed soul, and praise his worth in the present world which will guide him to the Good Lord in the next.'

Another interesting custom, said Wichman, was to fill the grave above the coffin with a layer of well-trampled earth; then a thickness of reinforced concrete of hard sea-shell, and finish with mounding the top with more earth in which a tree or flowers would be planted. He did not give a very satisfactory reason for this, but said: 'Just a custom, I suppose it prevents the earth collapsing too soon and breaking open the coffin below, or some say it has something to do with the early fear of grave-robbing . . .'

Exham invited us to share his normal midday *hangi* at his house with his family. On the way we passed a weather-beaten old man leaning on a stick by the wayside. He did not look up at us as our vehicle noisily overtook him.

'That's old —, a neighbour of my parents, a quarrelsome brute even today. When younger he hated my father, and refused to come to Father's burial,' growled Exham. 'Any able-bodied neighbour who neglects to help with a burial need not expect to be honoured and feted when he dies!'

Exham's wife was enchantingly handsome, and plump-bosomed above her moderate waist and large buttocks, the latter decorously hidden by a grass skirt. But fatness is much admired among Polynesian islanders, and not altogether for the reason a white man may suppose. The ability to lay up fat early in life in so-called primitive societies subject to periodic drought (or cyclones) resulting in famine has meant that the plumper individuals survive hunger longer than the lean ones. An ability visibly successful and genetically developed in certain African tribes, notably the Hottentot tribes of South Africa.

As Darwin noted in *The Descent of Man*, 'It is well known that with many Hottentot women the posterior projects in a wonderful manner; they are steatopygous . . . In some parts of Africa the men are said to choose their wives by ranging them in a line, and by picking her out who projects farthest *a tergo*. Nothing can be more hateful to a negro than the opposite form.' Quoting Darwin in her book *Wild Lives of Africa* my friend Juliette Huxley comments: 'If, by a curious evolution of necessity, a Hottentot girl makes her bottom her larder, is it not nice and fitting that it should be recognised as a sexual attraction?' Juliette had just seen 'a perfect example of a steatopygous Hottentot girl: under her cotton dress her buttocks projected like a pair of footballs'. (This girl was employed at a Welfare Centre in Cape Town, and was stirring a cauldron of soup – a circumstance likely to add more fat reserves to her splendid buttocks.) Elsewhere I have read that such a bustle-like posterior has significance in child-rearing – the extended rump makes a fine saddle for the growing infant to ride in comfort, clinging to a sling around its mother's shoulders.

As we rested in the shade of orchard trees, somewhat comatose after the delicious feast, one of Exham's senior friends swapped tales of the old way of life on our respective islands – ours in Wales and New Zealand. Simon Tariki Te Tula had been born on Aitu, remote northernmost of the Cook Islands. He had worked on steamships world-wide but was happy to return to die in the bosom of his family on Rarotonga.

'They will lay me deep in my native soil close to where my brother is buried. I also will be held down by shell-concrete under a mound of earth. Not – as they used to say – to prevent anyone digging me up, but because it is the custom to do so for the sound reason that the concrete prevents the weight of earth and water crushing the lid of your coffin. I remember how splendid my dear brother looked dressed in fine white linen shirt, black jacket and lava-lava, calm and peaceful in his coffin before he was lowered to his last rest on earth.'

A posse of children, who had been playing island tennis over a ragged fishing-net stretched between two avocado pear trees, were marshalled to entertain us with their version of the traditional song-and-dance of the island. The little maidens, hibiscus in their hair, naked to the navel in grass skirts, wriggled their lissom hips as they gyrated in imitation of their senior sisters, equally naked save for their *brassières des fleurettes* – breast covering of flowers (in French *fleurette* also means sweet nonsense), who were to entertain us nightly in the popular taverns and meeting-houses with traditional song-and-dance.

'A hundred years ago,' said Tariki Te Tula, 'our Victorian missionary elders would have been horrified at the sight of so much naked female flesh in posturing dances. And just a few of us oldies still scowl at such freedom today, remembering how we were forced as youngsters to cover our nakedness with trousers, skirts and blouses imported by the London Missionary Society pastors – probably at a good profit – from cold, rainy England where we might have been glad to wear them. It's taken us long to shake off that LMS yoke, to which faith we in Rarotonga have so long been loyal. The Catholic and the chapel faiths are here, but make little progress. My cousin Exham will take you to see our little cathedral, the nineteenth century LMS church, built of stone, just outside our village city Avarua.'

Next day being Sunday, Exham drove us to the service in this sombre building where, as in so many Polynesian churches, the sexes are segregated. There are side alcoves with benches for children, and visitors (foreigners) are relegated to the rear pews. Which pleased us, as we could study the scene and smile unseen at its spectator delights: the stately beauty of white-garbed and hatted matrons and mature maidens so upright of bearing (due to carrying heavy objects including water-pitchers balanced on their heads), the starchy propriety of the men wearing black jackets and lava-lavas – some wore trousers but all had their large bare feet encased in polished sandals.

From the infant benches came subdued chatter and giggles, to the small embarrassment of older children who were expected to keep order there, or if a small child was too noisy, to remove the offender from the church. The sermonising and prayers were evidently boring, but the singing was good and heartily enjoyed by all.

Certain favoured old dogs were permitted to enter the church, and nose their way towards where their owners sat. One tired old creature stretched out full length in the aisle nearest to the lay-preacher, occasionally raising its head to stare at the pulpit. Presently it got up, yawned as if bored and shambled out of the church, peeing against the open door as it departed.

The dark church smelt sweetly of the fragrance of frangipani and hibiscus, the altar and pulpit massed with tropical blossom and fern fronds.

In the churchyard, among the ranks of ugly stone crosses filling God's acre, the substantial raised tomb of the late Prime Minister of

Rarotonga, Albert Henry, recently buried, was almost hidden by fresh flowers.

'Albert Henry,' explained Exham, 'was politically more notorious than famous, but people have forgiven him his frailties which made him resign in the end for manipulating – it is said – the island's finances for his personal benefit, subsidised as we are by our protecting power New Zealand. Our chief ministers have never been paid an adequate salary, yet Albert Henry's thoughts – and I knew him well – were ever with securing the island's prosperity. I hope the Good Lord notices that not a day passes but fresh flowers are laid on his grave . . .'

Monday, 26 October was Gospel Day, a public holiday. We were directed to witness the pageant at Nuku village on the east coast of the island. Sunday-schools and other groups competed to act, in home-made costumes of boisterous design and colour, in sundry historical and biblical plays. We watched spellbound the *Trial and Crucifixion of Christ* taking place on the Nuku football field (rugby is preferred to soccer, as a more genuine battle). This was followed by *Captain Cook's discovery and landing on Rarotonga*. Then *The arrival of the first missionary*, Williams of the LM Society, impersonated by yesterday's pastor who read what he said was the original of the first sermon to the pagan islanders, only our 'Reverend Hon. Kokaya' spoke in English, whereas I believe that pastor Williams of the last century taught the islanders in their native Polynesian, of which he was a scholar.

After this agreeable surfeit of exuberant pageantry, accompanied by the unrestrained shrieks of joy and despair by the critical relatives of the actors, we escaped with Wichman and his charming wife Jancey to buy vegetables at a relative's farm in rich volcanic soil long planted with rows of fruit-trees, flowers and orchids – an export enterprise. A herd of milch cattle browsed beneath the orchard trees, and a flock of sheep, both tended by a small boy naked to the G-string around his loins, and playing a wood-wind pipe with some skill.

'This place, with its fine estancia-type house, is an example which your New Zealand government likes to point out as a showpiece of modern management of this island for financial profit,' was Exham's comment as we sipped a sugary island home-made wine on the veranda, and discussed the new trends of life in the Cook Islands.

It had been hot and humid all day, though we were wearing only shorts and sandals, and a sombrero. Torrential rain set in as Exham unloaded us at our beach lodging – the Tavern Tamure. A thunderstorm cleared the air at dusk, and we swam as usual in the coral lagoon which surrounds most of Rarotonga. But after supper on came the dancing girls and young men.

It is the custom that the young dancers may not sit down and take alcohol with visitors, and generally in those Polynesian islands we have visited alcohol is forbidden in village homes. But the dancing and singing is endemic and enjoyed by all as good clean fun. The sexes usually perform separately in groups, the tattooed men adopting warlike stances, grimacing, leaping and spinning, some holding staff or hoop, then slumping on the floor when the young women come forward to articulate their graceful synchronised movements of arms, legs and wriggling loins, as the old songs are sung.

As a polite concession to visitors there may be an interval when the actors select partners from the audience, and caper a few steps to a Polynesian hornpipe or Roger de Coverley on the juke-box. But it was noticeable that if you were dragged forth from your seat, your island partner held you firmly in the ring of his or her arms – no nonsense of laying your cheek or body against his or hers. And on one evening with a crowded house a prize was offered to the visitor judged most successful – the reward being a ticket to fly around the island in the only private plane.

On our last night an old woman dressed as a witch in a long Mother Hubbard gown and steeple hat suddenly glided into the hall, and began to imitate the young bottom-wriggling belles, more and more frantically thrusting her backside all ways, so that her costume gradually slipped down, helped by the young maidens grabbing at it. The laughter grew hysterical as she became more naked, and her old-woman's moustaches went awry before falling off altogether.

A moment later the master of ceremonies struck his bell. It was close to midnight, and amid a storm of applause the ugly witch stepped out of her disguise and removed her steeple hat with a low bow towards the visitors, revealing the substantial matron she was, holding firmly to a flower-decorated bodice covering her ample bosom, a grass skirt miraculously in place below her belly-button.

Perhaps we were prejudiced by the warm hospitality we received, without hint of monetary reward, but we became convinced that the majority of the islanders live happily in the present, accepting their leisurely existence and the bounty of the tropical land and sea as natural. While they profess gratitude to New Zealand as their protective power, they are not enamoured with the New Zealand way of life when they visit and work in her cities. Recently they turned down an application by a NZ building consortium to build a high-rise tourist hotel overlooking the coral reef.

Few stay for good after working in Auckland (warmest climate of New Zealand cities.) They told us it was too cold, and there is a lingering prejudice among the white (Pakeha) people that Cook Islanders are socially inferior. It is a fact that in general immigrants born in the Polynesian islands of the Cooks, Samoa and Fiji are considered inferior, and even the indigenous Maori, after 150 years or so living alongside European settlers in New Zealand and freely interbreeding with them, do not mix easily with the newly-arriving Polynesians.

'Most of the Maori and Pakeha of New Zealand today are intellectually ignorant of the natural courtesy and kindness of we Rarotongan, Samoan and other Polynesian races living in the small islands of the open Pacific,' said Exham. 'It is a kind of fear and hostility which goes far back in history to all tribes, white, brown or black who fought, and still fight, for living space where people multiply beyond the capacity of the land to feed them. In Polynesia, including New Zealand, populations colonising small Pacific islands reached that limit within a very few centuries. If you read Captain Cook's diaries, he saw that the natural cure for overpopulation was war and cannibalism, or emigration of the surplus young people to other islands. Hence the despatch of warriors and their fertile young women (Wahines) to search for new islands to colonise – or fight for.'

Historian Te Tula walked with us to the beach at Ngatonga (Place of the South Wind), a natural sandy harbour where a metal plaque declares that the 'Great Fleet' of catamarans (double canoes), each with a central thatched dwelling cabin for women and children, set out from this point to colonise Aotearoa in about 1375. 'Of course,' said Te Tula, 'there had been earlier voyages by exploring warriors seeking fresh islands, and it is said that New Zealand was first discovered by the legendary great explorer Kupe, who, returning to Rarotonga, like Odysseus to Ithaca, gave his people a glowing account of the new great island, as well as explicit sailing directions on how to reach *Tiri-tiri-te-moana* – Gift of the Sea. It is said that Kupe brought home with him dried moa meat and tough flint-hard *pounamu* or greenstone, so hard that axes made of it are still in use today. Greenstone also proved ideal as a *mere*, a sharp-edged hand-weapon for smashing the skull or removing the scalp of your enemy . . .'

But all tools on Rarotonga were of volcanic stone, bone, wood or

vegetable origin. 'When the first of our people left Malaysia and
sailed east into the open sea – at least two thousand years ago – they
brought with them no metal tools, but only their skills in wood-
working and weaving, and their tradition of oratory under their wise
leaders the *Ariki*, who ruled over the common people with a firm
hand, yet with dignity and kindness. Daily life was governed by what
is still called *tapu*, a word the Pakeha has corrupted into *taboo*. It
applied to many things, designed in the first place to maintain the
power of the Ariki chieftains by forbidding a commoner to lay hands
on his property, his weapons, or his food. These could only be
touched by his own sons or wife, with his permission. Tapu was a
good system whereby the Ariki for centuries had inherited the
chieftainship, and learned the wisdom of their leadership, acceptable
to the rest of the tribe because of the training the Ariki gave to their
sons and daughters in all the main arts of the Polynesian civilisation:
courage and humanity at all times, ability, use of wisdom in debate
and elocution on the *marae* – the tribal meeting-place – and acceptance of the skill in war and oratory of the more intelligent of the
younger men, which were promoted accordingly.'

So we talked there on the Ngatonga launching beach with this
learned man, ranging back over the centuries into the ancient religion
of the Rarotongan (Cook Islands) people which was carried to New
Zealand as long ago as 800–900 AD (proved by modern carbon-
dating of the first settlements, their artefacts and middens containing
moa and human bones). The Maori religion at that time did not
include the acceptance of original sin, or of the idea of supreme
happiness in the hereafter following piety in the life on earth. The
Polynesian seized 'joy as she flies' in the present, contented if he or
she could achieve *mana* (tribal respect) through skill, courage and
obedience to the Ariki within the community. There was an afterlife,
but it was not the heaven or hell of Christianity taught by the first
English missionaries. It was simply a place where the spirit lived on.
After death the spirit left the body and sought sanctuary in the ocean
of Kiwa, the site of departure in Rarotonga being the most northerly
point. In New Zealand this was Cape Reinga, where the spirit
plunged into the arms of the Dawn-Maid (the great Lady of Darkness) who was keeper of the Underworld.

'Cape Reinga looks north-east towards Rarotonga over an empty
ocean,' commented Te Tula, 'so perhaps the legend of the spirit
returning here had some substance, for the currents of the Coral Sea
and its trade winds favour a returning canoe, rather than one seeking

Aotearoa. Anyway I think the old legends a much more agreeable form of religion than that brought by missionary Williams. Before he came the Cook Islands had no written language, all history was learned by rote and passed down by recital of the names of our ancestors and principal Ariki and their achievements, back for almost sixty generations. If we allow twenty-five years for each generation it works out well with the belief that the first Polynesians colonised our Oceania islands about AD 500.'

'Here at Ngatonga, as at all major departure points of great expeditions,' said Te Tula, 'a large stone was carved with the symbols of Tangaroa, God of the Sea, and buried with smaller stones to indicate the direction the canoes must take to reach their planned destination. This main stone was the *mauri*, containing the life force of the voyagers safe for their return. Usually the expedition would embark at dusk, so that the stars of Rangi would guide them in the right direction. Navigation of the great Pacific Ocean was long known to our people, and exact sailing directions were handed down from our elders to the younger steersmen, who carried with them a Rangitira wise in the knowledge of all fixed and moving stars, and of course the periodic changes of the trade winds, the path of the sun by day and the moon by night . . .'

Te Tula was somewhat bitter about the arrival of missionaries, and at his home in Avarua showed me a book of old photographs by James Siers, lately published and containing a painting of Williams landing in the Cook Islands, with the comment that the missionary's first act was to order the wooden graven image of Tangaroa, God of the Sea, to be burned.

'They say Williams was a God-fearing man of high principles, but with no comprehension of our religion of *mana* and *tapu* and respect for the gods of the sea, earth, sky and other natural elements, which our Ariki and Rangitira (priest, literally sky-chief) believed and taught us to pray to. Williams impressed us with the written word of the Old and New Testament, of Adam and Eve in the Garden of Eden, talking to the Lord God of Heaven. Not really very different from the story of our beginning, for we were born of the meeting of Rangi (which is heaven or sky) and the earth mother Papa. Their children were the young gods Tane, father of the forest and creator of the flowers, and Tangaroa, god of the sea, and Tawheri, father-controller of all winds.

'All these young gods became restless when they grew up, and jealous of Papa's love for her husband Rangi. They conspired to tear

Rangi from the arms of his beloved wife Papa, and banish him forever to the sky. From his heaven Rangi looked down in sorrow upon his wife far below, and wept tears of rain at intervals. The dew and mists of Papa Earth are also the signs of weeping of the separated parents.

'Tawheri favoured his father, and joined him in the sky with his Pandora's box of winds. Gentle Rangi, looking down from the sky, admired his son Tane for creating great forests, and beautiful flowers and birds of many colours to enrich and clothe the land (his wife Papa). Tane was seeking to atone for having separated his parents. Having thus clothed his mother so handsomely Tane placed the sun and moon in the sky, so that Rangi could see more clearly – by night and day – his wife. In addition Tane gave his lonely father a robe of scarlet to put on at sunset or sunrise, as he pleased, and a basket of stars – the Milky Way – to brighten the hours when the moon had joined the sun on her monthly journey around the earth . . .

'But Tawheri remained jealous, and every now and then he would leave Rangi in the sky, sweeping aside his father's cloud-tears, and attacking Tane's forests with great gales. He stirred-up his brother Tangaroa, god of the sea, peacefully living with his grandchildren – Ikatere, father of fish, and Tutewehiwehi, father of reptiles, and drove them apart. Tutewehiwehi fled to Tane and the land for shelter, and Ikatere retreated under the sea with his large brood of children.

'Only Tumata-uenga, god of future man, stood firm, refusing to bend before his jealous brother. Tu was the Wise One, knowing that Tawheri would soon tire of his senseless attacks, including hurling his waves against Tane and his mother Papa. And when at last the sea was still again, the children of Tane launched their canoes from the land and captured the fishes which are the great-grandchildren of Tangaroa . . .'

Thus spoke Te Tula, declaiming the story of Maori gods learned as a child. 'It was time to people the forests with human beings. The gods were not satisfied with creating trees, flowers, birds, fishes, lizards, frogs and the little dragon Tuatara. They decided to create a complete woman from the warm soil of mother earth. This done, Tane gave her life by passing his breath into her lungs, and when she grew up he mated with her. They called her Hine-ahu-one, that is, Woman-created-of-earth, and she bore Tane two daughters. The younger one, named the Dawn-Maid, fled from her father to avoid incestuous union with the only fertile man on earth. She took refuge in the Underworld of Tangaroa where she forever gathers the spirits of her sister's descendants for safe keeping. She is known to all Polynesians as the Great Lady of Darkness . . . Then Tu, wise god of the future and of war, created Tiki, the first mortal human male, and so began the generation of man on earth.'

So much for Te Tula's description of the genesis of man, which he claimed was more interesting and just as credible or incredible as the legends of the Old Testament of the Bible. As a student of both Testaments, he found the Lord God depicted in the Old Testament as intolerably biased. ('Why did he favour Abel above Cain, so driving Cain to kill his brother in despair? Whereupon the Lord God put a mark on Cain as an outcast and told him that he would suffer hardship in his tilling of the soil – it would yield thistles and weeds, and Cain was henceforth condemned as a fugitive and vagabond by this jealous Lord God of the Bible, which Williams forced us to accept.')

Back in his home Te Tula showed me early black-and-white photographs of the people of the Cook Islands taken in the missionary era some eighty years ago, showing them unhappily grave in European clothes covering the whole body, and never a flower in the hair of the young women. Such decoration was sinful, as was the brewing of *kava* (*kvas* in Samoa), a narcotic drink made from fermented coconut juice. All wooden carvings representing the pagan gods were burned and the energy of the community directed by Williams and his deputies in the other inhabited islands to the building of large churches, using trimmed blocks of the only stone – native coral. These missionaries introduced a code of strict laws of private property and behaviour, which they enforced by enlisting church-going native men as police.

'Of course there was a rush of strong young men to take up the blue uniforms imported from London. Like the young Rangitira of our pagan days, they saw the opportunity to pay off old scores upon transgressing neighbours, a form of *utu*, that is revenge for insult in the past.

'These were the infamous "blue laws" by which the newly-appointed police could and did beat offenders black and blue, and impose heavy fines. Among other duties each household had to contribute a tithe (one tenth) of its produce of orchard, garden and sea to the church, a heavier tax than ever an islander had paid to the Ariki chief of old. Thus our traditional way of life and ancient system of food production shared equally with every family in the village was soon changed to producing cash crops saleable to the increasing number of trading, whaling and copra-collecting schooners for coin, bullion or bills of exchange. The same sad story in every Polynesian community. The people were forced to adopt a religion they did not want, but in addition the arrival of these ships and their white crews brought the horrible diseases of white civilisation – we had no built-in resistance to influenza, syphilis, tuberculosis, diphtheria, and so on. Some of these were encouraged by the necessity of wearing European dress, which in our climate was suffocating and insanitary.'

'So you haven't a good word for the London Missionary Society's efforts to civilise your people?' I asked. 'I have read that Christianity put a stop to Polynesian cannibalism.'

'But at what a price!' said Te Tula cheerfully. 'By the way, we only ate the bodies of our warrior enemies slain in lawful battle. After all, it was one way of reducing populations on overcrowded islands. A war was healthy in that respect, for peace and plenty followed. But the arrival of Christianity and its priests resulted in a severe decline in population from the diseases it brought, and among our exports thereafter were our young people, some seized by force and made to slave in plantations or on ships, for little or no wage. It was a time of the expansion of your British Empire, and Queen Victoria was as keen as any other monarch in acquiring – seizing – land before the German and American imperialists got there first . . .'

Germany and the United States had carved up Samoa by the time that Britain made the Cook Islands a protectorate in 1888, which together with Fiji they held with a British Governor in both, until 1901, when New Zealand's imperialist Prime Minister Seddon persuaded Britain to permit the Cook Islands to be annexed and its inhabitants granted New Zealand citizenship. At last in 1965 the Cook Islands returned almost full circle to self-government, electing their own Prime Minister, and a general assembly of twenty-two members. Every four years there is a general election, the winning party electing a Premier and a cabinet of six ministers.

Exham Wichman, younger than Te Tula, had less leisure to reminisce about the history of Rarotonga. He was too busy to sigh for the good old pagan days.

'Not so good at all, really,' said Exham. 'Women were just machines for producing babies, even after the missionaries arrived. Sons were especially desirable, to be trained for war. Daughters were less valuable; if they were in any way imperfect or ugly, they would be quietly thrown into the sea at night, or so I have read. Everything has changed since we gained our independence under our present free association with New Zealand. The new health clinics they helped us to set up here in Avarua teach our wahines modern methods of limiting the family. Polynesians love babies – we needed daughters to look after crops – and still do. But today every intending bride can be happy about her sexual contact with the man of her choice. Both partners understand the need for precaution against unwanted pregnancy, both before and after marriage. No longer can a man dictate who his daughter must marry, nor may a man have more than one wife. The women and girls are at last free of male domination, and although we have fewer babies, we are all the healthier and happier for that . . .'

Exham had promised to guide me to climb the steep central forested volcanic peak of Rarotonga, which I had longed to do ever since seeing the graceful snow-white tropic birds glide in from the sea to their nests hidden in the sheer cliffs of the mountain. There are two species here; both have two tail feathers almost as long as their long pigeon-like bodies, in total about three feet long. The red-tailed tropic bird flashes its scarlet streamers high up in the sun as it swoops in mutual courtship flight. The slightly smaller white-tailed species is snow-white save for a black crescent on its wings.

I knew both, for these truly-named tropic birds range oceans in all tropical zones, wandering far from land, occasionally perching to rest on a masthead spar, otherwise normally on the wing except when plunging upon surface-shoaling fish. Their legs are extremely small, like those of the aerial swifts, swallows and kingfishers which fly direct into their nest-holes. Exham knew them by the whaleman's name, bosun-bird, from the fancied resemblance of the long tail to a marlin-spike used by sailors in splicing rope.

But Exham was extremely busy just then, with influxes of tourists who paid him to be conducted on round-island tours. He kept putting me off each morning when I felt fresh and ready to climb before the noonday heat set in. I pleaded:

'There is also the chance that I can find one of the rare petrels which formerly bred in holes on most of these inaccessible volcanic peaks, where their remote craggy situation saved them from predatory man and other enemies.'

'True,' replied Exham. 'As a boy I often climbed after the burrowing sea-birds. But it is very difficult today. The path has fallen away in our heavy monsoons. You have to be one hundred per cent fit, and well-armed with a cutlass to cut through the jungle, and a pickaxe to cut steps . . .' Thus Exham warned me, puffing and blowing at the very thought of so much exercise. He was out of condition, poor man – I considered.

On the next morning, seeing the opalescent long-tails gliding high in the rosy-tinted dawn sky, I determined to go it alone.

At first the approach slopes were agreeably verdant through cultivated plots. The upward path bordered ripening crops of kumura, taro, yam, dwarf banana, kapok and lesser root-crops, sheltered by breadfruit, walnut and avocado pear trees, livened with shrubs of tree hibiscus, purple-and-white frangipani, canna and other lilies, and festooned with the deep blue morning glory convolvulus – this runs wild everywhere on the island.

The cultivated ground ended rather abruptly at the first steep shoulder under the mountain, where the dense wild jungle began. It was important, I told myself, to follow the stream which nestled through a valley above me; it would guide me on my return, better than my pocket compass might.

But after a few hundred feet of tortuous climbing the stream dwindled to a trickle and stopped altogether where it issued from a small concrete reservoir. So did the streamside path.

I sat down on the concrete edge. I could hear distantly the

tantalising song of a little brown bird I had hoped to see – the endemic Rarotongan reed-warbler. This is a species of the world-wide *Acrocephalus* super-species which has long colonised most continents, including Australia, yet on reaching remote Polynesian islands has settled down to become completely sedentary and in such isolation has got larger or smaller and changed its dull plumage somewhat. Rabid taxidermistic collectors rave over a new insular species, and have not seldom been responsible for exterminating some. But I had no such predatory thought as I recognised the song of this reed-warbler familiar as a summer voice in Britain, but which hid itself so completely in the Rarotongan jungle.

It seemed to be the only bird singing, no other small birds could I hear. But gone-wild jungle fowl crowed at rare intervals, as I marched upwards, wielding my cutlass, trying to follow a track marked with the slots of a wild pig.

I was by now in a bath of sweat, which attracted hordes of mosquitoes and smaller biting insects to my scratched naked skin, bleeding from wounds inflicted by unyielding branches of this young jungle. (It had been burned at intervals, hence its vigorous regrowth, and was no longer a forest of lofty trees with an open glade easy-to-walk floor.)

Buzz of cicada and hum of mosquito were the only other sounds, save for a distant murmur or coo of the now rare endemic pigeon – or was it the even rarer fruit dove? I could not tell, and was in no mood to enquire further. Shamefully I retreated down hill, beaten by the biting insects and stifling heat.

Miraculously this torment ceased when I reached the open air of gardens watered by the mountain stream. A Rarotongan woman offered me a ripe paw-paw!

So much for my ambition to scale Rarotonga's lofty peak. History records that the islanders formerly harvested numbers of the plump young *titi* (fledgelings) of the *Pterodroma*, sometimes called gadfly petrels, substantial enough to make tender good eating. From long isolation the gadfly petrels have developed into unique insular species on their remote volcanic peak homes throughout the tropical Pacific from Hawaii to the Easter and Juan Fernandez Islands, and south and west to the high-peaked islands of the Coral Sea and New Zealand.

Very few of these little islands have not been ravaged by man and his introduced camp followers, especially cats, rats and mongoose. Only a few petrels can survive, like the tropic birds, by nesting on the crags and crowns of mountains inaccessible to ground predators. From the crags a few of these fledgelings may accidentally tumble down into the villages and gardens during a monsoon blow, when, too fat to be ready to fly to sea, they are eagerly collected as a delicacy for the islander's table.

There are no sparrows on Rarotonga, and the only land bird at the time of our visit was a tiresome foreigner, the Indian myna *Acridotheres tristis*. It was originally introduced for its appetite in devouring grass and other grubs attacking crops. Which it did so efficiently that, as it multiplied to its present large numbers, it began devouring ripe orchard fruit. It is now accused of destroying all the smaller endemic island birds by raiding their nests, flinging out the eggs or young, although, as the myna is believed to be strictly vegetarian, it does not usually devour these. Mynas pair for life and are dynamic in defending their feeding territory, driving away all other small birds. Killing nestlings of these seems to be a facet of that territoriality.

Ornithologically disappointing, our holiday in the Cook Islands was blissful from the contagious happiness of the islanders, and the pleasure of swimming in the coral lagoon and its sun-warmed shallows alive with darting fish of many species, edible sea-slugs, octopuses, clams, sea-urchins, abalone, and other gastronomic delights.